Tiger Woman

on

Wall Street

*Winning Business Strategies from
Shanghai to New York and Back*

Junheng Li

New York Chicago San Francisco Athens London Madrid Mexico City
Milan New Delhi Singapore Sydney Toronto

1 2 3 4 5 6 7 8 9 0   DOC/DOC   1 9 8 7 6 5 4 3

ISBN   978-0-07-181842-1
MHID   0-07-181842-1

e-ISBN   978-0-07-181844-5
e-MHID   0-07-181844-8

This publication is designed to provide accurate and authoritative information in regard to the subject matter covered. It is sold with the understanding that neither the author nor the publisher is engaged in rendering legal, accounting, securities trading, or other professional services. If legal advice or other expert assistance is required, the services of a competent professional person should be sought.

—From a Declaration of Principles Jointly Adopted by a Committee of the American Bar Association and a Committee of Publishers and Associations

Library of Congress Cataloging-in-Publication Data
Li, Junheng.
   Tiger woman on Wall Street : winning business strategies from Shanghai to New York and back / Junheng Li.
      pages cm
   ISBN 978-0-07-181842-1 (hardback)—ISBN 0-07-181842-1 (hardback) 1. Li, Junheng.
2. Capitalists and financiers—United States—Biography. 3. Capitalists and financiers—China—Biography. 4. Investments. 5. Success in business. I. Title.
   HG172.L523A3 2014
   332.6092—dc23
[B]   2013026111

McGraw-Hill Education books are available at special quantity discounts to use as premiums and sales promotions or for use in corporate training programs. To contact a representative, please visit the Contact Us pages at www.mhprofessional.com.

This book is dedicated to my father, who gave me a strong mind;
to my mother, who taught me perseverance;
and to my grandmother, who exemplified resilience.

It is also dedicated to Middlebury College,
for teaching me that life is an art, not a science.

Contents

CONTENTS

Author Note

The opinions, analyses, and comments in this book are my own personal views based on my experience and research from public sources that I believe to be accurate and reliable.

For the companies I analyze, my team and I spend a tremendous amount of time collecting intelligence on their businesses by, among other things, online data mining and tracking and on-site customer surveys and reviews. To analyze the raw data collected, my team and I employ proprietary technologies and methodologies, which I believe give me a unique insight into the performance and prospects of the companies I review.

I hope that what I have written will provide my readers greater insight into and a better understanding of investing, especially in China, but readers should not take what I write as investment advice—they should do their own independent research or consult with their own investment advisors before making any investment or trading decisions in the United States, China, or anywhere else.

AUTHOR NOTE

I have based this book on my recollections of my life and my work. Some names and identifying characteristics of companies and individuals have been changed. All conversations are based upon my best recollections and should not be taken as verbatim transcriptions.

Introduction

WHEN I WALK INTO ANY BUSINESS GATHERING, I AM AWARE that all eyes are on me. I don't say this to be vain. As a Chinese woman living and working in the financial capital of the world, I know that my presence provokes conversation. People want to know my opinion on China's economic surge. They are curious about my journey from Shanghai to New York. They often ask if I was raised by a tiger mother and where I stand on the tiger parent controversy. They are endlessly curious about China and the Chinese ways of business and life and what I think of them.

I was born and raised in Shanghai, the commercial and financial center of mainland China. My childhood and adolescence mirrored the rise of capitalist China in the 1980s and 1990s. My parents, like everyone else in their generation, were survivors of the Cultural Revolution, the starkest period in modern Chinese history. That movement left a burn on the nation's psyche, the impact of which is still felt today and will be felt by many generations to come.

I had what Western critics would call a brutal upbringing, raised with strict discipline and harsh consequences. My father's tiger-on-steroids parenting style neither broke nor made me, but I do carry the memories into my adult life.

Somewhere between the Hollywood movies my father and I watched together and the Voice of America radio broadcasts we listened to together, I latched onto the American concepts of individualism, freedom, and diversity. My thirst for an American life drove me to pursue an American education. I accepted an offer for a four-year scholarship to Middlebury College in Vermont in 1996. At Middlebury I encountered a universal code of ethics for the first time in my life, and it has proved to be an important principle in my career in finance—especially where Chinese investments are involved.

My experience at Middlebury was also the first time I was exposed to the concept of an idea-based rather than a knowledge-based education. I was challenged to think and not just memorize—to recognize the *how*, not just the *what*. Study took place in collaboration, not isolation. I began to recognize on a deeper level something I never could in China: American values are not based on clichés of freedom and individuality, but rather on the importance of independent thinking, the courage to question the norm, and the belief in universal ethics.

At Middlebury, I became an avid student of the market economy. My endless curiosity about and passion for economics were both philosophical and personal. My study of economics has helped to cultivate a critical mind and a precise logic to understand how the world works—not just regarding monetary exchange, but also the role of government and citizenry in an increasingly global world.

* * *

In 2000, I graduated summa cum laude in economics, and I accepted one of the job offers I got: to work as an investment banking analyst at Credit Suisse First Boston in its New York office. A year later, I was recruited to join Franklin Templeton Fiduciary to help launch an international small- to mid-cap fund focusing on developed markets in Asia. In 2002, I enrolled at Columbia Business School to get my MBA.

Soon after Columbia, I joined Aurarian Capital Management, a long- and short-equity hedge fund known for its investigative research into under-covered and under-researched companies. I focused on the technology, medical device, and renewable energy industries globally, and I worked my heart out to become an expert on a myriad of complex and controversial investment subjects.

At Aurarian, I learned over and over again that an investment can be profitable if and only if the marketplace misunderstands and misprices part or all of the company's businesses. A stock analyst's job is to explore and develop variant views from the marketplace. If there are no variant views, the stock is considered fully priced and therefore is not interesting for investors seeking alpha, an above-the-market return.

While working on U.S. stocks first, I started to witness waves of Chinese companies raising capital in the United States. As I followed a group of listings closely, I noticed a lack of skepticism toward Chinese companies on and off Wall Street—in corporate America, among the general public, and among the mass media around the world. As the unchecked enthusiasm for Chinese stocks gained momentum, I saw a bubble forming and inflating.

The process of the bubble forming, and later bursting, is a result of classic push-and-pull dynamics: if there is a buyer, there is a seller. Greedy and lazy investors play off immature companies that have questionable ethics and practices, whose stocks are pushed out to the market by private equity investors, packaged by bankers, and cross-checked by auditors, accountants, attorneys, and other institutional managers. Most of these players are American-born.

* * *

The world's general lack of cynicism about China got me excited. I launched JL Warren, an independent research firm, in 2009 to plug the gap between the corporate and commercial reality in China and curious investors in America, leveraging my combination of a Chinese background and Wall Street experience.

The idea of an independent research firm came from years of observation that traditional sell-side research is inadequate for serious investors who invest heavily in China. Despite the theoretical presence of a Chinese wall, sell-side research continues to serve the banks' underwriting and advisory businesses. The desire to preserve existing relationships and develop new ones in the investment banking area creates an inevitable bias in a bank's research products that institutional investors can hardly rely on for investment purposes. Analysts are constrained from candidly expressing their views.

The need for unbiased research is even greater in the field of China-focused research as China's importance in the global economy has surged.

China makes or breaks the state of our global economic recovery and what comes afterward. As China goes, so goes the global economy. If China sneezes, the rest of the world catches a cold. For global institutional investors, the stakes of getting China right are high. So is the need for fact-based, meticulous, and accurate research.

I am fascinated by China, not just because it is my home country and I am emotionally and practically vested in it, but also because it is vastly complex. Complexity always intrigues me. Because of its unique structure—it is still a command-based economy, but it is bolstered by market instruments—China offers the chance for endless decoding, learning, risks, and challenges. And consequent opportunities.

4

INTRODUCTION

Most of the public domain commentaries on China's economy, companies, and businesses are simplistic, characteristic of the American media, in which sensational sound bites are far more important than nuances. These attitudes have left the United States with black-and-white opinions about China. With this book, I want to share my work and to plug the gap between what I see as the reality and the perception on Wall Street about China.

My conviction that the market is not efficient—the underlying premise of this book—contradicts one of the great canons of modern finance theory: the efficient market hypothesis of Eugene Fama. Inefficiency exists because accurate information takes time to travel and surface; analysis and human intelligence are subject to errors and biases by investors and fraud by management.

In the case of China, inefficiency prevails. This book aims to show you how mindful investors can profit from market inefficiency.

* * *

America is the strongest nation in the world in terms of its economy, military might, and influence in global affairs. Yet it is also among the youngest. This combination of its number one ranking and youth makes America consistently cocky but also insecure about falling behind. Washington's deep political divisions over fundamental and philosophical beliefs have been stagnating its political system and stirring doubts about whether America will continue to lead the world in the twenty-first century.

At the same time, China has emerged and appears to be a formidable competitor. Energized by the return to capitalism, its 1.3 billion people are demonstrating great manufacturing prowess and are modernizing at an astounding rate. But if you look beyond the surface of its impressive achievement, you will see what China has yet to develop: the rule of law, a functional and effective business and financial infrastructure, an imaginative and innovative workforce, free independent media, and social mobility driven by merit, not by class, ethnicity, and family background. Until the software—the quality of its citizenry and society—matches the government-led hardware of infrastructure buildup, China is far from constituting a credible threat to America.

At the same time, China is essentially caught in a prison of its own success: the staggering and unprecedented achievement of lifting 500 million people out of poverty in a bit more than 30 years. This achievement is based on a single economic mode—that of mass production of low-value manufacturing products, along with plenty of government-led investment in massive infrastructure projects. In the process, China has singularly focused on GDP growth at the expense of profitability, innovation, R&D, and productivity.

Today, that growth model has stalled. Excess capacity has been built in many sectors. Low pricing power has put pressure on corporate profitability, while the lack of R&D and innovation hinders Chinese companies from moving up the value chain and increasing, or even maintaining, global competitiveness. China is kept afloat by taking on more corporate and government debt.

The Chinese economy has become increasingly inefficient, driven by weak corporate governance, a historic misallocation of resources, and a political process hamstrung between an itch to westernize and a desire to remain a Communist regime. Those deficiencies will become more pronounced and damaging as China's economic growth slows.

* * *

Although it's a cliché, *do your homework* means there is no shortcut to sustainable wins in the market, in business, and in life. For investors, doing your homework means reading the company's filings and understanding the products, services, and people (including their families and mistresses) you invest in. Keep in mind that losing money is worse than not making money. Dare to be a contrarian, and if your view is the market view, move on to find an idea with which you can find an edge. There is never a shortage of ideas for a curious and able mind.

To participate and catch up in the global competition, China's policy makers must drastically improve corporate governance and transparency; continue market reform by allowing more foreign ownership and competition; and make banks lend on commercial criteria only, not for and on behalf of the government. To be a global player, one must respect established global standards, compliance, and regulations.

Just as there is no shortcut to sustainable profit in the market, there is no shortcut to corporate growth and to building a structurally sound economy. Today, China is at the tipping point, where the lagging quality of its institutions and people poses serious threats to its further economic growth.

* * *

For the 16 years I have lived away from China, I have been consumed by work—first academics, then a demanding career. While my family back in Shanghai has always been unconditionally supportive of my work and any pursuit in my life, I have spared little time for my parents. For that, I live with guilt every day.

Tiger Woman on Wall Street is a way for me to describe and explain my life and work since I left Shanghai in 1996. I want my parents to know that I have inherited their courage, discipline, and perseverance—and that I thank them for what and where I am today. With a tremendous amount of hard work and infinite curiosity, I am now an independent thinker, savvy investment professional, and humble student of learning.

My parents' parenting—although tough by any standard, Western or Asian—was an expression of selfless love and anxiety, the outcome of China's cultural traditions and its modern historical tragedies.

While I now live out my American dream in New York City, I will never forget who and what made me.

CHAPTER 1

Tiger Dad, Tiger Daughter

SLIVERS OF WOOD BORE INTO MY SKIN, MY BACK ACHED, AND my shins throbbed with pain. I had been forced to kneel on a washer board in front of my father for more than an hour while he drilled me on the multiplication tables, and the wooden ridges were digging so deeply into my legs that I could barely think.

"Eight times six!" he barked.

"Uh . . ."

I must have taken a beat too long to answer, so he slapped me hard across the face.

"EIGHT TIMES SIX!" he repeated.

"Forty?" I ventured.

"Stupid, useless girl!" he yelled, and slapped me again, even harder this time.

"Baba, I know it! Forty-eight!"

On and on it went, until well past dusk. I was beginning to bleed, but there would be no respite until I completed the entire multiplication table without hesitation. I was expected to spit out the correct answers like a machine. Dad was determined that I get these basic mathematic lessons down cold, and as far as he was concerned, the best way of teaching was through a brutal system of punishment and reward.

It was not unusual for my father to take this zealous tutoring too far. He believed it was the only way his daughter would gain an edge in China's highly competitive education system and get ahead in the world. Others might call it torture; he called it tough love. Later in life, he figured, I would understand and even thank him. But right then, there was to be no sparing of the rod.

I was just three years old.

When Dad decided the drilling had sunk in, he lifted me off the washer board and brought me to a nearby park where I could run around and play. At the park, I felt so liberated that I dropped my father's hand and took off, sprinting across the grass. By then, it was so dark that I couldn't see in front of me—the public park authorities turned off the lights after 8 p.m. to save electricity. The groundskeepers had just mowed the lawn and erected barbed wire to protect the grass. I ran straight into it.

The barbs pierced my stomach's tender flesh and blood started to blossom, staining my blue dress. Dad scooped me up, took me home, and cleaned my wound, the pain flaring as he dabbed rubbing alcohol on my punctures. When I screamed, his face flinched. Then he said something I have never forgotten: "Pain is just weakness leaving the body."

Dad tucked me in, then sat next to my bed until I fell asleep, touching my forehead from time to time and checking my injuries. In that bittersweet moment, I knew he cared for me. If anything, that fierce love was why he always demanded nothing less than perfection. His high standards for me were just part of his language of love that got lost in translation.

* * *

Throughout my childhood, his militaristic drills and beatings were almost a daily routine. If I displeased him for any reason, whether it was for coming home late after playing games with the neighborhood boys or stumbling as I played a tune on my accordion, I would suffer a whipping from his leather belt.

As brutal as he could be, I never once doubted that my father loved my younger sister, Jasmine, and me more than anything in the world. He would do little things for us, small love tokens like leaving toothpaste on my toothbrush for me before heading to work in the morning or preparing special breakfast foods. He always rose early to make breakfast for Jasmine and me; he was a stickler for proper nutrition, especially when it came to his children. When the monthly budget was strained, he would eat less so we could have more. If I were facing an important day at school, such as a big test or an accordion recital, he would prepare two eggs poached in hot milk. But I never liked the taste of egg no matter how good it was supposed to be for me. Once, Dad spotted me spitting it out the moment I left the apartment. After that, I wasn't allowed to leave until I finished chewing and swallowing right in front of him.

If I did something that pleased him, like scoring at the top of my class or winning a speech contest, he would wake even earlier than usual and bike 20 minutes to his favorite dumpling joint to bring home my favorite pan-seared pork buns and curried beef soup. Every time I saw pork buns for breakfast, I knew that I had made him happy. Poached eggs and takeout pork buns were luxury breakfast items at that time—a real splurge. And they were all for my sister and me. Dad would sit in the corner of the living room and eat his rice porridge separately, a contented look on his face.

Dad never spoke the words, "I am proud of you." He didn't have to. It was obvious. "One day you will understand why I'm so hard on you right now," he told me once. "All I do is to prepare you while you are young and moldable, so that you will have a bit more control of your destiny when you grow up."

CHAPTER 2

Working in the Gold Mine

New York, Spring 2005

W HEN I FIRST SAW JASON GOLD, HE WAS CARRYING HIS DRY cleaning into the office, a gleaming glass and steel money fortress on Fifth Avenue, right next door to Harry Winston's New York flagship store. He made a good first impression: he seemed energetic, sharp, and youthful, with a ready smile. His dark eyes were alert and penetrating.

Jason was the founder of Aurarian Capital, a start-up hedge fund where I was trying to land a job. I was there for my first interview. After working for several years on Wall Street, I was ready for a new challenge. The ad for the position said the fund was focused on under-the-radar small-cap technology companies. I knew very little about technology—in fact, I didn't even understand what a computer motherboard was at the time—but I knew I could learn anything if I set my mind to it. I could not wait to learn the ropes of a start-up hedge fund by working my heart out.

Before my interview, I asked around on the Street about Jason's reputation. He had an impressive résumé graced with some of the most prestigious multibillion dollar fund names in the business. Before launching Aurarian Capital, he was a research director at SAC Capital, one of the world's largest multistrategy funds, run by Steve Cohen. He had also been a lieutenant to Dan Benton at Andor Capital Management. Both funds were known for their cutthroat cultures.

The people I spoke with described Jason as everything from a bulldog to ultimately a good guy. He was a devoted family man, but he also worked like a maniac and suffered no fools. I didn't mind working for a tough boss, as long as he would be fair and even-keeled: a balance I would soon learn that Jason personified.

During the interview, Jason pointed me to a seat by his office desk while he sat on the couch across the room. Only much later did I realize that the seating arrangement was a part of his signature interview technique. By lulling interviewees into an informal dialogue, he later explained to me, he tried to open them up to reveal their true selves.

"Tell me about yourself," Jason began, looking directly into my eyes, "How do you describe yourself?"

"Two words—curious and tenacious," I replied, without even thinking.

I went on to tell him that I inherited an insatiably curious mind from my dad—nothing turned me on more than learning. I also inherited his legendary tenacity, which meant I would never back down in front of challenges, ever.

"I also possess common sense, and I am resourceful," I added, listing the qualities I inherited from my mother. I explained how my mother shrewdly ran a household with limited financial resources. She would make the rounds at the farmer's market and would speak to dozens of vendors to ferret out the best deals. My mom was also a great listener, someone whom other people trusted with their stories and insights. She'd listen, digest, and then dispense sage advice with all that information. In my mind, that kind of instinct and pragmatism were much harder to teach than the ability to analyze a company's income statement.

As I talked, Jason observed my body language attentively, checking out how I made eye contact, watching my hand movements, and listening for pauses between sentences. When I told him about my experience coming to the United States with nothing but one suitcase and limited English skills, but then graduating at the top of my class at Middlebury and ultimately moving to New York City with two suitcases, he laughed. I could see recognition in his eyes. Despite being in the midst of a high-stakes interview, I felt relaxed. In fact, I felt understood and appreciated.

Then Jason's next question ambushed me. "What was your biggest failure?" he asked, watching my facial expression intently.

I paused, my mind racing, and had to answer honestly: "I can't think of any."

"This business is brutally humbling," he warned me. "You are graded by the market every day. You will make plenty of mistakes, which is okay. But I will not tolerate an employee making the same mistake twice."

Jason then launched into an explanation of the world of Aurarian. I knew this meant he was interested in hiring me, or he wouldn't have wasted his time. Aurarian, a name inspired by the Latin word for "gold mine," invested in small to mid-sized public companies in the high-technology sector. More specifically, the fund focused on companies with market capitalizations of less than $2 billion with patentable intellectual property. "These small businesses are the lifeblood of the U.S.," Jason told me. "Our decision to invest in them makes a difference to their growth and success."

It sounded exciting and compelling. I pushed for more information.

"Sell-side analysts write volumes about blue chip names like Apple, IBM, and Cisco," I said. "But they typically don't waste time covering small companies since the trading fees are so limited. So how do you research them?"

"Great question," Jason responded, nodding in approval. "I use the research tools I learned over the course of my career from some of the best investors in the business and apply them to the under-the-radar stocks. I'll train you on that, one technique at a time."

The interview was the beginning of a great working relationship. A few months after I started, the COO told me that Jason went back to the trading desk after our interview and announced, "I saw fire in this woman. She is a lion—she can get anything done if she wants to."

* * *

I certainly had had my share of challenges in life by that time, from Shanghai to Middlebury to New York. I was striving to learn new skills, solve problems, and meet people. And yet the pace of my life and the challenges it brought, no matter how daunting, were nothing compared with what almost every Chinese person of my father's generation experienced during the Cultural Revolution.

CHAPTER 3

Growing Up Under Mao

China, 1949–1976

I F CHINESE PEOPLE TOOK PSYCHOLOGY SERIOUSLY, DAD AND most others of his generation would probably have been diagnosed with some sort of anxiety disorder brought on by the traumas of living through one of the most terror-filled times in Chinese history: the Cultural Revolution.

The revolution began in the summer of 1966 as an attempt by Chairman Mao Zedong to reorganize and recentralize power within the government and shore up support among the people. He piggybacked off a student movement at the time, encouraging the antibourgeois beliefs of these passionate students. Within a year, the student movement had transformed into a national mindset in which anyone with "bourgeois" or "anti-Communist" backgrounds could be punished—intellectuals, monks and nuns, doctors, experts in any field, people who grew crops for their own families—just about anyone.

The wealthy and educated classes were considered not merely passé but rather a serious threat to the livelihood of the Chinese people. Everything one needed to know, contended the cadres (the public officials charged with advancing the revolution) who formed the core of the new party, could be learned in the country-side, from laboring alongside one's brothers-in-arms.

It was to this end that Mao forced 17 million urban youth out of the cities and into the countryside during the Down to the Countryside Movement. Colleges closed, and parents bade their children farewell, in some cases forever. Some students were killed. Others, like the countless girls who were raped by cadres, committed suicide. Relevant and accurate statistics from this era are impossible to find; only stories remain, and even those are murky. But the outcome was clear: the movement paralyzed China politically and left the entire country shell-shocked.

At the age of 17, Dad was stripped of his dream of going to college and was instead "reeducated"—that is, sent into the fields to hoe turnips. My grandfather lost not only his son to the coun-tryside but also the family's rice shop during a local purge of indi-vidual ownership. Although the official slogan claimed everyone was guaranteed an "iron bowl of rice," my father's generation remembers it only as a time of unfilled stomachs. The revolution spared no one.

Worse than the shortage of material possessions was the unpre-dictability and instability of a party in which there was no rule of law. People could disappear, be imprisoned, or be killed at the whim of the "Great Leadership." Far more common and disturb-ing than commands from on high were the betrayals of friends, neighbors, and even family members to demonstrate a person's loyalty to socialist principles.

But at the same time, China was oddly free. While the high ranks of the inner party rested in Mao's palm and while the treach-erous Gang of Four—Mao's last wife and her cronies—dangled the arts and media sector like marionettes, the central government had little to do with the everyday comings and goings of the common people. It was as if the government had constructed a metaphorical birdcage to house its people, songbirds that could sing as loudly as they wished, as long as they remained within that cage.

China's Red Guard was the most raucous of all the cage-born birds. Nearly every middle and high school in the country had a group of Red Guards, a title conferred upon students by local officials and even other students themselves. With Mao's blessing, Red Guard cliques erupted across the country in August 1968, competing with one another for control of their schools. On a good day, Red Guards would write revolutionary poetry and sing red hymns. At their worst, these students burned books, turned their parents in to the authorities, and lynched teachers.

Unbelievable though it may seem, Red Guards thought of themselves as innocent followers of a utopian ideology, brethren in a world free of classism and feudalism. My father was among them—until he spent time in the countryside. The Down to the Countryside Movement awakened him and millions of other Red Guards to the harshness of peasant life.

My father's delusions about life in China finally shattered when, as a young man in his twenties, he was confronted with the brutal reality of life in the Cultural Revolution. Everyone seemed to be a victim and an aggressor at the same time.

On one occasion, he went into a government office to submit some papers and was halted at the door by a guard.

"Identification card," the guard barked without looking at him.

When my father reached into his pocket, the man became agitated and pulled a gun on him, screaming reflexively, "Hands up! Hands up or I'll shoot!"

My father came within a hair of being executed on the spot. Yet he still had to have the last word: "If the people are indeed the master of the country, why are you trying to kill me?"

* * *

Dad was a driven, outspoken, energetic young man. He thought that most of his comrades were too brainwashed to hold a meaningful conversation, and as a result, he had few friends. While his peers indulged themselves with Shanghai opera—a slightly more tolerable version of Beijing opera—simply because that was the music on the radio, Dad bought a violin and taught himself to play. In secret, he convinced a professor friend at the Shanghai Conservatory of Music to give him extra coaching. It was his passion for music that kept him mentally stimulated in the absence of the advanced education he coveted.

Dad didn't do himself any favors by refusing to blend in or conceal his intellect. One night, as he was boarding the bus after a secret music lesson, a pushy stranger bumped into his violin. The man was a cadre, and he was trying to barge his way to the front of the line. Dad told him to wait his turn. When the cadre saw that my father had a violin, he charged him with "participating in an underground concert" and had him thrown into a basement cell by the Suzhou River near the Soviet Embassy.

Terrified as Dad surely must have been after spending a night in the cellar, he was actually lucky. Others were beaten or detained for weeks at a time, all depending on the mood of the cadres.

To this day, Dad struggles while talking about that period in his life. I know only a fraction of what he went through. But I do know that his independence and intelligence frequently landed him in trouble. Unlike most of his peers, he questioned everything, striving to lay claim to his own voice outside the Maoist rhetoric. He refused to be swayed by propaganda and read extensively, trying to understand why a revolution that intended to empower the working class instead caused such massive suffering and social upheaval. He used to tell my sister and me: "Don't ever blindly believe in anything. You brain sits between your ears for a reason, so use it."

My father finally concluded that the leadership fed the masses nothing but lies and that the revolution was no more than a political power struggle at the expense of the common people. He also decided that the one-party system would never be viable—a realization that, while obvious in retrospect, most of his peers failed to accept.

"If you give all the power to one person and there are no checks and balances, what can you expect?" he used to say. "Abuse of power is human nature." This hard-bitten cynicism was passed on from father to daughter, and it has lingered with me ever since. In my line of work, this attitude has been useful; but in his time, Dad's acute intelligence was a curse rather than a boon. In an environment where enlightened thinking and idea generation were not encouraged, ignorance was bliss.

Mom fared a little better during Mao's reign. While she, too, missed out on a college education and lost her youth to the countryside, she was allowed to return home to care for her sick grandmother rather than continuing to toil in the fields.

That was how my parents spent their youth up until Mao's death in 1976. When Deng Xiaoping took over not long after, everything changed.

CHAPTER 4

Window of Opportunity

Shanghai, 1976–1989

U NTIL DENG XIAOPING, A REFORMIST WITHIN THE COMMU-
nist Party of China, officially kicked off his Reform and Opening Up program in 1978, there was not much to do in one's daily
life. The schools had been closed for a decade. City children had
been sent to work on farms. Even when they returned to the cities upon Mao's death, there was still little to do but work one's
manual labor job, bike around town, and watch street-side games
of checkers.

Everyone was poor. It was not a point of shame then, because
we were all on equal footing. A concrete, one-story house with a
tile roof was the only choice of residence for many families. Public toilets were the norm. The streets bustled with bicycles and
some buses, but never cars. Not only was there very little private
property, but the idea of privacy itself was also alien. Neighbors
burst into each other's living rooms without knocking, and idlers

gathered around checkerboards to watch the games. Local communities, carved by the tight alleyways and open-air markets, formed the fabric of city people's lives.

Fortunately, my parents possessed remarkable survival instincts. By the time I was born, they had both secured stable jobs at state-owned enterprises. Mom was an accountant at a textile company, and Dad worked as a mechanical engineer at an automobile plant. Nevertheless, our family's resources were limited, so the fact that their spending was concentrated on me and my baby sister, Jasmine, who was born four years after me, served as a practical reminder of my parents' love. My parents each earned 36 renminbi (RMB) per month (a little less than $6 given the current exchange rate). Their apartment was paid for by their employers, or the "work units," as the state-owned companies were called. It cost 1 RMB a day to bring food to the table, amounting to about 31 RMB a month—a little less than half of my parents' combined income. The rest was spent on a nanny for Jasmine and on my private math and accordion lessons, which cost about another 8 RMB per month.

* * *

There was no such thing as quiet solitude where I grew up. My father, my mother, Jasmine, and I lived in a tiny two-bedroom apartment in Jing An District, a desirable neighborhood at the center of the city. Our apartment was on the second floor of a six-story building on Tai Xing Road, a noisy commercial street filled with bicycle and bus traffic, snack carts, and fruit vendors. The clamor of people bargaining constantly floated up to our balcony. "Fresh peaches, 2 jiao!" the stall owner would bellow. "No, 1 jiao—deal or no deal!" a customer would retort, and back and forth they'd go. We shared our balcony with our neighbors, whose doors were always open. I knew everything from what they were cooking for dinner to what their underwear looked like; everyone was always meddling in each other's business. All you had to do was stick your head out the door to snag the latest gossip.

It was a working-class neighborhood, but by no means were we impoverished. If anything, by local standards, we were living a comfortable, middle-class existence, largely thanks to my mother's shrewd housekeeping skills. Our home was always immaculate. She had a way of adding a few accents of lace and fabric here and there, subtle touches that made our home seem more refined than those of our better-off friends and neighbors.

My mother is lovely, tall, and slender, with porcelain skin and high cheekbones. Thanks to her innate elegance and the keen sense of style unique to Shanghainese women, her exquisite beauty seemed almost effortless. "There are no ugly women, only lazy women," Mom used to say; whatever favorable qualities you possessed, you had to use them to their fullest advantage, no excuses. Shanghai women enjoy the reputation of being fashionable, practical, and commercially savvy, and Mom took that claim to the highest degree.

I was tall, robust, and clear-skinned, with large, catlike eyes and long dark hair, typically bunched up into two pigtails. The neighbors called me "doll." My mother dressed me simply, but always in bright colors, in bold contrast to the navy blue Maoist outfits of the time. One of the happiest memories of my childhood was the time my mother presented me with a colorful butterfly-print dress on Children's Day, June 1, right before my accordion performance at school. It was my first short dress, hemmed just above the knee. Unlike the plain school uniform of a starched white shirt, blue skirt, and the Communist Youth League's Young Pioneers red scarf we all had to wear, this dress embodied everything that life should be, all the joy and freedom I so rarely enjoyed during the course of my childhood. The skirt flared at the bottom when I twirled around, like a flower opening in sunlight. I wanted spin around the stage at my accordion recital, just to mesmerize the world with the colors.

The woman next door, whom I called "Grandma," couldn't stop staring at me in my dress. My enthusiasm sent deep wrinkles across her face, branching out from a timeless smile. "This girl has a lot of fire inside of her," she would proclaim, to no one in particular.

* * *

I lived a charmed childhood—except when it came to my education, which dominated my youth. I was the constant target of my father's relentless, militaristic discipline. Looking back, I understand why. China's population topped 1 billion in the early 1980s, and the vast majority of this number lived in poverty. In order to break out of the cycle and succeed in China, attending a first-rate high school was obligatory. Shanghai had about two-dozen "flagship" high schools that could funnel their students into good colleges—two-dozen schools for 2 million children of high school age. Clearing the next hurdle would land you in a top-tier college in China that usually resulted in securing a plum white-collar job with a stable, above-average salary after graduation. Dad truly believed brute force was the only thing powerful enough to propel his daughter through this narrow channel of opportunity.

My father was essentially competing against 4 million other anxious parents (and 8 million grandparents). Nowhere was this more evident than in class, where the teachers were the greatest facilitators of a fierce competition that began in grade school. Each student's successes and failures were paraded in front of the entire class, and laggards were intentionally embarrassed when the results of our classwork and exams were posted publicly. If that wasn't enough pressure, our parents and teachers colluded to instill a fear in each of us that failure to excel in school would lead to a lifetime of poverty, since only the top students would be rewarded with decent-paying jobs.

My dad, obviously, had begun preparing me for those games much earlier. After being savagely drilled by him at home on almost all the subjects I studied in school, I didn't learn much from the teachers themselves. For me, going to class gave me the chance to leave home—and to show off. But I also got into trouble by interrupting and sometimes even correcting the teachers without solicitation. This was, of course, utterly unacceptable. As a result, I would often have to spend the rest of the class period standing with my back pressed against the blackboard. I didn't mind it; it may have been exhausting for my legs, but it was a breeze compared with the punishments my dad delivered. I actually liked the view of the class from the teacher's perspective, and I enjoyed making faces at the other students.

Despite my tendency to interrupt, I knew even then that the teachers liked me. With my consistently perfect scores, I was the ideal student to set an example for the others. At the same time, the teachers were concerned that indulging my brazen behavior would lead to a disorderly classroom. Order was the ultimate goal at school; we had to sit with our hands clasped and backs straight at all times. We always had to repeat what the teacher said verbatim, even mimicking her tone of voice.

In addition to remembering the rigid classroom environment, my other distinct memory was the endless stream of tests. We took hundreds of them throughout the semesters, the results of which were always announced in front of the entire classroom, from the highest to lowest scores, distinguishing the "good" students from the "bad."

My favorite moments were having my name called for first place. But the worst times were when the teacher called the name of my desk neighbor, Yianjie. Her name was almost always at the end of the list. Yianjie would then duck her head and suck mournfully on a corner of her red scarf. Good students were purposefully paired with bad students in order to mentor them. Yianjie and I were the perfect desk mates in that sense. She was a sweet, bubbly girl from a big cadre-filled family, but that didn't save her from the heartache of failing tests. I figured that her father was not hard enough on her.

Memorization, not creativity, was the key to academic success. One story we all had to learn was Hans Christian Andersen's "The Little Match Girl," which is about a poverty-stricken little girl who spends New Year's Eve trying to sell matches to passersby. Though chilled to the bone, she is afraid to return home where she knows she will face a beating from her father. So she lights the few matches she has left to try to keep warm. Tragically, she eventually freezes to death during the night.

There was one thing and one thing only to remember about the story: that although it was written by a Danish children's writer in the 1800s, China's Communist Party taught it as an example of capitalism's brutality and heartlessness. Capitalist class divisions exploited poor workers like her, and the little girl's very life depended on her commercial enterprise. It was a mouthful of a lesson, but after learning it once, you never had to memorize it again. This kind of lesson eventually became intuitive—it was a safe go-to answer on all our tests.

We rarely asked any questions in class. Very occasionally someone would whisper something. If the teacher didn't like the comment or the question, he or she dismissed our interruption, saying, "It won't be on the exam. Don't get distracted by a minor point."

Opinions were not required or encouraged. Instead, there were countless formulas, stories, and poems we had to memorize for our tests—which we were allowed to then forget so we could free up brain cells for future tests.

Cheating was rampant throughout grade school and high school. Sometimes we wrote formulas on the backs of our hands, sometimes on the surface of the wood desk. I would occasionally even tuck a piece of paper into one of my sleeves. None of us ever boasted about this behavior to each other in public, let alone confessed it to our parents or teachers. I suppose we subconsciously knew that cheating was bad. But I never felt guilty about it—I was just doing what everyone else was doing. Even at that young age, we all understood that class rank mattered more than the score itself. If everyone in the classroom cheated, the ranking of the scores wouldn't change—it simply inflated everyone's scores. If bad students hoped to climb up the class rankings by cheating, good students like me wanted to make sure we stayed on top. Understanding this made it easy for all of us to continue to cheat. No one wanted to become a victim by not buying into the system.

* * *

In 1978, Deng Xiaoping announced reforms that lit the fires of economic change. He designed and implemented a program that freed agriculture from collective control, privatized state-owned enterprises, lifted price controls, and opened up the economy to foreign investments. There was so much pent-up energy that when Deng waved his red flag and said, "Charge," there was no stopping the Chinese people from surging ahead.

By the time I entered grade school, just about everyone my family knew was becoming an entrepreneur of some sort, with most leaving their state-sponsored jobs to start up businesses of their own. But quitting wasn't always necessary. State enterprise jobs weren't what one would call challenging; by midday, most people shed the pretense of productivity and sat around drinking tea, smoking cigarettes, and gossiping. It wasn't unusual for the most resourceful among state employees to manage side businesses and fill up the remainder of their afternoons and sometimes evenings with outside appointments.

My father was bored with his job and disgusted with the cadres in charge of the factory. He often complained about the way they abused power, soliciting bribes and harassing female workers. He didn't have enough to do, so he spent most of his day in a quiet corner, reading and observing. His intelligence isolated him, so it was a godsend when freelance opportunities presented themselves. At last, Dad had a chance to fulfill some of his frustrated ambition.

He started looking around for real estate deals. His sister held an important position at a Shanghai water company, in charge of water allocation to construction projects. No building could be sold without water flowing in, so my aunt would give Dad the inside track, and he would become the contractor on major sites. The more construction sites that popped up in Shanghai, the less often my father could be found at his auto plant.

Meanwhile my mother left her accounting job and launched a garment import-export business with her colleague, a well-connected man with relationships with buyers in Taiwan and Japan. My mother served as a project manager and liaison between the foreign garment companies and the textile factories just outside of Shanghai, where they subcontracted production of their clothes. She kept a close eye on the factories so they wouldn't be tempted to shortchange buyers with cheaper fabrics or shoddy workmanship.

Graft in all forms was rampant; everyone was under the influence of short-term greed. The goal was to make as much money as possible as fast as possible. "Take the profit off the table while you can," Dad was fond of saying. "Nothing is long term in this country."

These changes in circumstances didn't take the pressure off me. I was still Dad's focal point, his special project. My parents had made it in just under the wire of China's one-child policy. My sister had been their second shot at having a boy, and when that didn't come to pass, Dad resolved to channel all his energy and frustrated ambitions into me, his firstborn. I was raised to be the son he never had.

Outwardly, I am very feminine. But inside I grew tough as nails. I refused to cry, and I learned to tolerate beatings the way a boy would.

Dad also taught me how to ride a bike and play sports. Of course, his teaching methods were no less extreme when it came to the physical arena than they were in the classroom. When I was just a toddler, he taught me to swim by equipping me with an inflatable ring and tossing me into the deep end of the public swimming pool.

"You won't sink—the ring will keep you afloat," he assured me while adjusting the ring around my waist.

"Okay," I croaked.

My voice was trembling, and I could hardly breathe; I was in the throes of an anxiety attack. I urged myself to calm down, because I knew any show of fear on my face would be taken as a sign of weakness, which would inevitably enrage him.

"Put your head in the water, but keep your eyes open," he commanded.

Duly submerged, I was confronted by an unfamiliar blue world, dappled with reflected sunlight. I was just a small child at the time, and the liquid silence below the surface completely disoriented me. I was terrified. I was certain I would drown.

My reward for surviving the water torture consisted of a trip to the yogurt stall. Chinese yogurt is nothing like the delicious treats Westerners are used to—it's lumpy, sour stuff, and it made me gag. "It's good for your health," Dad said, staring at me closely to make sure I swallowed it. "What doesn't kill you makes you stronger!"

As painful as some of my earliest memories are, I recognize that, in many ways, I was lucky that my father took the trouble to teach me how to swim and play the accordion. It was unusual for most Chinese parents at the time, and it lent me a certain edge. Unlike many of my peers, especially those who did well in school,

I wasn't just an assembly-line robot, memorizing facts and spewing numbers to get through school. Dad's lessons made me well rounded and creative, as strong in the right side as in the left side of my brain.

More often than not, my father's rages were completely disproportionate to any perceived transgression. His reactions to my music practice were a case in point. One of his favorite pastimes was listening to or playing a piece of classical music; I can still remember him standing by the window in the dimming evening light, playing "The Swan," his favorite piece by Camille Saint-Saens. The devotion with which he played afforded us a rare glimpse of his softer side, and even today, the sad strains of that piece can move me to tears. Music was Dad's way of finding freedom of expression without resorting to politics. It was nourishment for his starving soul, and he wanted the same for me.

This made him determined to transform me into a miniature maestro. But because we couldn't afford a piano, I was forced to learn the accordion. The wretched instrument was about two-thirds my size and weighed more than I did. I particularly hated the way the bellows would pinch the flesh on my thighs if I practiced sitting. But I had no choice. Dad engaged the services of one of the best instructors in the city for me, and she often came so early I'd wake to her sitting by my bed in the morning, waiting for me to get up so we could begin.

Music was so important in our household that on weekends my mother would prepare a sumptuous lunch for my instructor, an honored guest in our home. I enjoyed the feast but thoroughly dreaded what came after. Dad would tell us what piece he wanted to hear, and if I didn't measure up to his standards by the end of the day, I would receive yet another walloping. The performance could have been note-perfect, but it wouldn't have mattered. His reaction depended entirely on his moods.

* * *

However, as the economy took off, Dad had more to do with his time than worry about whether or not I'd pressed the wrong chord on his favorite sonata. And as I got older, I no longer needed him to tell me what I had done wrong. I had been admitted to a first-rate high school, and my ambition was all my own. Dad didn't have to discipline me—I was already hardest on myself.

CHAPTER 5

Dreaming of
a New Land

Shanghai, 1992

As the music began to swell and the credits rolled across the screen, I squirmed in my seat.

"Sit *still*, Li Junheng!" my father snapped. It was one of his cherished moments of cultural edification, and I was threatening to ruin it with my childishness. *Gone with the Wind* was one of the first foreign films to become popular in China after the Reform and Opening Up policy began in 1978, and my father, American history fanatic that he was, had been looking forward to seeing it for months. He had finally located a showing one Saturday on a college campus in Shanghai. All I knew about it was that the movie was four hours long. We were cramped in a small, dark room with about 50 other people, and I couldn't wait to be out in the sunshine again.

Then the film started, and I forgot where I was.

Vivien Leigh as Scarlett O'Hara took my breath away: with large jade-green eyes set in her pale heart-shaped face, her wavy raven hair, and a slender frame, she was both exotic and perfect in my eyes. She pulled me into a world foreign to my own, one of whirling hoopskirts and galloping horses, high-class culture and romantic trysts. More than anything else, she was too smart and proud to be subservient to anyone. Even in a system in which women did not have much freedom, she played the system to find her own way.

I had never seen a female character like her before: brave, unconquerable, and free. Scarlett's looks drew admirers in, but her brain and resilience were really her greatest assets. As she whirled around the dance hall in black mourning clothes, she and Rhett laughing at her "ruined" reputation, I smiled along with them. I had never seen anyone so free-spirited, liberated, and indifferent to how others viewed her. It was wildly different from the traditional Chinese tragedies and propaganda films I was accustomed to.

What came next was a scene that I could never forget. At the moment Scarlett faced her greatest adversity, she remained determined to fight and win, silhouetted against the setting sun:

"As God is my witness, they're not going to lick me. I'm going to live through this and when it's all over, I'll never be hungry again. No, nor any of my folk. If I have to lie, steal, cheat or kill. As God is my witness, I'll never be hungry again."

If my father felt me fidget again, it was not out of impatience; I was getting chills. The movie had been dubbed in Chinese and censored in certain parts, the sound was warped, and the celluloid was scratched, but it had still spun a spell on me. Scarlett awakened something inside me that lay dormant, yet to be explored. I wanted to be a fighter and winner. But first and foremost I desired freedom and possibilities. I did not know a lot about the world then, but I felt the calling of America.

Dad was unusually silent on the walk home. We walked for nearly half an hour before he realized that he almost missed a chance to drive another lesson into my head.

He said: "America is a special place. Opportunities exist in all circumstances, whether you are falling down or ascending. You will make it there as long as you work hard and be smart. It is different in China—we might be making more money now, but our psyche will always be burdened by too long and devastating a history."

I did not say anything, but I felt my father was right. Having just watched my first American film, I could not help but compare America with China. Yes, my future would have to be made in the United States.

The very next day I bought an original version of the book in English. With the help of both my father and a Chinese-English dictionary, I read *Gone with the Wind* from cover to cover at least five times that month, soaking up every word into the fiber of my being.

* * *

Maybe I also identified with Scarlett O'Hara because the world around me was changing, just as hers had after the war—and fast. In Shanghai, where I lived, the reform movement championed by Deng was beginning to take shape. Small family-run eateries and convenience stores started to pop up everywhere, as the government gave the go-ahead to private business.

The shift of labor from the farmlands to the factories that began in the 1980s accelerated into the 1990s. Parents parted from their children, leaving them in the care of their grandparents back on the farm, in order to make a better living in manufacturing towns. These migrant workers flooded the cities at an unprecedented rate, chugging along to the pace of "progress." That was the buzzword of the 1990s. Neighborhoods were razed and replaced with hulking malls; new factories rose up that employed entire towns but devastated the countryside and ruined rivers, all for the sake of progress.

Immigrants from the western and central provinces would stand on the street peddling hand-pulled noodles, whirling and pulling the dough until it was thin enough to be boiled and consumed. That was the goal of this era: consuming. Getting other people to consume what you had to sell. Grandmothers turned their living rooms into tailoring shops. Villagers poured into the city, offering homemade snacks for sale on every street corner. People sold cigarettes out of hastily constructed lean-tos and cooked noodles for strangers in their communal courtyards. Hundreds of identical all-purpose-goods stores sprang up, all supplied by the same distant producer of soaps, slippers, and sponges.

By the early 1980s, the authorities instituted a dual-track system for most goods produced at state-designated prices. Some goods were still sold under the quota system, but all surplus production could be sold on the market at a different price. For the government, this was the only way to shift the economy gradually toward market-determined prices. But it also created alluring opportunities for price arbitrage. Anything people could get their hands on—shoes, color television sets, rice cookers, all of which were novel at the time—could be resold on the gray market to make a quick buck.

In the city, privatization took place first in manufacturing, led by light industries such as textiles, apparel, shoes, home appliances, and consumer electronics. Then came housing reform. Before the mid-1980s, urban housing was almost all public housing assigned by the work units. These vast bureaucracies allocated apartments according to the worker's length of service, the worker's position, and the number of people in his or her family. But the flood of workers into the cities created an acute shortage of urban housing. In Shanghai, the average family was crammed together in an apartment about the size of an American two-car garage.

As private-sector businesses took off, state-owned enterprises saw their profits decline as they faced competition for the first time. The deregulation of prices, loose lending, and fast economic growth combined to push up the price of goods during the 1990s, and inflation reached a heady 27 percent in the middle of the decade. The government and work units decided that they could no longer subsidize housing for their employees. Around the middle of the decade, Beijing started to privatize the housing market by drastically lowering the purchasing prices of houses to encourage people to buy the units they lived in.

That was the cue my family needed to transform ourselves into capitalistic entrepreneurs adept at spotting the latest opportunities. We were not alone. The neighborhood gossip turned away from the checkerboards and instead toward making money.

This newfound energy permeated not just business, but all sectors. With consumerism came a proliferation not just of soaps and snack foods but also of Chinese hopes and dreams. The arts had bloomed soon after the death of Mao in 1976, and while Deng reinstated a fair amount of media control by 1980, the door to the birdcage was now ajar. New ideas flooded the country in the form of forbidden books, films, and images, invigorating the Chinese public—just as Scarlett O'Hara galvanized my dreams. Young people traded dog-eared paperbacks of "scar" literature, which expressed regret over the wrongs of the Cultural Revolution. And along the fringes of society, avant-garde poetry and painting found fans in the young and the middle-aged alike, for many of the middle-aged felt they had been robbed of their youth.

People were busy trying to make life better—to put the 1970s behind them.

* * *

For most of the 1980s, they succeeded. But this energy ultimately propelled the Chinese people right into Tiananmen Square on June 4, 1989. The protest was a call for democratization, but the event itself was about much more than that. It was the ultimate culmination of a decade of Reform and Opening Up, as people made the final push for their political freedom.

We learned from our relatives and friends who were in Beijing at that time that protestors carried banners that quoted new-age Chinese poets' expressions of personal dignity, individuality, and martyrdom. Just as the Germans had knocked down the Berlin Wall, the Chinese wanted to break out of their birdcage.

The world watched as tanks rolled into Tiananmen, putting an end to the fervor of the 1980s. But most Chinese didn't know what was happening, as the national media toned down their reporting of the "6.4 Incident," as the Tiananmen episode was called. No one knew exactly how many people were killed, injured, or missing. Even the Voice of America (VOA) radio program, the official broadcasting service of the U.S. government, which my father tuned into in an effort to get the real story, was so full of static that it wasn't much help.

The leaders of the Tiananmen protest—mostly intellectuals such as university teachers, students, artists, and political commentators—were imprisoned and exiled. Once again, Chinese people were taught a hard lesson in the dangers of having a "politically incorrect" opinion. "Do not challenge authority," the government was telling us. Creativity was definitely not appreciated.

I was in high school in Shanghai at that time. I knew people were gathering on the street to demonstrate, but I was not aware of any violence. I didn't realize how serious the incident was until Zhu Rongji, the mayor of Shanghai and a political liberal, held a surprise press conference broadcast on TV. His message was something like, "You can demonstrate, but make sure you go home by 5 p.m."

At the very end of his speech, he expressed sympathy for the students and demonstrators who were injured. As he was wrapping up, he choked, and we saw tears in his eyes. It was only then that we began to realize that the loss of life in Tiananmen Square was much greater than we had guessed.

Just like that, the dreams, aspirations, and artistic blossoming of the 1980s were extinguished. The crackdown made it clear that business would now be the only activity in which Chinese people could safely invest their energies. Under this unspoken "Grand Bargain," the Communist Party would continue Deng's economic liberalization. But political reform of any kind would be squelched instantly. The message was clear: as long as the Chinese people concentrated on getting rich instead of building a fair and transparent society, then they and their children would enjoy the ever-ripening fruits of this labor.

The creators of the Grand Bargain could not have foreseen that by shifting their nation's focus to solely making profits, they would create a culture bent on cutting corners. The Chinese learned to pursue short-term gain relentlessly at the expense of long-term sustainability and innovation, and their reward was a system rife with unfair and inferior commercial practices.

* * *

It isn't that the Chinese are born without creativity—far from it. The Chinese invented gunpowder, the compass, papermaking, and printing, among many other things. But under Communism, that creative energy was misspent finding ways to game rather than improve the system.

Consider a case involving a family friend of ours named Yang, who was a party member. An ambitious man, Yang never felt he made enough money from his job at a state-owned company. So he asked for sick leave. He used the time to launch a side career, scalping tickets to the concerts of popular singers from Hong Kong and Taiwan who had begun to tour the mainland in the early 1990s.

Scalping was a popular part-time job for many people at the time. People scalped everything from food stamps to consumer electronics—and made more money in an evening or weekend than their full-time jobs paid monthly.

Scalpers would buy up and hoard all the available tickets for a concert at the prices preset by the concert company. One or two hours before the concert, they all would show up at the gates and peddle the tickets—with big markups, of course. Scalpers had no inventory risks, since the ticket office colluded with them and would take back any unsold tickets. As long as the ticket office's number of sold tickets matched the money it had collected, the higher-ups never noticed the discrepancy, and everyone made a profit.

Scalpers were just one of the many suspect businesses that sprang up in a market where prices were set by the government. A command-based economy like China's created abundant arbitrage opportunities for gutsy people who weren't afraid to enrich themselves by screwing others over.

Getting rich was glorious, in Deng's words, but merely spotting good opportunities would not do it: you also needed to constantly be on the lookout to avoid being taken advantage of. For Dad, that meant keeping an eye on his migrant construction workers to make sure they weren't stealing the good tiles or mixing dirt into the cement. For Mom, that meant driving miles to visit garment factories to make sure the subcontractors weren't cutting corners with cheap textiles or shoddy workmanship.

* * *

One day, Mom came home from a factory that was two hours away from Shanghai, exhausted and frustrated. "Unbelievable!" she exclaimed. "They did it again. The managers told me that they spent 10,000 renminibi on new textile material. But there is no material. I asked around and found out the guys have been living it up in karaoke bars every night!"

A few weeks later, she had to close down the factory. When she went there to collect the valuables, there was nothing left—the managers had taken even the sewing machines with them.

Sketchy business practices happened all around us. For example, restaurants and other small businesses rarely printed the receipts that the government used to track sales taxes. Instead, they used only handwritten slips of paper. They didn't want to leave a paper trail that the government could use to punish them for skimping on their taxes. If a customer asked for a receipt, the restaurant would offer a free drink or even a discount on the meal instead.

Indeed, the practice of having multiple accounting books became commonsense strategy for businesses in China. One was the real book for internal use, one was for tax purposes, and one was for a business owner's wife to see. (There might have been one more set of books for the mistress as well.)

My parents taught me a much more valuable and practical lesson than any business school class ever could: in China, numbers don't mean very much. My parents never believed anything unless they had seen it with their own eyes—and, eventually, neither did I. Seeing was believing, and that meant that every penny we earned was a result of hard work and extra caution.

* * *

But all the corner-cutting and shady business practices were becoming downright dangerous—a fact that my family learned firsthand due to the death of my uncle.

"Little Uncle," as he was called, was my maternal grandmother's youngest child and her only son. He was a sales manager at Shanghai No 2 Toy Company. Smart and charismatic, he was one of the company's top sales people. I was Little Uncle's favorite niece, and he always brought me new toys when he visited on the weekends. Little Uncle's job frequently took him to distant, unheard-of towns to do business, and he was away most of the time. And as business picked up around 1994, his trips became more and more frequent.

But as Little Uncle continued to sell, his customers began to rack up debts to him. On one trip to a very rural area, his client took him out to dinner. They had a feast and drank a lot of rice wine (strangely enough, the company had enough money to wine and dine its supplier but not to pay its debts). Almost all business deals in China involve plenty of drinking and cigarette smoking, and so, as a good businessperson, Little Uncle was a strong drinker.

Apparently even strong drinkers have their limits. He went into a coma that same night and died in the village hospital a few days later. We didn't even have time to fly him back to Shanghai to get him help in a real hospital. The event was so sudden and unexpected that our family could only think of rescuing his body from the remote town. No one—not even my Dad—had a minute of rational thought to request an investigation or autopsy. It was not until a few days after his death that we all started to reflect on how this tragedy could have been avoided.

Little Uncle's manager showed up at my grandmother's home with a box of fruits and an envelope of cash. He promised my heartbroken grandmother that he would take care of her just as if she were his own mother. He left, and we never heard from him again.

This was the first loss that I experienced in my life. I remember the funeral, where I was dressed in black from head to toe and wailed for hours. We kept my grandmother away from the funeral; she was so disconsolate that we were terrified she might take her own life. There is nothing more painful than a parent burying a child—especially in China, where it is said that if you lose your only son, you have nothing else to live for.

Little Uncle's death left us feeling powerless, not unlike the way most Chinese people felt during the Cultural Revolution. Had Little Uncle been poisoned by someone who could not pay his debts? Or with corner-cutting becoming so rampant in China, perhaps the alcohol he drank was fake or tainted and his death really was an accident. Both scenarios should have warranted an investigation. But China's legal system played second fiddle to the progress of the economy; we had no legal recourse to pursue. Pressing charges would mean implicating someone—someone in a province that we didn't reside in.

Instead, the case got lost in China's bureaucratic black hole, somewhere between "out-of-province affairs" and "food and health inspection." Government workers avoided taking responsibility for our case and lawyers were so rare that we didn't stand a chance of finding someone to help us press charges. We were completely without options. Once again, an individual's life proved to be worth very little in the grand scheme of China's economic reform.

* * *

It was around this time that I first became intrigued by financial markets. The Shanghai Stock Exchange reopened in 1990 after having shuttered its doors for 41 years. The early days of the exchange attracted international media attention, and I watched the news segments on CCTV, the state-run TV channel, with fascination. The images of red-vested men hustling and bustling across the stock exchange floor appealed to me even before I knew exactly what they were doing. They looked sophisticated, fielding multiple phone calls at the same time and reading symbols and numbers off those big computer screens with a fluency I admired.

Compared with the staid, inefficient, and corrupt world of state-owned enterprises where my parents had toiled, capitalism in action was invigorating. As I watched the stock runners and traders on TV, Dad would mutter under his breath about how much money those "youngsters" made. I was drawn to the idea of a glamorous money business, and it wasn't just the money that fascinated me: it was also how busy and important the job seemed to be.

45

Whatever they did, I wanted in.

* * *

Despite the challenges and the risks, my parents' business savvy and can-do attitudes eventually helped them amass a small fortune. Today, they have three apartments in Shanghai, with a market value of a few million U.S. dollars—a level of prosperity that was unthinkable when I was a teenager. Back then, none of us could have imagined the economic behemoth China would become. Instead, we were focused on making our immediate circumstances more comfortable. One by one, my parents brought home the "big three" appliances—a washing machine, TV, and refrigerator. Once considered unaffordable luxuries, these household appliances had become the new must-haves.

We were immensely proud of our new imported household appliances, and we were happy to let the neighbors come over to admire our Japanese-made washing machine. Having a fridge allowed Mom to save time by making fewer trips to the farmer's market, and it saved me from having to make my regular trip to the ice cream store around the corner. For the most part, I was not allowed to watch TV except for a few American shows for which my dad had a soft spot, such as *Growing Pains*, *Falcon Crest*, *Hunter*, and *Superman*. He was always happy to let me familiarize myself with American culture through movies and television.

For my father, though, the family's rapidly rising living standard did not satiate his intellectual curiosity and need for stimulation. In fact, his most prized material possession was his compact radio. Every night, Dad indulged himself with news from America. As China transformed economically, one thing in particular did not change: the opaque media. *People's Daily* was still full of the great deeds of the Communist Party and the suffering of the rest of the developing world—the leadership's transparent way of making us feel better about our own struggles.

The Chinese have a phrase to describe being walled off from the outside: "like a frog in a well." Most people read *People's Daily* and did not look beyond the walls of China's well. My dad was different.

Through Voice of America, which began broadcasting news from the United States in 1942, Dad's cherished radio became the window through which he glimpsed the rest of the world. Whenever a politically sensitive topic came up on a Chinese radio show, we knew it would usually be interrupted or even completely blocked by the state. Any discussion of human rights, for example, meant almost instant static on the radio or TV. But with the VOA, there was a chance to get the real story (or at least part of it). So Dad decided to learn English, with the VOA as his teacher.

It was something Dad and I did together, and he did not have to force me on this one. It also became a useful tool for me to improve my listening comprehension, as I was preparing for the English exams that would give me access to my American dream.

One event that I followed intently on VOA was the 1992 campaign when Bill Clinton won the presidency. Besides the fact that I thought Bill Clinton was incredibly articulate and rather handsome, the rise of the Clintons from a humble background to the highest rank in American and global politics seemed to embody the quintessential American spirit. In my impressionable mind, America was a land with abundant opportunities for those who are smart, driven, and willing to work hard.

All this exposure to American culture only served to fuel my determination to get there by any means necessary. I was already well on my way. My father's methods were paying off, and by the time I made it into a top high school, he did not need to beat me into academic stardom. In fact, his tiger parenting eased up considerably as his business took off, in part because he had less time to focus on me. He didn't have to; he had already molded me into his perfect tiger daughter. Taking his lessons to heart, I learned not only to succeed but also to imagine what might come next for me.

Nothing seemed impossible for me. I made it into one of the top colleges, Shanghai International Studies University (SISU), which has a strong English language program. Because SISU funneled so many of its students into Western universities each year, I viewed the college primarily as my necessary stepping-stone to get to America. I spent most of my time studying for the test that would get me a full scholarship to a school in the United States: the TOEFL (Test of English as a Foreign Language) examination.

Although the economy was rapidly improving and people were visibly happier now that they had opportunities to acquire material possessions, many university students were eager to attend American colleges. American schools had the reputation of awarding generous financial aid to high-caliber applicants from around the world, which was important because a top American liberal arts college cost around $20,000 to $25,000 in 1996 when I applied, an astronomical figure to most Chinese middle-class families.

In the summer of 1994, after my freshman year, I signed up for an evening English prep course. I took a sample test before the class started; I got 480, which ranked me in the twenty-first percentile. At the end of class on the first night, I cornered the teacher.

"What is the minimum score I need to get a full scholarship from a good American college?" I asked.

"You'd need to get 600 out of 677," the teacher said, not looking up as he shoved papers into his bag.

"I am at 480 now. What are my odds of getting up to 600 in three months?" I persisted.

"Three months!" He looked up.

"I need to score above 600 in *three months*—what do I have to do?"

"Where there is a will, there is a way. Good luck, SISU lady."

The only way to reach my goal was to lock myself up and do nothing but study English. That night, I went back home and packed up everything I needed to withdraw from the world for two months. By then, my parents had bought an apartment in one of Shanghai's up-and-coming neighborhoods, which was anything but peaceful and quiet.

Shanghai real estate was booming, and with it came such relentless construction noise that it was impossible to study. Besides hammers, drills, and pile drivers, workers used giant hydraulic hammers to lay the building foundations that shook the ground beneath us. Migrant workers, with or without work permits or resident cards, toiled away day and night. Since Shanghai was so hot, they would sometimes sleep in tents during the day and then work in their underwear during the nights, drilling the whole neighborhood into madness. I still wonder whether my deep aversion to noise came from living in Shanghai during that turbulent time.

I returned to the SISU campus, empty for the summer, and locked myself in my dorm room. It was an austere room made of concrete, with no rugs or wallpaper; we slept eight to a room in bunk beds. Since I was the only student there that summer, I had a bit more space than I was used to and a desk all to myself. I would sit on that metal chair all day in spite of any discomfort, venturing out only for a few scraps of food when I was growing faint from hunger.

The campus was about an hour and a half from downtown Shanghai. Out in the suburbs, it was eerily quiet. Not only were the drills and jackhammers a distant memory, but even the lively murmur of students was absent. The cafeteria opened only once a day and served a handful of insipid and unappetizing dishes that would have been appropriate for a prisoner. For two months, I lived on cabbage and watermelon.

Studying or not, I probably would have spent the day in my dank concrete dorm room anyway. The summer heat hung heavily from a sky that was increasingly gray and polluted by industrial activity. I took a cold shower every evening—we didn't have hot water—and as soon as I put my clothes back on, I was sweating again. The only relief from the heat and my studies came at dawn, when I woke up naturally. The air was fresh at that hour, and campus felt peaceful. I never allowed myself to get too comfortable for more than a few minutes, but the cool stillness of dawn gave me one of the very few moments of pure joy I felt during the day.

Every morning, I took two 3-hour TOEFL sample tests. I would then grade myself, analyze my errors over and over, circle every English word I didn't recognize or understand, look them up in a newly bought dictionary, and hand-copy the definition next to the word. I marked each word I looked up in the dictionary, and by July the dictionary bled with black ink.

In the afternoons, I read English novels. My reading speed needed a big kick if I ever wanted to finish the test on time. So I trained myself to read fast, focusing on the first and last sentences of each paragraph and then skimming the middle to look for key words. I knew many people read novels for pleasure, but my method was mechanical, my goals too specific for it to be pleasurable, with the exception of *Gone with the Wind*. Reading that book was a treat to myself, and sneaking in a chapter here and there reminded me why I was so willing to suffer.

After my reading session, it was time for evening class. It took an hour and a half by bike to get back to the inner city, so I had to leave around 4:30, when the sun was at its worst. There were almost no cars on the streets then, only a sea of bikes in an endless wave of heat. I swerved through masses of gray and blue uniforms, racing through the areas where the sun beat down and slowing in the shady stretches. By the time I got to the classroom, my clothes were stained with sweat, but I wasn't embarrassed. I was even a little proud that my dedication was visible in this basic, bodily way.

I grabbed a seat near the front of the room and waited to stop sweating. It was a huge auditorium—so big that TV screens hung in the middle of the room to broadcast the class to students in the back and corners. Seating was first-come, first-served, and those who came late would end up sitting on the floor or windowsills. My teacher was one of the center's most popular instructors. Because his students typically scored well on the TOEFL classes he taught, hundreds of eager students had signed up to take his class.

At the time, attending class was the closest thing I had to socializing. After it ended, it was back to the dorm for more vocabulary review.

* * *

After a few weeks of this grueling schedule, Dad came by the evening school to check up on me. When he first saw me, his eyes grew wide with alarm.

"Junh, what's happened to you? You look sick and starved!"

There was no mirror in our dorm, so I had no idea what I looked like to others, though I had noticed my clothes becoming looser. In fact, I was red as a tomato from sunburn and emaciated from my watermelon diet. I had always been thin, so losing 11 pounds made me look skeletal. By then my TOEFL score hovered around 630, so I didn't mind.

I don't think Dad could quite believe the intense and focused monster he'd created. From then on, my father or mother would stop by twice a week to deliver a dinner box stuffed with something nutritious, like chicken or smoked fish. The delicious food seemed to shake me out of my malaise. After a few minutes of ravenous eating, I would sit and savor what had just happened, staring at the empty tin bucket. I then biked all the way back to my dorm and collapsed onto my bed by midnight.

I was running on fumes. To make my dream happen, I had to work that hard. For Chinese people, logic and math are easy topics, but English is tricky. Since I never had the opportunity to practice English in real conversation, my listening comprehension was poor, and I found slang to be baffling.

The only other human being I had contact with that summer outside of class was Catherine, a brilliant and equally driven girl. By pure coincidence, she'd planned to take the test at the same time as I was. While it was comforting to realize that I wasn't the only one slaving the summer away, in my mind I'd turned her into a "frenemy," measuring myself each day by her progress. I always made a point of getting up earlier and going to bed later than she did.

Catherine brought out the super-competitiveness in me. I was already aware of this cutthroat tendency of mine, but this experience with my unwitting rival reinforced it. In many ways, she served as a more effective propeller than my father did.

I vowed to nail the TOEFL, and I did. After receiving 640 on my TOEFL in the spring of 1995, I applied to a dozen liberal arts colleges in New England. I was determined to attend this type of school, seeing it as a place where I was likely to be the only Chinese student on campus. It was my intent to spend four years studying hard and absorbing everything I could about the United States and its culture.

Just a few months after I submitted the results of my TOEFL test, Middlebury College in Vermont granted me early admission— plus an annual renewable $23,000 financial aid package. My rival Catherine got a similar package from Wellesley.

The college admission came like a sigh of relief. Everything in my life had prepared me for this admission. Oddly, the America I knew was still a distant stranger, a land I had become obsessed with through movies and the VOA.

But far from being scared to leave, I thought that the more different my new home was from where I grew up, the better.

CHAPTER 6

An American Education

Vermont, 1996

MAKING THE 20-HOUR JOURNEY FROM SHANGHAI TO BURL-ington, Vermont, may have been the most important event in my life, but my grand arrival to the United States was greeted with silence. It was the middle of the night when I landed, and the airport was nearly empty.

The cultural differences I encountered at Middlebury College presented far greater challenges for me than learning a new language and living a different campus lifestyle. The hardest changes lay in the social and ethical rules that governed the campus. At Middlebury, there were different expectations of how to behave in and contribute to the classroom and community.

Everything ideological that my Chinese educators had taught me about America—that it was a depraved society of selfish capitalists—was simply false. My American education gave me a chance to do something I had never done before: to discover my personal principles and to choose a career path. For the first time, I was allowed and encouraged to make decisions about my own life.

Looking back on my two disparate experiences in education, it is clear how the United States and China got where they are today. Competition was fierce in Chinese schools, but we were spoon-fed information. Our teachers wanted us to do well so that they looked good, and they ensured this by holding our hands through endless testing. At college in America, the professors wanted me to do well, but at the same time, they cared about me as an individual. The long comments they took the time to write on papers, tests, and assignments are a testimony to that. My American professors also pushed me outside my comfort zone by teaching me to consider the *how* and not just the *what*. For someone like me who had to work her way out of an authoritarian system with hundreds of millions of competitors, these changes were not just opportunities; they were privileges. Without that push, I could not be the analytical thinker that I am today.

* * *

When I applied to Middlebury, I intended to inundate myself with every American experience I could. I certainly got that right: I could not have ended up in a place more different from Shanghai than Middlebury, Vermont, which forced me to make nearly constant adjustments.

Growing up in Shanghai, I hadn't noticed that I was living my entire life surrounded by concrete and steel—there was nothing to compare it with since I almost never traveled outside the city. At Middlebury, I was shocked when the green mountains on all sides of the campus suddenly blazed red in autumn and then faded away with the winter. I took the first hike of my life in those mountains, which was also the first time I had ever walked any considerable length on unpaved ground.

I immediately recognized that Americans behave differently from the way Chinese people do. I found them strangely intimidating because they smiled a lot and looked you directly in the eye—something that rarely happened back in China.

My fellow students were also apparently experts at lounging. I couldn't help but stare every time I saw this phenomenon, and it was everywhere: students were lying on the grass, sprawled out in student lounges, milling about in the hallways, and sitting in the dining halls after meals. Even though they had books open in front of them, they were often talking to their friends.

It was frustrating to watch this form of "studying" and still not be able to outperform them in class discussions. The American students spoke in class with such ease. While I certainly did well on my TOEFL, I could not really speak English confidently, so I usually kept my mouth shut. But they would talk for more than a minute at a time, sometimes several minutes, completely unrehearsed. I spent most of the first semester watching them as if I were watching a farce: they would interrupt and challenge the teacher, and the teacher would reward them with a smile and encouragement. This show was almost opposite from what I had experienced in China, where the teachers were the masters who ruled the classroom.

Later, an American classmate shared with me his insights: we pay high prices for a college education in the United States, he said, making us customers of top-tier education. The students were, in a sense, entitled to be the masters of the classroom.

* * *

During the first week of my freshman year, I was shuffled from one orientation event to another, clutching a folder with my name on it that contained an events schedule inside.

One of the event listings said: "Saturday, 3:30 p.m., Mead Chapel: Honor Code Ceremony." I imagined this was yet another welcome event. I was in no position to deviate from the schedule, especially since this event was starred as *MANDATORY*—a word I had learned in my TOEFL class.

The honor code turned out to be one of the oddest things I had to learn about American education. It was a contract that all students were required to line up and sign. It was essentially a promise that we would not cheat on any assignments. Later I was told it was called a pledge. The pledge also applied to witnessing such behavior; failure to report a cheater could result in one's own expulsion or suspension along with the culprit. Big deal, I thought. Of course we're not supposed to cheat. But how was this piece of paper going to stop anyone?

In time, I learned the enormity of this contract. For example, a few Chinese upperclassmen warned me that so-and-so had been kicked out of school for something called "plagiarism."

This plagiarism was a very tricky thing to wrap my head around. In China, we learned by copying down what the teacher said. To study, we copied from the book, over and over again, until we had it memorized precisely. Sometimes, my teachers in high school would green-light us to copy out of the book on tests, because even the teachers knew that no normal kid had the capacity to memorize the large amount of information the test required.

Even having the book was still a challenge, because we were under time pressure and had to know exactly where everything was. But this collective behavior of copying from books didn't change the ranking of grades: the students who studied the most still did the best. What others called cheating, we just considered a means to an end. Simply put, copying from the book was never considered wrong—if anything, it was the only way to be right.

At Middlebury, on the other hand, tests were not proctored. It was shocking to learn that the professors were not even allowed to be with us. Sometimes we took tests home with us. At the top of each test and paper, we wrote, "I have neither given nor received unauthorized aid in the completion of this assignment" and then signed our names. This was all strange to me, to say the least. The school was so strict on cheating and yet took no measures to police it—something I came to learn firsthand.

One semester I enrolled in a large mathematics seminar—the kind held in an auditorium where the professor wouldn't notice if you didn't show up for a month. But I attended every class and couldn't imagine why anyone would bother skipping.

Apparently Nikolai, one of my fellow students, had a different opinion. Nikolai was also an international student, like most of the other students in the math seminar I was taking. In fact, the majority of the math and economics classes were made up of international students. Nikolai was a big blond Russian, tall as well as broad. He was always trailed by a few smaller-looking guys. His wavy blond hair swung across his brow, and his chin pointed up when he walked, likely to ensure that he was always looking down at everyone else.

I probably would not have even noticed him except that he took several bathroom breaks during the first test. While it was obvious he was cheating, I was mostly mad at him for not being more discreet about it. Didn't he know we were required to report cheating? I just put my head down and hoped that someone else would do it. I focused on my test.

On the second test, he did it again. This time, he brought his textbook to the bathroom with him! Of course, there was no teacher in the room to notice him, but you could tell from all the uncomfortable shifting noises around the room that other people had noticed what was going on. I decided to bite the bullet. I finished my test quickly and went to the professor's office to hand it in.

"All set?" he smiled as I walked in. I always thought that was a weird English phrase. "Yep," I smiled back, nervously. "Also, I . . . I think someone might be cheating." He took off his glasses and looked very serious. I couldn't back out now. "How do you know?" he asked. "It was Nikolai," I told him. "He keeps leaving the room to go to the bathroom. I saw him take his textbook with him. It's just really obvious."

He put his glasses back on. "Yes, I did notice he was doing remarkably well for not having attended most classes . . . you do realize that this is a very serious offense and that you will need to testify in front of the academic committee?"

I had not thought that far ahead, but I said the default American word *okay*.

In the dining hall a few days later, I felt someone standing over my shoulder as I filled up at the coffee machine. It was Nikolai.

"Grades not good enough?" he sneered. "You afraid of me outdoing you?" I was in fact terrified of him—mostly physically. I put my head down and scuttled out of the dining hall.

Every time I walked past his table for the next few weeks, he made an obnoxious snorting noise. His cronies laughed and threw me arrogant glances.

At the committee hearing, I repeated what I had said in the professor's office—most of it at least. "So you saw him leave several times during the test?" a woman behind the desk drilled me. "Did you ever witness him cheat?"

"No," I replied as I looked down. "I saw him leave several times during the test—during both tests—but I'm not positive that he cheated. I just saw him leave and come back."

After the hearing, my professor approached me. He was very disappointed that I had not shared the bit about Nikolai taking the textbook with him. "I was too scared!" I quaked. "What if he came after me?"

"Junh, it is breaking school code to omit this information," he explained. "We all have the responsibility to report unlawful actions. Now that I know you left something out, this puts me in an awkward position too."

"Am I in trouble?"

He sighed. "No, this case is over. Nikolai will get red-flagged but not suspended. Just please think about the fact that you assisted him in breaking the honor code. All right?"

As if Nikolai and his gang's dining hall jeers were not bad enough, I was racked with guilt for months to come. I've heard that Asian societies are shame based and Western (Christian) societies are guilt based. I really cannot say how true this philosophy is, but I do know that this was the first time in my life I had ever felt so consumed by my own wrongdoing. It was strange how everything before that moment of guilt seemed like an innocent time in my life.

It was only over time that I realized that the goal of the honor code was to establish a system of trust—or create a social norm—in which all of us would make conscious decisions about right and wrong. Since we were not monitored during the exams, the onus of upholding honest behavior fell completely on the individual. We were expected to know what was right and to help carry it out.

That's why, in comparison with the Chinese system, Middlebury's honor code was much cleverer: it relied on self-regulation. In that sense, the honor code was one of the very first examples of how effective freedom could be. In China, our teachers had vaguely informed us not to cheat, then didn't really care what we did. Since the teacher—the authority—didn't care, naturally neither did we. At Middlebury, however, I was the one responsible for my own moral compass.

It might be hard to understand how difficult it was for someone not used to making choices to suddenly have to make a very important decision like this. But dealing with this challenge played a major role in my personal development. This dawning of my own moral awareness was a significant step in my life—something I may never have realized if I had remained in an authoritarian society.

To Live

One Friday night, I was in the library photocopying some class materials when I noticed a poster on the bulletin board that was printed with Chinese characters. A beautiful woman with high cheekbones was looking stoically outward. Printed above her in both English and Chinese was the phrase "To Live."

At the bottom, it read: "Nominated for a Golden Globe, this astounding tale has been banned in the PRC for exposing the tragic side of Mao's China." The movie was produced by Zhang Yimou and starred Gong Li, the most controversial cinema duo in China at the time. The former was China's top director, the latter China's most glamorous actress, and they were also rumored to have had an affair. I rarely took nights off from the library, but this piqued my interest enough to make an exception. I packed up my books and headed to the school's auditorium, which was very close to the library.

As the movie began, I was instantly drawn into the turbulent world of mid-twentieth-century China. The first scenes depicted the fall of the Nationalists to Communist forces, and I watched the initial joy with which the newly "liberated" China turned hopeful eyes onto Mao and the beginning of his Great Leap Forward. I witnessed the members of a happy family, reinvigorated by the socialist promise, gladly contribute their efforts to the new political campaigns. I then wept as one tragedy after another unfolded around them—as their son died at the careless hands of a party cadre and their daughter because there were no doctors to tend to her during childbirth as the doctors had all been imprisoned as "intellectual criminals." It was a story of how an innocent family was ultimately powerless in a sociopolitical system. The parents were then left with no children of their own; only their son-in-law and his new baby remained. After the movie ended, my head was heavy from weeping for three hours in the dark. The movie's narrative was so devoid of emotion that I felt I had to compensate for its matter-of-fact delivery by crying my eyes out. I was too exhausted to return to the library afterward.

Instead, I called home that night. I wanted to hear my father's voice. I felt I had a new understanding of the intensity he had used to prepare me for life, starting when I learned my multiplication tables perched on the washboard and when Dad threw me into the swimming pool to force me to float. The Cultural Revolution must have scared him, and he had been terrified to leave me unprepared for my own adulthood.

Mom picked up the phone. Dad was not home.

"Mom, what was it like to live through the Cultural Revolution?" I asked, after exchanging a few pleasantries. There was only silence on the other end of the phone. "The Cultural Revolution is long over now," she finally answered in a quiet voice. "We have all moved on. What is the use of lingering in the past?"

Mom then asked how my studies were going. I assured her that I was studying hard, then quickly wrapped up the conversation. I was tired but restless, and I decided to take a walk around campus.

Strolling down the path, listening to the crickets in the grass, I could not keep the movie out of my mind. The family lost a son and then a daughter; yet somehow the story ended with everyone smiling at each other. They were still hopeful that the society that had caused their pain would also bring them relief and that a bright future was still in store.

I wondered whether this could be the attitude that sets Chinese people apart. We have a long history blighted with disasters, the Cultural Revolution being just the most recent example. But that period of suffering did not result from an external attack like the Japanese invasion of China. It wasn't a civil war between political parties, either, as when the Nationalists fought the Communists. It was a time when best friends and sometimes even family members sold each other out in order to fulfill a leader's wishes. And rather than discussing these dark times, China had collectively chosen to move on so the people could just forget about it. This is how Chinese people choose to deal with their very own dark history and to "move on."

I was in America now, and I was grateful for that.

* * *

It's unclear what career path I would have been allowed to follow had I remained in China. In America, where you can make your own destiny, my choice became obvious. You could describe my relationship with economics as love at first sight. I sat in on an Intro to Macroeconomics class during the first week of classes, or "shopping week" as it was called, and was smitten after just a few lectures.

My passion for the subject was practical, philosophical, and also personal. Since my own family benefited from a rapidly transforming economy, I wanted to learn more about how and why China had transformed itself. I saw how people were more charitable in America than in China, which made me curious to learn how this behavior was connected to wealth and freedom.

Concepts that were steeped in deductive reasoning and free of ideologies were very compelling to me—especially given that economic principles help explain how much of society interacts. In China, I had been taught that socialism is superior to capitalism (despite the obvious disasters in China's recent history, which our textbooks conveniently glossed over), because a socialist government takes care of its people as long as the people follow its rules—the way parents reward their children as long as the children behave. But now that I was in the United States, studying economics allowed me to see the capitalist system around me with a new clarity.

The invisible hand was one of the first theorems that drew me in. This metaphor, first conceived of by Adam Smith in the eighteenth century, describes how society as a whole will benefit from everyone acting in her or his own self-interest. This world-changing concept suggested that the market can naturally replace the government in its ability to coordinate a multiplicity of individual choices and make many key societywide decisions.

"Does the market always work?" I remember asking in one class. Class participation was part of the grade, which gave me the incentive to speak up.

"No, it doesn't," my professor answered. "But it works better than all the other alternatives we've thought of."

Each class I took taught me something new, and I began to realize that economics was intellectually stimulating, ferociously logical, and highly practical. I was shown a new world where things made sense. I tore through the classes offered by the department: political economy, game theory, econometrics, monetary theory, and financial markets. I could apply the lessons I was learning immediately through the decisions I was making in my own life.

For example, I learned about *opportunity cost*, a concept that I think about, use, and live by every day. The opportunity cost of a choice is the sacrifice of the foregone value of the next best alternative that is not chosen. For example, the opportunity cost of my becoming an economist would be the rewards I could have reaped from becoming a doctor or a lawyer.

Then there was the law of *diminishing marginal utility*. The term describes the economic concept where the pleasure, benefit, and utility from consuming goods and services diminish as the amount of consumption of those goods and services increases. I experienced it every night during study sessions, when the first bite of Cheez-Its and Oreos tasted heavenly, but the last one usually made me feel bloated and a little sick. In this case, each additional bite gave me less and less pleasure.

There was also *game theory*, an approach to understanding (and therefore predicting) human strategic interactions—whether and when to cooperate, compete, or withdraw. Today, a dozen years later, I apply game theory principles to analyze and predict the strategy of many Chinese companies and businesses I research, particularly when it comes to understanding a price war.

Beneath all the equations and charts—what I think of as the scientific appearance of economics—is the study of human behavior. While the scientific appearance scares many American kids who are intimidated by numbers and unfamiliar symbols, my rigorous math training enabled me to see through to the core of the subject quickly. In fact, economics was closer to social studies than anything I had encountered before in my propaganda-driven education.

* * *

Studying economics also helped me realize that I was destined for a career working on Wall Street. But while I was mastering the theories behind the market, I knew I needed some practical hands-on experience as well. So I applied for and received an internship at M Capital, a prestigious, multibillion dollar, multistrategy hedge fund run by a Middlebury alum. My job was to help an equity fund manager in analyzing transportation companies—just the sort of high-rolling opportunity that I was hoping to get in on.

M Capital is headquartered in bustling midtown Manhattan. The entire office was set up as an open trading floor, with most people sitting in front of three or four computer screens. I sat in the back next to a "quant trader"—someone who used a lot of math to calculate and execute profitable trades.

For two months, I attended meetings and painstakingly scribbled notes on airlines and on shipping, trucking, and cruise companies. While I was enthralled by this whole new world of stocks and the market, the people and culture of the firm were equally fascinating. If my intensity was considered off the charts at Middlebury, I felt mellow compared with the traders and analysts at M Capital.

Part of the draw of that environment was that it was first time I felt being such a work addict was socially acceptable. I did not have to explain myself to anyone; in fact, it was expected that everyone work as hard as the next person and remain single-mindedly focused for the grueling hundred-hour workweek. This was something I excelled at, and it made me excited to have so many new acquaintances of the same mindset. The fact that it involved the field of global economics was more than enough to keep me hooked. I was starting to fall in love with this kind of workplace and this lifestyle.

After my summer internship at M Capital ended and my senior year began, I was intent on returning to Wall Street after graduation. I had caught the New York bug and couldn't wait to return.

* * *

As my time in college drew to a close, there were only a few courses that stood between me and my future on Wall Street. I still had to fulfill two humanities credits, required classes that I had put off since my freshman year: history and art. I chose a class called History of Renaissance and Modern Art so that I could kill two birds with one stone.

Up until that point, my interaction with art had been minimal. I could not name any famous pieces of Chinese artwork, as my education had mostly revolved around science and math. I had been to an art museum only once, in New York during my summer internship. As I wandered around the hulking building, listening to other people's comments on the pieces, all I could muster were the adjectives *pretty, nice, weird, scary*—like a child trying to speak in an adult's world. I hoped that with this class, I could at least learn to talk the way other people did about art.

That art class turned out to be my hardest class yet. The textbook we used was Helen Gardner's *Art Through the Ages*, and I struggled every time a name like Ghiberti or Brunelleschi popped up, not to mention Cailebotte, Baselitz, the Louvre, and Die Brücke. I felt like I should be getting a foreign language credit on top of the history and art one.

But the memorization wasn't the hardest part. When the professor urged us to analyze and explore the aesthetic elements and social contexts so that we could understand "art for art's sake," the course very nearly became a game over for me.

As the final exam approached for my art class, I became as anxious and jittery as an ant on a frying pan. I sought out the professor in her office, bringing the voluminous textbook and my even thicker notebook along with me. I began telling her how difficult and confusing the course was for me. In China, I said, everything we were taught in school had some specific message or ideological function. Chinese students studied stories, films, or artworks because of their underlying message, whether the selfishness of a government official or the piety of a daughter to her parents. But in this class, I never felt as if I figured out the right answer to the teacher's questions.

She smiled sympathetically and flipped to a painting by Picasso of an old man playing a guitar. "Have you even heard of art for art's sake?" she asked me. "True art is divorced from any moral or utilitarian function. It can have a message, or it can exist without one."

She told me that what made a painting "good" was up to the viewer. She explained that people often considered a painting such as the Picasso in front of me great because it provoked an emotional response in them. "Don't think of art in binary terms of good and bad," she said, looking into my eyes. "Think of how it affects you."

In the end I received a B in the class, but I didn't mind much. I felt as if I had gained a distinctly different way of looking at the world around me, part of my Americanization: analyzing my surroundings through emotion as well as through deductive reasoning.

In China, I had been taught tomes on what to think but never how to think. Questioning and commenting on things were considered signs of idiocy. Thinking back on when my elementary school teacher taught us "The Little Match Girl," I remember being told that it was an allegory for the selfishness of a capitalist society, and suddenly my education seemed incredibly easy. Sure, I had slaved to memorize all that information, but I never had to think about why it was important to do so.

That conversation with my professor has stayed with me vividly to this day. The concept I learned from that discussion—that learning how to think was just as important as or even more important than learning what to think—has been hardwired in the back of my brain ever since.

Other concepts are permanently etched there, too, such as *results versus method* and *logic versus emotion*. Success cannot be solely about one or the other. Both are needed in order to create something of value, whether it is a work of art, a research paper, a relationship, governance—anything.

In short, I was finally learning to see the complexities in the world around me—something that would have a massive impact on my Wall Street career.

CHAPTER 7

Wall Street 101

New York, 2000

I REALIZED MY DREAM OF WORKING ON WALL STREET IMMEDI-ately after graduating from college, when I was recruited by the investment bank Credit Suisse First Boston. I moved to New York City to start my job as an analyst.

My first apartment in the city was in Murray Hill on Thirtieth Street between Park Avenue and Lexington Avenue, 10 blocks from my office. I chose the apartment's location strategically because I knew how much time I would be spending at work.

I walked into my first day of work on lower Madison Avenue in June 2000. The building was impressive, with a cafeteria, a full-service print shop for the copious marketing materials the bank produced, a fitness center, a spa, and hair and nail salons. A line of limos waited outside of the building 24/7 to ferry bankers to the airport.

I called it the "prison," or sometimes, when I was feeling generous, the state-of-the-art prison. The whole idea behind this full-service institution was to maximize the hours the employ-ees stayed inside the building. The setup worked well: at Credit Suisse, a 90-hour workweek was considered easy.

As a sell-side analyst, I devoted 80 percent of my time to pre-paring pitch books—the deal proposals that senior bankers used to market the firm. I often found myself at my desk at 3 a.m. still working on the books, changing periods and commas in presenta-tions, adjusting the font size from 10 to 12, and switching the font color from green to blue, then to greenish blue.

My first weekend at Credit Suisse, I was called into the office at 6 a.m. on Saturday to compile financial profiles on a dozen fiber-optics communications companies. I slaved in the office for 20-plus hours, as Saturday turned into Sunday. Then I was informed that the project had been made up, just to test my work ethic.

It took me about a week to come to what now seems like an obvious conclusion, something that is as true in China as it is in the United States: bankers are ultimately no different from used-car salesmen, except for the bankers' fancier suits. Bankers are paid to stoke interest in the market and close transactions—the bigger the deals and the faster they close, the better. They have no incentive to care about the consequences of the deal or even whether their clients lose or gain in the long run, because they only make money by closing the deal itself. I realized that the glamorous investment banking profession is the ultimate relationship business; it's about whom you know more than what you know. I wanted a career where my analytical ability could set me apart from my competi-tion—and drive how much money I could make.

* * *

I got my opportunity in the spring of 2001. I was recruited to join Fiduciary Trust International, one of the oldest money manage-ment firms in the country, to launch a stock portfolio that would be investing in Asia. I became a stock analyst, tasked with researching and identifying small and fast-growing companies in the developed markets of Asia and then buying stocks at attractive prices in whatever market they were listed, be it Hong Kong or Tokyo. My performance was benchmarked against the index of that specific market. I covered Japan, Hong Kong, Singapore, South Korea, Australia, and New Zealand.

I spent my first few months on the job learning how to decode the flood of investment information on my Bloomberg terminal, while also fielding dozens of calls from brokers, analysts, and market strategists from Goldman Sachs, Salomon Smith Barney, Nomura, CLSA, and others. It seemed as if everyone had stocks to peddle. Back when I was at Credit Suisse, my job had been to make these calls to help sell a company to individual investors or corporate acquirers. Sell-side analysts are paid to be optimists, dressing up a company to maximize the odds of completing a transaction. Thankfully, I was now on the other end of the phone and free to be my analytical self.

One undeniable perk of working for a big asset management firm was the almost-unlimited access to analysts, conferences, industry events, and management meetings. Since firms like Fiduciary Trust place a large volume of trades with brokers, and therefore pay high commission fees, we would gain extra privileges as preferred clients.

A few months into my new job, I was flown to Asia to visit companies, which was a critical component of the stock-picking process. Fiduciary had a rule that we wouldn't buy a company's stock until we visited the company on its own turf. I once flew to Tokyo, for example, and researched a company that owned pachinko parlors by using my corporate account to play a few hours of the pinball-like betting game. I also visited consumer electronics companies in Seoul; real estate conglomerates in Hong Kong, where I was invited to attend a horse race with one of the CEOs; and medical device companies in Sydney.

Working for Fiduciary was an interesting ride, and it gave me my first exposure to the investment world, along with skills that later helped me in my hedge fund career. But I was starting to run out of steam. I had been on an adrenaline high for years, slaving through college and working nonstop while traveling around the world. I felt as if I had been running on a treadmill since the first day I arrived in the United States, and I needed a break. I decided to take what young people on the Street called a "paying vacation." So I applied and was accepted to Columbia Business School in New York City.

The World of Hedge Funds

While I did take some interesting classes at Columbia Business School, made friends, and relaxed a bit compared to working, the biggest advantage was having the free time to acquaint myself with a very entrepreneurial Wall Street business model: the hedge fund.

On the surface, hedge fund managers picked stocks just the way I had in my former job. But the mostly young men who ran these funds seemed sharper, hungrier, and more eager to bet big than anyone else on Wall Street. The high-stakes hedge fund world was just more entrepreneurial. It was becoming increasingly common for talented analysts and portfolio managers to leave their jobs at more established firms to start their own funds. Since firms were springing up and shutting down all the time, the industry appeared fragmented and chaotic compared with the more traditional world of mutual funds. But the more I learned about the hedge fund business model, the more it made sense why so many people were drawn to running their own fund.

Mutual funds and hedge funds are different animals, with distinct purposes and cultures. Mutual fund managers charge their clients a percentage of their total assets under management, with management fees typically ranging from 0.5 to 1.5 percent. The performance of the fund is then benchmarked against other indexes that track the performance of the market as a whole. If the Standard & Poor's Index rises 8 percent this year, for example, and a mutual fund delivers a 10 percent annual return, that mutual fund is considered to have performed well. As long as a fund outperforms the market—even when the market is down and the fund loses money—investors are generally satisfied.

But things work much differently for hedge fund managers, who are incentivized to deliver absolute returns regardless of the market direction. Investors expect a hedge fund to deliver a positive return even when the S&P goes straight to hell's basement. To get that kind of return, investors have to pay a lot more to the talented "hedgies"—shorthand for hedge fund managers—than they would to a mutual fund manager. Hedge fund fees have two components: a 2 percent management fee on the total assets under management plus another 20 percent in performance fees, with performance defined as the return on the fund's portfolio.

For example, let's say a hedge fund manages $100 million of assets, including stocks, bonds, or other securities. The manager makes a 2 percent management fee, or $2 million, regardless of his or her performance. Typically that $2 million would be spent first on operating expenses such as office rent, a research budget (including the subscription fee for the Bloomberg terminals and other data and research providers), trips to attend conferences and visit companies, and salaries for analysts and staff.

The fund then makes another 20 percent on any appreciation of the assets under management. Let's say, hypothetically, a fund delivers a 10 percent return on its investment of $100 million and the fund earns $10 million. Then 20 percent of that return, or $2 million, would be distributed among the team as bonuses, along with funds from the management fees left over from operation expenses. In time, I came to see that the smaller a fund is, the more focused the managers are on generating positive returns so they can earn that extra 20 percent fee.

One strange quirk of the business is that hedge fund managers also typically invest in the same fund they are managing. They are general partners, meaning they run the show and have full liability for the acts and debts of the partnership. General partners can invest in their own fund or not, but in either case they can stand to lose everything if their operation goes under. In contrast, investors are limited partners, meaning they don't have control of the partnership and are liable only up to the amount of their investment. I always thought it unwise to put one's financial and human resources in the same basket, but more often than not investors prefer or even expect their money managers to have some "skin in the game" to prove their commitment to delivering strong returns.

The hedge fund world seemed to be fiercely competitive, a place where, in theory, the best and smartest survived and thrived.

It sounded like my kind of workplace.

* * *

When I joined the Aurarian team in 2005, it felt like I became part of a new family. It was a small operation with only four people: CEO Jason Gold (whom I had interviewed with), a trader, a marketing officer, and me. Our four desks were clustered together, facing one another in the center of our office. There was still a sense of privacy, however, since each of us had four enormous computer monitors staring back at us. Given the close quarters, it wasn't a place where anyone could keep a secret or catch up on errands like paying a Con Edison bill or booking a dinner date. Even our phones were interconnected so that anyone could patch in on a call at any time, with or without notice.

Jason and I in particular kept in constant contact by talking and texting throughout the day and night on our BlackBerries, instant messaging on the Bloomberg terminal, calling over the phone, and, of course, peeking around our monitors to speak face-to-face. Our close proximity made it easier for Jason to train me personally on the secrets of his unique methods of investigative research, which he had perfected at SAC Capital. The process involved interviewing the senior management of target companies, then cross-checking information with third parties to verify what those senior managers had said.

The team would initially identify targets by meeting with the senior management of companies, attending trade shows and conferences, and screening stock charts on our Bloomberg terminals. We called ourselves a "bottom-up" investment firm, which meant that we chose companies by analyzing their individual businesses rather than using strategies based on macroeconomic trends and government policies.

When we identified possible targets, we would begin digging into the background of the company and the credibility of its management team. To do so, we would talk with customers, suppliers, competitors, regulators, and government agencies.

On paper, this method might not seem unique. But Jason was truly rigorous in how we went about it. When I worked at Fiduciary, for example, I would make two phone calls to verify the legitimacy of a business model. But at Aurarian, I had to make at least 10 calls to complete the same task.

Jason was adamant that I master all the investigation techniques he had learned at SAC. His former employer used to hire ex-CIA and ex-FBI investigators as consultants to teach analysts how to effectively interview management teams. Known as "elicitation techniques," these methods were used to discreetly draw out additional information from people without raising any suspicion that you were after specific facts. Jason trained me in the same methods: how to relax interviewees, how to monitor nuanced shifts in body language, when to speak and when to pause to induce information, and how to phrase my questions.

Jason would entertain us from time to time by sharing some of the stories that showed how effective his techniques really were. For instance, he told us about how one particular company's CEO was calm and collected when he was delivering a well-rehearsed presentation. But when Jason started to ask difficult questions, the guy exposed a nervous tic, slipping his shoe on and off one of his feet. Another story involved a CFO who, as Jason's due diligence questions got more intense, began drinking from an empty cup of soda. Then, when Jason asked another tough question about the company's liquidity, the CFO started dusting an empty chair with his fingers.

"Those are the sort of cues you need to look out for," he told me. "It's about 'the tell,' as they say in poker."

He went on to explain how, when people are under stress, they give off different body signals than what he called their "baseline." You establish someone's baseline by observing how they typically carry themselves and then see how that changes when they are subjected to various stimuli.

Since the fund made investments across many sectors, we had to learn an overwhelming amount of industry-specific knowledge to make each investment. In order for me to truly understand the potential of a company, I needed to essentially become an expert in the industry it operated in. In my time at Aurarian, I headed up investments, both long and short, that ranged from wireless semiconductor chip manufacturers and human resource software companies to drug addiction treatment providers and spinal surgical device makers.

* * *

Jason was an effective mentor, and he taught me the art of research in stages so that I wasn't completely overwhelmed. My first hands-on experience was with phone calls. To show—not just tell—me how to do it, Jason would patch me into conference calls he led, where I could listen in with my phone on mute. He would then instant message me while he was talking to fill me in on his thought process. He would ping me to explain why he asked the questions he'd just asked, why he interrupted the answer of the person he was talking to, and when to read between the lines. I found it hard to keep up with this process at the beginning and often found myself lost in the jargon. But over time I realized that decoding conference calls was not much different from decoding TOEFL exams; you really don't need to be proficient in the entire English language to score well on the TOEFL, and I knew I could master the essentials of this language as well.

Jason insisted that we all use the same formula when we conducted each early round of our due diligence calls.

"Don't get off the phone," he cautioned me, "until you are well informed of the following: What are the products and services they sell? What differentiates them from their competition? What does the competition center on? Do they have a management team in place to execute the business plans? Do I trust the management with my money? If I invest in their business, what is my expected return?"

It was a steep learning curve, and I had my fair share of screwups. One particularly memorable mistake came during a call with a lifestyle and fitness media company based in Colorado. I had a call with the CEO scheduled for just after lunch. One of my coworkers had ordered in burgers for everyone so we could eat at our desks. By the time of my interview, the heavy food—plus the sleep deprivation that came from pulling an all-nighter researching the reviews on this company's yoga products—began competing to knock me out.

"Joe, can you please walk me through your strategy in building the online yoga community and how you will realize the synergy with your core business?" I asked him.

As Joe, a legendary consumer-branding-guru-turned-entrepreneur, started his pitch, my eyelids became heavier and heavier, and his words bobbed about in my head.

"Yuppie interests . . . yoga video . . . social media" was about all I took in.

I wasn't sure how long my eyes were closed until I opened them and saw Jason towering over me, arms crossed, shooting daggers from his eyes. It had been too long.

"Hello? *Junh*?" Joe was saying into my headset.

"Yes, Joe, that's fascinating stuff," I stammered, then sat straight up and plunged into jabber, asking directionless questions, one after the other, until I could shake off the fog.

I blew the call, and I knew it. Worse was that look of death from Jason, something that would haunt me for months to come. At that moment, I decided to give up eating a proper lunch altogether. Rather, I subsisted on nothing but vegetable juice and raw almonds, a habit I have continued to this day. It might sound austere, but it's an effective formula that keeps my body and brain at peak performance throughout the day.

Despite the steep learning curve, it wasn't long before I was working the phones like a champion. But calls could only do so much to get to the truth about a company's prospects. It was also critical to see and experience the product in person.

Case in point: Once I figured out a creative way to check out a cosmetic laser company. The business had a new product that performed laser-assisted liposuction—an outpatient procedure offered at medical spas. The procedure is designed to disrupt fat cells and tighten tissues by inserting a laser through a tiny tube to melt and liquefy the fat before extracting it through another small tube. What could be a better way to learn the efficacy of body contouring than by experimenting with it myself? So I made a visit to the Medi Spa on Madison Avenue, which was just around the corner from our office.

"I'd like to book a liposuction treatment," I told the receptionist.

She sized me up quizzically from head to toe, "What area would you like to treat?"

"My tummy?" I attempted.

I was worried that she wouldn't believe me because I was so thin. But the receptionist didn't bat an eye, presumably because the clinic already had plenty of inquiries from skinny Park Avenue socialites. This treatment was effective on any perceived flaw, which meant it was a great fit for the abundant number of narcissistic perfectionists who lived on Manhattan's Upper East Side.

The nurse told me that the earliest available appointment would be in six months—the treatment was that popular. The procedure was minimally invasive, meaning patients could be in and out within an hour and the recovery was much faster than the normal liposuction procedure. Not surprisingly, that meant that lunch slots were fully booked.

That visit piqued my interest. I followed it up with a trip to Las Vegas the next week to attend the Aesthetic Show, an annual industry event where companies showcase their latest products. It was impossible to miss the buzz that this liposuction machine generated among the doctors, sales reps, and manufacturers. The line waiting outside the company's booth was five times longer than at any of its competitors' stands.

After reading through two studies and comparing my own financial model with the Street projections, I figured that the company was going to beat everyone's expectations. I advised Jason that we should buy and accumulate the stock. Not long after, when the popularity of the laser liposuction treatment soared, our investment generated a handsome return.

This may sound like a way to make quick and easy money. In reality, however, it takes rigorous analysis to dissect a company and determine its strengths and weaknesses. As we saw with the laser liposuction company, one new product could establish its leadership in the cosmetic surgery industry and therefore influence a stock's performance. Our job was to find ways to fill in that piece of the investment puzzle. Over time, these habits helped my natural analytical ability evolve into an intuition, a gut feeling for separating good investments from mediocre ones.

Short Selling

I first learned about the concept of short selling in business school. Unlike going long on a stock, which means you are betting that its value will increase, a short sell means you are placing a bet that a stock will lose value.

When most people think about short sellers, images of ill-willed capitalists and pernicious market manipulators who bet against a company's success or even against its survival come to mind. These conclusions are groundless, uninformed, and entirely wrong. Shorting is critical to maintaining the integrity and enhancing the vigilance of the capital markets.

In essence, short sellers are the market watchdogs who indirectly encourage transparency and disclosure by exposing the dark side of company management. Since regulators are usually a few steps behind, short sellers represent an important self-correcting mechanism in the market. They also directly help investors minimize their risk by helping the market correct itself and by adding liquidity to the market through their trades.

Shorting stocks is difficult both because the market has an upward bias and because managers usually do their very best to preserve their companies' stock prices. By and large, national economies, labor productivity, and therefore corporate earnings go up, not down. In an adverse environment, managers can also do a variety of things to boost their share price, such as buying back shares or paying dividends.

When shorting a stock, investors are effectively expressing their negativity about a company's business model and the management team's ability to deliver on its business goals. In a short sale, an investor "borrows" a stock at a cost. If a stock is heavily shorted, the borrowing cost can be almost 100 percent per year. In this case, unless the investor is highly confident that a catalyst—an event that triggers a movement in the stock—will soon cause the share price to sink, the short is probably too expensive to be worth pursuing.

Investors who take short positions need to follow the activity of their peers closely. If an investor who has shorted a stock believes its value is going to rise, he or she will buy shares back to limit losses, known as "covering a short." But if an increase in the value of a stock encourages many short sellers to do this at the same time, that can push up the share price further and force other short sellers to liquidate their positions to avoid big losses—a situation known as a "short squeeze." Therefore, I would make sure I was well informed on a stock's short interest (which is also reflected in the cost to borrow) as well as the management's dividend and buyback policies before starting any short position. I also never shorted any stock without a well-defined catalyst in mind.

Since the lowest price for a security is $0, the maximum return for a short position is 100 percent. On the other hand, the downside for the short seller is theoretically unlimited. If a stock does really well—if its share price doubles, triples, or quadruples over time (think Google, Apple, and Amazon, to name a few)—that creates virtually unlimited risk for short sellers, who can lose 100 percent, 200 percent, or even 300 percent of their investment. The opposite is true for those who long the stocks: their downside is limited to 100 percent, but their upside is unlimited. To manage the risk of that downside of shorting stocks, most funds impose stop-loss disciplines. For example, at Aurarian, we had a stop-loss rule of

30 percent, which means that if a short or long position moved up or down by 30 percent, the position would have to be covered immediately—if Jason, the portfolio manager, deemed it appropriate, that is.

In reality, the execution of these rules is almost always subject to the discretion of the fund's managers. And to manage risk, portfolios would always use options and other derivatives to protect their downside, in addition or as an alternative to the stop-loss rules. I had experienced multiple cases where shorts exploded in my face but, just the same, my short thesis didn't change and sometimes even grew stronger. Instead of covering, I added to the position, after carefully reviewing the situation and discussing it with the portfolio manager. To manage the risk, I would write calls—the right to purchase the shares at a specified price within a specified period of time—to mitigate the downside.

To short-sell effectively, one has to distinguish between companies and stocks. "A good company doesn't necessarily imply a good stock and vice versa," Jason would repeat, until he was convinced it had been drilled into my head. "A stock has a life of its own, and it is different from that of a company. You will be trained as a stock analyst."

What Jason meant is that the market constitutes a near infinite number of participants who each have a different view of what's happening. A stock's price reflects the collective view of its worth—its so-called market valuation. The collective view is based upon the consensus of the company's future earnings potential, which the company can beat, meet, or miss, typically with predictable consequences for its share price.

In order to properly value a stock, therefore, an investor needs to develop his or her own independent view on the earnings potential of the business. Those who investigate a company with care can often develop a more accurate projection of the company's future earnings than the market's herd mentality. It's only worth making a trade, however, if you have a significantly different view than that of the collective. The more your opinion deviates from the norm, the bigger the arbitrage opportunity becomes.

By shorting a stock you are effectively expressing your opinion that the business has a risk or flaw that the rest of the market doesn't yet see. That's why shorting is essential for price discovery—a process or mechanism of determining the price for a security, which is a primary function of the market.

To further complicate the issue, there are two types of short candidates: hypes and frauds. Hypes deserve to be brought down to earth. Frauds need to be exposed and busted. When you can identify a stock that is a combination of hype and fraud, you have the potential to hit a home run and land a big payoff on one of your bets.

A Big Little Short

In the spring of 2008, the market was flooded with deals to be made on "green" energy stocks. The sector was white hot. One Friday morning, a broker called me to pitch a "clean-tech" stock (a fancy name for green energy) that we'll call Sunlight Systems. The Wisconsin-based company made light fixtures and had carried out a successful initial public offering (IPO) in December 2007, which was oversubscribed many times over. As a result of all that demand, its share price jumped from $13 to $21 on its first day of trading.

Sunlight's management team marketed the company with a narrative that claimed it had a proprietary light fixture that reduced electricity consumption and saved its customers lots of money in the process. Its lofty valuation suggested that its management's pitch resonated with investors who were hunting for additional clean-tech plays in the wake of prior rushes to scoop up solar and wind stocks.

To end the conversation on a high note, the broker added: "John Rogers, a longtime friend of the president of the United States, is one of its largest investors."

I hung up the phone. I knew from my experiences in both Shanghai and New York City that when people rely on name-dropping, it often means their argument is lacking. In my business, making money depends on the ability to develop a variant or contrarian view from the consensus. You have to break free from the herd and be comfortable operating as a loner. And if people were buying Sunlight merely based on a celebrity recommendation, there might be an opportunity in moving in the opposite direction.

One Sunday afternoon, I came into the office as a part of my weekend routine. I loved to work in the silent office with no one around, with only four big screens staring at me. As I was flipping through Sunlight's IPO memo, a slew of red flags caught my attention. First of all, Sunlight marketed itself as a "demand response" company—a trendy term meaning that it would be responsive to the needs of the electrical grid. Since none of Sunlight's competitors made similar claims, it was an important point of differentiation. But as I read and reread the description of its products, I still couldn't figure out what the secret sauce really was that gave this stock its premium valuation relative to its competition. In fact, the information the company provided on its technology was paltry at best.

I soon found other alarming clues. The CEO (let's call him Manfred) was a high school dropout. Prior to founding Sunlight, his main experience was as a salesperson for a large industrial company. After he started his own company, he hired his wife to be director of operations with an annual salary of close to $1 million—despite the fact that the company was unprofitable. I smelled trouble.

That afternoon, I posted a question on LinkedIn, the professional social media website that I often use as a research tool. "I am looking for recommendations for lighting fixtures for a large commercial storage facility," I wrote. "What's your opinion on Sunlight?"

The following Monday morning, I received a long e-mail in response to my question from the CEO of one of Manfred's main competitors, someone I'll call Ernie.

"They make tons of claims and love to reference their patent portfolio but in the end they have a cookie cutter, one-size-fits-all solution," Ernie wrote forcefully. He explained that more than 60 U.S. companies made high-intensity fluorescent lighting fixtures that were similar to Sunlight's and that this competition was putting pressure on all these companies to lower their prices. He also shared the contact information for several of Sunshine's distributors.

It all started to become clear to me. Sunlight was operating in a commodity business, and the competition was cutthroat. However, to get a high valuation in the stock market, the management decided to spin a clean-tech story by making false claims about how its proprietary light fixtures reduced electricity consumption. They were lying. I had seen this act before, but not to such a blatant degree.

But before I pulled the trigger to short the stock, I needed more data points to confirm my conviction. So I dialed up Sunlight's distributors and pretended I was a purchasing manager looking for lighting fixtures for several large industrial warehouses in China. When a representative from Sunlight's largest distributor picked up the phone and, after my introduction, began ripping into the company, I was stunned. "Their fixtures are extremely low quality, and their hardware and software are incompatible," the man on the other end of the line told me in his midwestern accent. "Their bulbs also break frequently during shipment."

"That's terrible," I said. "But how do they manage to sell so much? Their revenue has been growing nicely."

"Those guys massively discount their products every three months or so," he said. "And the CEO is great at marketing. He goes to the trade shows and tells people that his bulbs save more energy than others and that he has intellectual property that no one else has. But we talk to our customers every week, and I don't think anyone who has used their products has bought from them again. If you want to buy anything of quality, I'd advise you to stay away from them."

Competitors often bad-mouth each other, but I had never seen a distributor bash the products he carried. I knew I was close to finding a home-run short. After the phone conversation, I borrowed and sold a small short position of the stock at $12 a share.

Three weeks later, Sunlight reported its quarterly earnings. Its revenue came in a staggering 15 percent below the average estimate that banks on Wall Street put out. Its earnings missed Street estimates by even more, as the company's profits suffered from the pressure put on it by low-priced competitors. According to the company's balance sheet, its inventory and accounts receivable both shot up significantly—meaning a higher percentage of the company's sales came from extending credit to customers than from selling products and collecting its money in that quarter. The stock started to retreat but didn't collapse. Together with the trading volume, this signaled to me that the die-hards were giving the company the benefit of the doubt and hoping this dismal performance was a one-time event.

The next day, analysts started to publish notes defending Sunlight and dismissing the poor performance as a slip-up that could be fixed in the near future. After all the work I had done on the stock, I knew it was not a misstep but a sign that management was cooking the numbers. My conviction was that the company was guilty of "channel stuffing" to meet Wall Street's expectations. In other words, it was discounting its bulbs significantly toward the end of each quarter, which its distributors called "promotional sales." Since the products were of inferior quality, distributors were not able to sell what they bought from Sunlight. As a result, inventory piled up. However, since the products had already been shipped from the manufacturer to the distributors, Sunlight recognized the revenues although its products had not actually been sold through to the final customers. This scheme is one of the most common methods that companies use to cook their numbers. When I added them up, these red flags all pointed to the fact that the company would soon be experiencing a severe deceleration in its sales.

Out of curiosity, I called up one analyst who had issued a strong buy rating on the stock.

"What's there to love about this stock?" I asked him. "It seems like terminal cancer to me."

"Well, you know, they are working on the pipeline . . . a bad quarter doesn't mean something good won't happen in the future," was his lame answer.

"Why don't you upgrade it when good things indeed happen?" I tried to be polite. "For now, it's a crapshoot. And you are recommending a crapshoot to the Street?"

"Yeah, but . . ."

Over time, I learned that "Yeah, but" is a typical defense when an analyst can't downgrade a stock he or she knows is bad. Sell-side analysts are often caught in a tricky position: they run the risk of sabotaging the bank's relationship with powerful companies if they express negative opinions about a stock. Because of this conflict of interest, their ratings always have a positive bias.

"Know your enemies and know yourself and you will not be imperiled in a hundred battles," Sun Tzu wrote in *The Art of War*. The conversation with the analyst gave me extra comfort that I was way ahead of the crowd in my due diligence, and I added on to my position. In the following three quarters, Sunlight missed its estimates again and again. Eventually the Street's sell-side analysts were all forced to downgrade the stock, and its price collapsed to about $3. Since I borrowed the shares at $12, I made a respectable 80 percent profit in less than a year.

Short selling is not hard. It just takes independent thinking and a lot of groundwork to analyze any difference between the company's underlying business and its perception in the market—as well as the guts to bet against the market. After that, it is all about having the patience to watch as the movie plays out on its own.

CHAPTER 8

Learning, Burning, and Crashing

ONE SUNDAY IN THE SUMMER OF 2007, I WENT TO BEST BUY TO perform "channel checks"—analyst-speak for a third-party investigation of distribution channels to verify how well a product sells. This time, I bought my research partner and boyfriend, Andrew, to join me in playing the role of a married couple shopping for a GPS gadget—to help us navigate from Manhattan to our weekend house in Vermont, no doubt.

I had met Andrew, an Irish-born American from North Dakota, at a colleague's party. Tall, fit, and blue-eyed, Andrew was a senior investment professional at a multibillion dollar hedge fund founded by two former Goldman traders in the summer of 2003.

I remember our first conversation at a cocktail party at a mutual friend's apartment in Manhattan. We didn't get along too well: Andrew took the opposite view on a medical device company that I liked, claiming that its heart monitoring technology was ineffective in predicting heart failure. The disagreement led to a dinner at which we planned to exchange research notes on the company. The dinner went very well. We realized that despite our drastically different conclusion on that particular investment, we had a lot in common. After the non-date date, we quickly became best friends and close colleagues. In 2008, we got married, just about a year after we met.

Most of the dates Andrew and I went on did not take place in restaurants or theaters. Instead, he would accompany me on field trips and to my office over the weekend to brainstorm investment ideas or help me build financial models. Andrew knew how to entertain me—not with flowers and lavish gifts, but with endless intellectual stimulation. For us, a trip to Best Buy to analyze and discuss new tech products was not unusual.

We were there that day to investigate Garmin, a U.S.-based tech company that made only one type of product, portable navigation devices, including the global positioning system (GPS) devices that people kept in their cars at the time. The company was at the top of my short list. To help it keep its shelf space at stores like Best Buy, the company relied heavily on spinning out new models for its navigation devices, with various features or in different colors. Garmin had a strong brand name that allowed it to charge high prices, but my suspicion was that competition would soon push into the segment, bringing prices down. That could trigger a collapse in Garmin's stock.

By now, I was a seasoned technology investor, enthusiastic about all gadgets and technological devices. I would often go to this Best Buy store in Noho (a neighborhood in New York City north of Houston Street) to check out the latest technology gadgets. On the corner of Houston and Broadway, it sat on prime real estate in one of the priciest shopping neighborhoods in New York. The Noho store was buzzing on the weekends, which provided plenty of material for real-time field research. To get an idea of what consumers thought of a product, I would chat with the shop assistants; compare features, reliability, and prices among different models; and eavesdrop as other customers discussed what they wanted to purchase. Sometimes I would even jump into their conversations, asking whether they favored certain models over others. This was harder to do by myself than with Andrew. My all-American boyfriend—with his nonthreatening, midwestern manner—always put strangers at ease.

After an hour of this research on Garmin, I decided to conclude my field trip before someone caught on to me and realized my true intention. One salesperson became suspicious when I was grilling him on different models of wireless routers. He thought the product company had sent me to monitor sales in the store. Since then, I only went to that Best Buy on Sunday, his day off.

"Did you learn anything new?" Andrew asked.

I pulled him aside to be discreet. "I'm afraid that the competition is getting tough for Garmin. TomTom and Sony are coming after it aggressively."

"How do you know?" he said.

I told him that Sony's latest model cost $200—one-third of Garmin's—and offered very similar features. The sales guy had also told me that TomTom, Garmin's European competitor, and Sony in Japan would both introduce more affordable models with virtually the same features in just a few weeks. I believed this competition would be the catalyst for a profitable short play.

Andrew was intrigued by my passion for gadgets like GPS devices. Once out of the store, he told me that my eyes had been shining as I shared my analysis. I told him it was because I had spotted something that the Wall Street analysts glued to their financial models had not yet noticed: Garmin's sales cycle had peaked. Garmin's stock also had a price/earnings ratio of 20, far more than that of most technology companies with only one successful device. That's why I was excited.

"But their latest models look really cool," Andrew said, reminding me of the slim pink model I had picked up.

"Do you really expect consumers to pay $400 more for a pink device they leave in their car?" I asked him. One tip that Jason had drilled into me was that, in the fast-evolving technology business, hardware companies that depend on spinning out different versions of a single product always get crushed. Dell, Palm, and Nokia had all suffered this same fate: they created products that captivated consumers, but eventually new market entrants created enormous pricing pressure, which in turn killed their profit margins. One could go long on these stocks for a limited window of time, when they were growing their market share. Eventually, however, they all became credible shorts.

Later that year, Garmin marked the entrance of a competitor that would prove even tougher than TomTom or Sony. Google launched the second version of its mobile maps application in November, a technology that quickly made even the sleekest and cheapest GPS clunky and obsolete. People began pulling out their smartphones to look for directions, and demand for stand-alone GPS devices sank.

* * *

For four years at Aurarian, as I said, I worked like a maniac without realizing it. I became a CrackBerry addict—slang for someone attached to his or her BlackBerry at all times. I had to be ready to answer e-mails at any time of the day or night. Jason would message me with random questions on everything ranging from the newest laws on Internet gambling to changes in the tax credit status for geothermal companies. These requests disrupted many dinners and workout sessions, not to mention my sleep. But I loved the constant intellectual stimulation of covering so many industries and the challenge of zipping through these requests. I got into the habit of typing out my thoughts (fearful that I might forget them) as they came to me. More than once, a truck almost hit me when I was crossing a street and typing notes to myself or to Jason.

My typical day started at 5:30 a.m., when I would head to the gym. I would get in four miles on the treadmill while simultaneously watching CNBC and reading that day's *Wall Street Journal*. By 7:30 a.m., I was in front of my four computer screens, glancing through the news headlines for the companies in our portfolio. I would then spend most of my day talking to companies—ones we were invested in, ones we were interested in investing in, and everything else in between, including competitors, customers, and suppliers. I never really ate lunch, but rather snacked on nuts and fruit throughout the day to ensure my energy level remained high and steady at work. My brain usually crashed around 6:30 p.m., so I'd go back to the gym for a short workout to recharge.

If I didn't have a business dinner, I would do more work from home. I would either work on my financial models on my laptop (it was hard to model during the day in a busy office), comparing the assumptions and earnings estimates in my own model with those of the Street analysts, or speak with contacts in China before calling it a day.

I also spent countless hours on the road. When it comes to researching companies, seeing is believing, and I traveled extensively to company headquarters to meet investment targets on their own turf. Unlike broker-sponsored investor conferences, which usually take place at posh locations, some of the industrial companies our fund was interested in were based in places in the United States so remote that many Americans had never been to them.

These memorable trips included a visit to North Dakota to see a company that claimed to have a technology to convert animal waste into ethanol. I remember standing in an animal waste processing facility in February, half of the building open to the air despite the subzero temperatures. I toured the facility and chatted with the company's site engineers for a few hours to understand the technology and its commercial applications. I was underdressed in my New York fur coat, freezing my butt off. Many of the workers—clearly entertained to see my fur coat among their usual sea of Carhartt overalls and work boots—asked to take a picture with me.

Another time I traveled to a frigid Duluth, Minnesota, to check out an iron ore company's on-site exploration firsthand. I spent several days on various sites hanging out with the construction workers. At the end of the trip, I developed a nasty skin rash. I'm still not sure whether it was from the hard hat, the rubbery turkey sandwiches I ate for lunch and dinner a few days in a row, or the sheets from my aging motel.

My obsession with work came at a sacrifice: I wasn't exactly living the lifestyle of an average young professional woman in Manhattan. That didn't bother me, though. At Aurarian, I was obsessed with learning about stocks and the market, and I put in insane hours, with my signature intensity. As a result, I had established a reputation as a winner—a stock picker with good eyes for home runs. I was run down physically but very satisfied with my career.

I was beginning to understand why this business belongs to the young and hungry. To succeed in this business, one has to operate at peak condition 24 hours a day, 7 days a week, for a simple reason: globalization means that the investment universe is in action 24/7. Asian markets open just a few hours after the U.S. stock market closes at 4 p.m., and in between investors can trade the European markets. There was never any time for boredom or idle reflection, as the work never ended. There was always another stock to nail, another company to visit, another analyst to call. The intellectual stimulation never stopped, and neither did I.

Investing in China

By 2006, it was hard for anyone on Wall Street to dismiss the surge that was going on in Chinese IPOs. Being a prudent investor who had never been to China, Jason initially avoided Chinese stocks. "It's still a Communist country, after all," he would say. "I don't want to wake up one morning and find the company I invested in being nationalized." He knew there were good momentum plays among Chinese companies, but he didn't have the stomach for the risks that went with investing in an emerging market. This view was not uncommon among more conservative investors at the time.

At a certain point, however, dealing with China became unavoidable. Aurarian was a small-cap fund focused on innovation of all sorts—high technology, medical devices, and green technology were our specialties. China was becoming well known as the world's factory, making everything from MP3 portable music players to solar panels and wind turbines. Production of all kinds of critical goods was shifting to China, especially in the two sectors I followed closely, semiconductors and green technology. With cheap labor and low costs, Chinese companies seemed destined to put their American competitors out of business.

At the time, the third wave of Chinese companies was invading U.S. capital markets. The first wave of Chinese IPOs began coming to U.S. markets in the 1990s. These companies were state-built empires in strategic industries such as insurance, energy, and telecommunications, monopolies constructed with generous government funding and protection. They had gone public not of their own volition but as part of Beijing's "go-out" initiative to list state-run businesses overseas. The idea was that the IPOs would bring improved business practices to the companies while also building China's image abroad as an economic superpower.

The second wave of Chinese companies hit U.S. exchanges in the early to mid-2000s. These firms were sexier than their predecessors because they operated in hot industries such as technology, consumer products, and media. These companies sought out American markets to raise capital and obtain the prestige of a

U.S. stock ticker symbol. Many went to the United States because they were as-yet-unprofitable high-tech start-ups and therefore couldn't satisfy the listing criteria of the Chinese exchanges, such as having three years' minimum profitable operating history. For those companies, Nasdaq was a suitable listing destination, as it brought together high-risk, high-growth companies and offered an investor base that was experienced and willing to bet on innovative business models for a potentially big upside.

Names like Baidu, Ctrip.com, and New Oriental Education & Technology quickly became Wall Street darlings due to their industry-leading positions and the familiarity of their business models. During their IPO road shows, these companies were pitched as "the Chinese Google" or "the Chinese Expedia"—except, given the size of the Chinese market, they were expected to soon dwarf their U.S. equivalents. These were terms every U.S. investor could understand and was all too willing to pay a premium for. Most of these Chinese IPOs debuted successfully, and their managers returned home as heroes armed with handsome market capitalizations.

Many companies in this second wave of IPOs were in certain restricted sectors, such as technology, media, education, and healthcare, in which Beijing limited or prohibited direct investments from foreigners. The Chinese companies used something called the variable interest entity (VIE) structure to circumvent that rule and gain access to international capital markets.

The structure is essentially a series of contract agreements that give foreign investors control but not technical ownership over companies operating in China. Since equity holders do not actually have a claim on the company's underlying assets, the structure is inherently risky. The risk is often compounded by worries of China's opaque legal system and weak law enforcement.

One incident in early 2011 shook investor confidence in these structures, which some estimate apply to nearly half the Chinese companies now listed in the United States. Alibaba, the largest e-commerce company in China, transferred ownership of its online payment system Alipay to a Chinese domestic company held by Jack Ma, the founder and CEO of Alibaba. Yahoo, which owned more than 40 percent of Alibaba shares via a VIE structure, claimed that it was blindsided by Ma's move, which was done without the approval of Alibaba's board. The incident alarmed foreign investors because it set a high-profile example of the inherent risks in investing a company while its underlying assets are at the discretion of management and the Chinese state. Prominent investors such as David Einhorn at Greenlight Capital sold their shares in Yahoo immediately after the dispute broke out.

* * *

The third wave of Chinese IPOs, which rushed to join the party on the American exchanges around 2006, presented problems of its own for investors. At the time, China's private sector was gathering momentum, and a slew of some 400 smaller companies, so-called piggybackers, rode in on the high tide of U.S. investor optimism toward China. Among this group were many small Chinese companies that snuck into U.S. exchanges through backdoor listings, in which a company injected its assets into a listed but defunct shell company, thereby getting listed with less regulatory scrutiny from the SEC than it would have experienced in a standard IPO. This group was dominated by mom-and-pop businesses that often dealt in commodities, such as agriculture or resources. Many were located in rural areas, making it hard for investors to do due diligence. Today, many of these companies have been delisted—some voluntarily, after being taken private by management or private equity funds, and some involuntarily, after failing to comply with SEC requirements.

Getting listed in the United States is a pricey undertaking, and the application process requires jumping through a lot of hoops.

But for many Chinese companies, it was worth the effort. Smaller Chinese firms typically sought out an American exchange listing, and especially a coveted Nasdaq ticker symbol, for the prestige. Getting listed on an American exchange was glorious, to modify Deng's phrase—it was a sign these companies had made it. Once listed, they could also use their stock as a currency to compensate their employees and to acquire other assets and businesses.

By the mid-2000s, cautious attitudes like Jason's were rare. Most investors were climbing over each other to get a piece of the next Chinese offering—"market tested, SEC approved." It didn't matter that most of them didn't know the first thing about China. They simply recited the mantra that China was the world's fastest-growing economy and consumer market and that it was finally open for business. It seemed like a once-in-a-lifetime opportunity to buy in at the bottom of a huge economic wave, and most people I knew on Wall Street jumped in headfirst. But few suspected that their enthusiasm for these get-rich-quick plays was helping to inflate an investment bubble similar to the dot-com boom and bust America had seen only a few years prior.

Touring the Factory to the World

I took my first trip to mainland China as an investor in the summer of 2006. Despite Jason's strong resistance to investing in China, I managed to convince him that the firm wouldn't be able to avoid analyzing Chinese businesses, even if we didn't invest in Chinese stocks. Many U.S. businesses had exposure in China or competed with Chinese firms, and knowledge of the market was growing increasingly vital. Plus I suggested that Jason should make use of me as a resource, being a China native. He saw my logic, but he insisted we stick to companies with market capitalizations of more than $500 million, leaders in their respective businesses in private sectors. He also warned me to thoroughly investigate management backgrounds to mitigate the chance of us later discovering that we had invested in firms run by crooks or gangsters.

One company I wanted to research was called Active Chip, a Chinese company that made chips for MP3 music players. Active Chip completed an IPO in 2005, and within less than eight months, the stock shot up from $8 to $12, a handsome 50 percent return that seemed to validate American investors' love for the China factory story. By tapping into China's wealth of cheap and competent engineers, Active Chip undercut its major U.S. competitors, Sigmatel and PortalPlayer, and drove them to the verge of bankruptcy. At its peak, the stock exemplified a popular belief—later proved to be naive—that the rise of Chinese manufacturers would bankrupt American companies and steal millions of American jobs.

Something caught my eye on its financial statement: Active Chip spent almost nothing on R&D—only 2 percent of its sales, which is unusually low for an emerging tech company. That told me that its chip had little to no real value in terms of intellectual property, and the company was not investing in new product development.

I went to see the company's brand-new office building, one of those fortresses of steel and concrete that had sprung up in the sci-fi-inspired skyline of Shanghai's new Pudong District. The floor-to-ceiling windows in the CFO's office looked west, out over Pudong, the river, and the colonial buildings where Shanghai's opium traders had once been housed. The CFO told me that the company's low R&D budget was commonplace in China. The main reason was the loose enforcement of China's intellectual property laws. "It doesn't pay off to spend money on intellectual property," he explained. "It can be reverse-engineered overnight. In the United States, you could take a violator to court. But in China, the judge will simply rule in favor of whoever gives a higher kickback."

Over time, I started to realize that this was the reason for China's notorious lack of innovation. The culture of lawlessness meant many companies feared having their products reverse-engineered and copycatted. So Chinese companies spent much less on R&D than their American peers, stifling industries where innovation drives revenue growth and market share, such as technology and healthcare.

During the same meeting, I learned of a fascinating development—something that no American portfolio manager sitting in a fancy office on Fifth Avenue would have ever imagined. Active Chip had just acquired a team of engineers from Taiwan with the goal to develop a new chip for video players. But the merger went badly. The two groups of engineers—the mainlanders and the Taiwanese—clashed for cultural reasons, the CFO told me. I could guess why: in Taiwan, Chinese mainlanders are despised for having no manners or sophistication; in the mainland, Taiwanese are looked down on for being harsh bosses and cultural elitists. The Taiwanese see themselves as the more professional Chinese, more civilized and in sync with the modern world. They have little patience for Chinese mainlanders, who, having grown up in a post-Communist, not-quite-modernized country, are often perceived as crude and unprofessional. Add in nationalist sentiment—the fact that Chinese mainlanders are taught from childhood that Taiwan is a Chinese province—and little room is left between the two sides for cooperation. Regardless, the merger didn't generate the intended synergy but instead compromised morale and productivity.

When I left the meeting, I immediately arranged a call with a small private semiconductor company in Shenzhen that was rumored to have snuck into the market by selling chips similar to the ones Active Chips made but at a 30 percent discount. During the call I confirmed that the small company was willing to sacrifice short-term profitability in order to win a piece of the market—a death knell for Active Chip's profitability.

A fierce price war did indeed follow. Starting in September 2006, Active Chip reported four consecutive weak quarters. The company missed analyst earnings estimates and revised its revenue guidance downward for three consecutive quarters. Two years after its IPO, the stock dipped from its peak of $16 to below $3, around its cash balance per share.

Ferocious competition was a recurring theme for many of companies I visited, whether they made semiconductor chips, medical devices, or solar panels. Every market has examples of small companies delivering superb growth and profit margins in their early stages. But once they get to a certain size, their success attracts competition. Since few Chinese companies have defensible intellectual property, their products are often commoditized before they have the chance to scale up and establish their brand equity and franchises.

This combination of low barriers to entry and ferocious competition means Chinese companies are typically not buy-and-hold investments because their profits are not sustainable. However, some of them can be compelling trades in the early stage of their product cycle. For investors in Chinese companies, it is critical to figure out early on how far a company has progressed in its product cycle and monitor its developments and competitive landscape closely. This trend holds true for all "commodity companies"—businesses that make goods or services that are hardly differentiable from each other and compete on pricing rather than features—in emerging and developed markets. That's why I frequented Best Buy to track price changes among GPS gadgets week by week and why other American semiconductor analysts spent more time in the evening calling Chinese companies to check their prices rather than creating financial models. Even the best financial model instantly becomes inaccurate if competitive dynamics change.

My trip dispelled another myth, that of China's green-tech innovation. Many investors in the United States heard the awesome data on how many solar panels and wind turbines China was producing and believed that the country was leading the green-tech revolution. I thought so too until I started researching the sector firsthand.

I visited several solar facilities, nestled in the industrial landscape that stretches for hundreds of miles west of Shanghai. The companies tried their best to show off their labs and "proprietary technologies," but it soon became obvious to me that they were following the same low-cost manufacturing model as any Chinese button or sock manufacturer.

These companies took advantage of hefty amounts of government stimulus, cheap labor, and lax environmental regulations to pump out "clean-tech" products and ship them overseas. They were rushing to grab market share by offering cheap prices, just as with any other low-value-added Chinese factory story. Few of the turbines and panels I saw were actually installed in China; when they were, they often didn't work or were never attached to the electrical grid.

Years ago, when polysilicon, the raw ingredient for solar panels, cost 10 times what it does now, some Chinese companies boasted about their ability to use large amounts of recycled polysilicon in their cells and thus lower their costs. My contacts told me that they actually had droves of laborers sifting through the floor sweepings at polysilicon factories and hand-picking out all the leftover material. This manual process was hardly a defensible innovation worthy of being labeled high-tech. Instead, it was just another example of a Chinese company relying on cheap local labor to boost its production yield—tactics that its competitors could easily adopt as well.

China's green-tech companies became known not just for lacking intellectual property but also for stealing it. One famous case was American Superconductor Corporation (AMSC), a Massachusetts-based company that makes operating systems for wind turbines. The company had a profitable partnership supplying operating systems for wind turbines to one Chinese wind turbine manufacturer, Sinovel. But then one day, some AMSC employees visiting China saw a Sinovel wind farm operating a version of their software with an expired code. The American company had encrypted its software to stop working if its clients didn't pay a renewal fee. Clearly, Sinovel had breached these defenses.

One of AMSC's employees who had access to the software code was ultimately tried and convicted for selling company trade secrets to Sinovel. The Chinese company had given the employee a six-year employment contract worth $1.7 million in return for the codes. AMSC lost far more than that. The U.S. company was so heavily dependent on its relationship with Sinovel that its revenues dropped 90 percent. Its stock price also plummeted, falling from $44 in January 2010 to less than $5 in September 2011.

After Chinese solar and wind turbine companies bankrupted almost all their competitors globally, they finally took a dive themselves in 2011. Just like any other sector the Chinese government had supported or intervened in, the clean-tech industry faced severe manufacturing overcapacity that ultimately triggered the collapse of solar product prices and made the businesses unprofitable. Suntech Power, one of the world's largest solar companies, dissolved into bankruptcy in early 2013. Senior creditors took over the company, and equity holders saw the value of their shares fall from roughly $50 in 2008 to only $0.50 as Suntech filed for bankruptcy.

Ironically, this was all made possible by China's hefty government subsidies. On the one hand, the subsidies lowered costs for domestic manufacturers and allowed them to win market share. But ultimately they damaged their businesses by creating excess capacity in the market. The situation worsened in 2012 as the United States and the European Union passed antidumping actions to protect their markets from low-priced Chinese products. In December 2012, the Chinese government finally decided to withdraw subsidies to solar companies that were not yet profitable. The industry is now undergoing a massive restructuring, and many Chinese manufacturers have filed for bankruptcy.

No Longs, Only Shorts

I met with more than 30 companies during the two weeks I spent in China, a typically exhausting schedule that hedge fund analysts call "speed dating." What I learned did not inspire confidence. After doing exhaustive research, I had to confess to Jason that I couldn't find a single company to fit into Aurarian's long book. Our fund only bet long on companies with sustainable business models and proprietary technology, which ensured that competitors faced a high barrier to entry and the company could maintain a stable or rising profit margin.

Of the Chinese companies I saw, larger companies in big cities with proven operating track records were clearly the lesser of two evils for U.S. investors. The small ventures in rural areas had a hard time recruiting and retaining talented employees, and many of their executives were amateurs. Still, there was nothing I liked enough to invest our clients' money in. China lacked the commercial infrastructure needed to conduct business efficiently, and average labor productivity and management talent lagged behind the West as well. Instead, I found dozens of companies that had succeeded based on mass production and cheap labor, with their products well on their way to being commoditized. Many of them were perfect short candidates, and I convinced Jason to trade some of them.

I saw an interesting dilemma. No country in the history of human civilization had progressed as fast as China over the past 30 years. The country had transformed from dirt poor in 1980 to what was today effectively a middle-income country. But in some ways, China had become the victim of its own success. Chinese people at all levels of society had grown used to this rapid pace of transformation and come to see it as a goal in itself. Everyone from corporate managers to local government officials was racing to build empires.

Despite this rapid growth, the nature of economic activity had not evolved. China's success was almost entirely driven by mass production in low-end industrial manufacturing sectors and by economies of scale. Modern China was stalled in that model, wanting but unable to move up the value chain from its cheap-labor production model. Moving up that chain would require a serious and difficult effort to establish the rule of law (not to be confused with the rule of lawyers, which is sometimes the case in the United States) and political and regulatory transparency.

When I asked Chinese managers about their goal for their companies, more often than not their answer was that they wanted to grow as fast as possible. In comparison, most executives at American public companies would say they were working to generate quality and sustainable profits for their shareholders. To do so, American companies invest in research and development as well as human capital, including training their staff and cultivating a corporate culture. Chinese companies, on the other hand, often seem eager to see their growth outpace their ability to manage the company, even though this might hasten the company's demise.

This mentality of building an empire in one day seems to be deeply rooted in Chinese society, from government to individual business owners. Perhaps China changed too fast—after all, the country experienced a magnitude of economic growth in 30-plus years that had taken the Western world from the eighteenth to the twenty-first century to complete. China's institutional growth, including the rule of law and checks and balances on the single-party central government, has not kept up with the economic gains. That incompatibility continues to hinder China's progress up the global value chain. Meanwhile, other emerging economies are catching up, eroding China's position as the world's factory by offering even lower labor costs.

The Financial Crisis Strikes

The year 2007 was a good one both professionally and personally. Jason and I were a winning team, and all our hard work began to pay off. In 2007, our fund delivered a more than 60 percent return to our investors—an achievement that led *Institutional Investor* magazine to call Jason one of most promising emerging managers in the business.

The next year led us into much choppier waters. As did many other people on Wall Street, Jason and I foresaw the crash of 2008, but we weren't prepared for the magnitude of it.

Jason had seen the signs of an imminent housing crisis first-hand in 2007, as he traveled to Los Angeles and Florida to visit companies we had invested in. While driving his rental car up the coasts, Jason noticed just how many unfinished real estate projects and rows of McMansions stood empty on newly cleared plots far from city centers. This scene clashed with the public perception that both demand and prices in the housing market had nowhere to go but up.

As we know all too well now, housing purchases were fueled by widely available bank credit. Appreciating property prices and easy money sparked a gold rush, and many Americans bought properties that they couldn't afford, just because the banks were willing to lend them the money. The banks then repackaged the mortgages into their latest white-hot financial innovations and sold them to investors who bet on the continuous appreciation of the housing market. Major U.S. financial institutions created complex, often deliberately misleading financial instruments, such as mortgage-backed securities and other derivatives, which Moody's and Standard & Poor's then minted with inflated credit ratings.

During the peak of this housing bubble in 2006 and 2007, the Wall Street firms were so hungry for mortgages to securitize that they started accepting mortgages without any documentation about the borrower's creditworthiness. These subprime loans were often called "liar loans," because the borrower didn't have to verify his or her income through W-2s, income tax returns, or other records.

The proliferation of mortgage-backed securities backed by liar loans planted the seeds for the financial meltdown that began in 2008. These financial instruments, while seeming to decrease the risk financial institutions faced, actually complicated their balance sheets and ultimately served to burst America's inflated housing bubble, creating unforeseen risks to the broader economy.

In financial terms, an asset bubble forms when the market value deviates from the underlying intrinsic value. Every bubble must burst; it's a matter of when, not if. Jason and I believed that when the housing crisis occurred, the contagion would hurt all sectors of the economy, and consumer discretionary spending would be one of the first things to fall. We began building short positions around the thesis that the housing bubble had inflated consumer purchases of appliances and electronics and that once the housing bubble popped, those consumer stocks would crumble.

Our reasoning went like this: Between the early 2000s and 2006, homeowners saw the value of their property expand significantly compared with the amount of their mortgages. The environment of rising home prices and low interest rates encouraged people to refinance their homes and draw down on the equity, which they spent in turn on consumer discretionary items they otherwise couldn't have afforded. So the housing bubble had effectively fed a broader bubble in the consumer economy. If the real estate bubble popped, stocks of high-end retailers and makers of consumer electronics were certain to suffer from volatility. We decided to ready a list of short targets and be prepared when the market took a dive.

Our thesis proved to be entirely correct. But while our short positions worked out well for us, our longs suffered as banks clamped down on their lending to corporate America. In 2008, we were heavily invested in early-stage green-tech companies in the United States that relied on debt financing. Once banks tightened access to credit and eventually cut it off for small companies, some of our largest holdings—many of them apparently great technology plays—went belly up.

A good number of these companies produced the latest technology in the green energy space. But just like most green-tech companies, they were in the exploratory phase and needed incremental financing in order to commercialize the technology for mass adoption. We call this kind of a company a bull-market story, since its potential for success is tightly linked to the overall strength of the financial market. When the credit markets completely shut down in late 2008, these promising young companies were cut off from the funds they needed to operate, and many soon ran out of cash and declared bankruptcy.

Aurarian made money from our short positions, but we lost even more from our green-tech holdings. Like many others on Wall Street, we anticipated the housing crisis but underestimated its scale. While our performance was still in line with the market, those losses took their toll. We could have survived the storm if we were bigger—but we weren't.

The financial market meltdown triggered a crisis of confidence among investors. Redemption—where investors pull back their capital—accelerated, especially for small funds like ours. A group of conservative Swiss gentlemen were our main investors. Despite having earned a 60 percent return with us in 2007, they decided to withdraw their funds due to the uncertainty of the market. That spelled the end of Aurarian. It didn't take long for us to decide to return the money to our investors and close down the firm.

The entire city of New York was affected by the collapse of Wall Street. New Yorkers felt the shock waves in all aspects of our daily lives, from a plummet in prices in the high-end condo market to the closing of restaurants, fashion boutiques, and nail salons in the banking district. In the months and years that followed, many of my professional colleagues and personal friends saw their Wall Street careers interrupted, in many cases for good. Some friends took pay cuts as large as 90 percent. One good friend went from a $12 million guaranteed package at a major investment bank as a lead healthcare analyst to a $200,000 base salary at a private brokerage firm.

The banks all entered austerity mode. Banks slashed paychecks, benefits, even office amenities. When I worked at Credit Suisse, they would offer us free Starbucks coffee; after the financial crisis, my analyst friend at Goldman Sachs said the only things the firm's cafeteria gave away for free were plastic utensils. Research analysts worked for a fraction of what they used to make and felt lucky to have a job. Research budgets shrank, due partly to skyrocketing compliance and legal expenses for banks after the Dodd-Frank banking regulations were signed into law in 2010. Analysts had less money to visit companies and attend industry events, giving them fewer resources to acquire good data on given industries or companies. As a result, the quality of sell-side research suffered.

By comparison, China weathered the financial crisis well. In 2009, the Chinese economy was still heavily dependent on exports, and China almost immediately began to feel the negative effects from plunging demand in the West. So the Chinese government acted quickly: to stave off the impact of the global financial crisis, China pulled its stimulus trigger and released a $4 trillion package for large fiscal projects.

Almost immediately, railroads, bridges, and airports began expanding from the country's busy coast to the less populated center. Cities threw up infrastructure projects both useful and frivolous, from new highway systems to Olympic-sized gymnasiums destined to stand empty. Industries such as steel, cement, heavy machinery, and infrastructure construction led China's recovery. After dipping to 6.1 percent in the first quarter of 2009, real GDP growth rebounded to 11.9 percent one year later.

The world was impressed, and China envy was in full swing. Commentators everywhere forecast the decline of America, and some even went as far as to make the case that state capitalism should be the new model for the modern era.

Starting My Firm

After Aurarian closed down, Jason quickly launched a green-tech company developing something called the organic rankine cycle, which converts the heat from biomass, industrial waste, and geothermal sources into electricity. He was determined to make back the money that he lost from investing in green tech by going into the industry himself.

I was not going to leave Wall Street. I was too interested in stocks and the financial markets to go anywhere. By that time, I had developed a strong reputation and a Rolodex of contacts. Being an Asian woman in a white male-dominated world also helped me to stand out. People noticed me and my questions at various conferences, field trips, and industry events. I wasn't sure what my next move would be, so I took some time off to travel, learn to surf, and get some much-needed rest, after having worked so intensely for five years.

Both my dad and my husband encouraged me to start my own China-focused business. They thought the timing could not be better. I had both a highly desirable China background and Wall Street training and could therefore run between the world's two hottest markets with ease. Dad said that if he could start and run a business successfully without a Columbia degree, I could definitely do it with my cutting-edge Wall Street training. Two of the most important people in my life were assuring me that I had the perseverance, drive, and intelligence to do it. So I decided to give it a shot.

I could do two things: I could raise money and start a hedge fund on my own. Or I could utilize the investigative approach that I had mastered from Aurarian and set up an independent research firm to advise the investment community. After weighing both options, I decided to launch an independent research firm. I named it JL Warren—*JL* for my initials and *Warren* for the name of the street where I lived at that time.

Initially, JL Warren provided premium fundamental analysis to investors on a project-by-project basis. Over time, I expanded the platform to offer real-time data and knowledge-based research on Chinese businesses and multinationals doing business in China, mostly to sophisticated institutional investors. My research is not meant to compete with traditional sell-side reports but to supplement their qualitative reports with much more detailed raw data and and unbiased, variant views on stocks.

My career entered into a new and exciting chapter. However, my personal life didn't weather the crisis. It turned out that neither my dad's tiger parenting nor my Wall Street education in stock picking had equipped me with the skills necessary to deal with marriage.

As my engagement with my work deepened, my relationship with Andrew went from good to bad to irreparable. The day I signed my divorce papers in the fall of 2010 was the worst day of my life and marked the hardest lesson I have had to learn yet. I still pray every day that I, as well as the people around me, never again repeat my ignorant and painful mistake.

CHAPTER 9

The Red Party:
Instant Alpha

New York, 2010

I'M NOT SURE WHETHER IT WAS A NEW YORK THING, BUT OFTEN when I told people about my recent divorce, they would respond with "congratulations" or "let's go out and celebrate a new chapter." I would laugh in response, but inside I still felt a clawing and persistent pain. I deeply felt that my divorce was a personal failure—a big one.

Once again, work provided me with a psychological escape. Having China back on my radar was a welcome and much-needed distraction. Crunching numbers, scrutinizing charts on Bloomberg terminals, and attending long conference calls with company management teams dulled the pain. That was partially the reason I found myself at an IPO road show in the New York St. Regis Hotel in September 2010.

It was a wet and blustery day, one of those storms that turn the city streets into rivers and ruin a banker's Ferragamos. I had expected a low turnout at the road show, but the private dining

room of the plush hotel was packed with eager investors. Everyone was excited to hear what the executives of Global Education and Technology (GET), the latest buzzworthy China play, had
to dish up.

"I hope you enjoy the meal," a Chinese man in a stiff suit said
in stilted English, gesturing toward our roast chicken and fall root
vegetables. He then smiled and switched to Mandarin.

The purpose of the meeting was to persuade New York's banking elite to invest in the IPO of a small business that was booking
$50 million in revenue that year and growing at a rate of 30 percent.
GET had chosen to float its shares on the New York Stock Exchange
for its prestige, although Manhattan was thousands of miles away
from Beijing, where the firm conducted its business. The company
claimed it deserved a spot among several other Chinese companies
that had become Wall Street darlings. The suits in the room were
duly and easily impressed. This was the midst of what we called
the Red Party, a time when just about every Chinese asset seemed
as if it would go up in value forever. What a party it was!

The company's presentation was so well rehearsed, it felt like a
recital. The CEO started with a brief introduction of his business in
Mandarin. His bankers simultaneously translated the speech into
imperfect English laced with heavy Cantonese accents. I'm not
sure who was harder to understand. After the CEO finished, he
deferred to the CFO, who was also his wife, for the rest of the presentation. Her Canadian college degree paid off as she whipped
through the PowerPoint, gliding through the predictable questions
and deftly anticipating curve balls. There were at least two bankers stepping in to help her provide the right answers. Not that it
mattered— everyone in the room was clearly desperate to buy
stock in this Chinese growth play, the latest investing sensation
that seemed destined to print money for years to come.

Luckily I had an advantage over the other bankers in the
crowd. My old friend Peter Winn had gone to China years ago

with nothing but a Wharton MBA—and no Chinese. But through pluck and intelligence, he had become the founder of one of the largest private education companies in the country. In a nation where the upkeep and enforcement of contracts depends more on one's personal network than the law, he became an absolute expert in doing business and became extremely well connected. Peter built the China operation for English First, one of the largest and most influential language training brands in China.

With as little subtlety as I could get away with, I contacted Peter on my BlackBerry as I leafed through the voluminous IPO documents and listened to GET's presentation. Even though it was the middle of the night in China, his e-mail quickly set me straight.

"Do they have business outside of China since they call themselves global? And what technology do they have?" I wrote.

Peter e-mailed back immediately. "It is a mom-and-pop shop, a husband and wife team. They don't have much presence outside of Beijing. They get a tax break by including the word 'technology' in the company name."

Good old Peter. After 15 years in the China trenches, his business sense was better than that of most natives. And from his description, GET's business was pretty lame.

Five seconds later, another e-mail from Peter came in. "Mom-and-pop operations can make money in the Chinese education sector, but GET is not a scalable business." He clearly had a lot to say about his industry of expertise. "Their bankers told them to raise money to grow, but they don't have any clout outside of Beijing. You need to apply for a new license each time you enter a different city. That takes relationships and seamless execution, which I know all too well they don't have."

After the lunch, as I was passing through the lobby, I spotted Brian, a portfolio manager friend at a $5 billion multistrategy hedge fund. "Hey Brian, are you crashing the Red Party as well?" I asked jokingly.

He was familiar with the term we used for all of the fabled opportunities of still-Communist China. "It's a party you can't miss," Brian replied in a serious tone. "Everyone and his mother are looking at and buying China. Don't miss the boat."

"I thought you were a stock picker, not a chaser of hype," I said, prodding him further.

His face lit up at my challenge. "There's nowhere else in the world where you can find growth right now, and the money we manage needs to be invested somewhere," he countered. "If not, investors will think we're not smart enough to be their money managers."

Brian went on to tell me about two other education companies that were expected to list the following week. When I asked him which ones he liked and why, his answer was telling: "I can't really tell one from the other, but I'll put an order in for all three of them. Education's got to be hot, right? The one-child policy in China and all."

"Uh, right," I said. It seemed I had done more due diligence on which American college to apply to than he had done on these supposedly hot education companies in China.

This presentation, like so many before it, had told me all I needed to know at that moment: *caveat emptor,* buyer beware. I thought of how the dot-com bubble had built up investor hopes to such dizzying heights, only to crush them in the spring of 2000. Peter had spent a decade and a half building his company into an empire. It took him years and many mishaps to learn to navigate the legal and cultural intricacies of doing business in China. How could so many bankers, living on the other side of the world and knowing so little of China, be so greedy, lazy, and careless as to take an unfamiliar Chinese company at its word?

While I had decided not to invest in GET, it turned out to be a successful IPO. But soon after, the stock started to retreat as the husband and wife team missed its revenue targets over and over again.

* * *

Scenes like the one at the St. Regis had become common in New York by that time. China's seemingly unstoppable economic growth through the global financial crisis impressed many American investors, and Chinese companies were eager to cash in on this sentiment. In 2010, as many as 41 Chinese companies floated their shares on U.S. exchanges—making up more than a quarter of the year's IPOs, up from 18 percent in 2009 and 13 percent in 2008. China-based IPOs posted an average return of nearly 30 percent, compared with approximately 19 percent among all IPOs over the same period.

Investors hurried to lunches like the one at the St. Regis not just to learn about the company that was being touted, but also to test the waters to see how hot an IPO would be. A big crowd indicated that the IPO was likely to be oversubscribed—meaning that investors wanted more shares than were available to buy—and therefore that the stock would "pop," or soar up from the IPO price. Investors could then offload their shares for an "instant alpha," a quick effortless profit for the lucky bunch who managed to get a piece of the deal.

The lunch also gave investors face time with the key underwriters, the banks that would sell the company's shares to the public during an IPO. To get a piece of a white-hot offering, small funds and individual investors had to be sure they were at the lunches. And if the temperature was really hot, as almost all Chinese IPOs were at that time, merely showing up at the road show wasn't enough. Desperate would-be investors had to write thoughtful thank you notes afterward and persistently call their brokers at the underwriting banks, providing their feedback on the lunch and reiterating their interest.

Altogether, this was some serious bowing and scraping. But the investors had to do it. Otherwise, unless they worked at a multibillion dollar fund, they wouldn't get a piece of that instant alpha.

All this hype created a lot of converts, drunk with blind faith in the China growth story. But one peculiar character stood out the most. In my mind I nicknamed him "Knucklehead."

Knucklehead was an ancient guy who came to all the IPO lunches, rain or shine. He was born and raised in New York and had lived there all his life. He had never been to China and didn't speak a word of Chinese, but he had a passion for everything about the country. He raved about Chinese paintings, slurped soup dumplings with relish, and had an obvious appreciation for Chinese women. But above all, he loved Chinese stocks—especially the pops.

Knucklehead caught the China bug from Baidu, the homegrown search engine that now dominates the Chinese market. Baidu's stock popped 354 percent on its IPO debut in August 2005, the kind of instant alpha not seen since the dot-com boom 15 years before. From that day on, Knucklehead made sure that his butt was in a chair at every China IPO lunch.

I first met him at the lunch for Youku, a video site that was being billed as China's YouTube. I was surprised to see him attending the road show for an Internet company, a sector that usually appeals to a younger crowd. It wasn't until later that I learned that he didn't use e-mail and could barely find his way online.

At one point during the lunch, he leaned over to tell me that he owned Baidu. "What a great stock," he said loudly. "I bought it at $27.5. It's a five-bagger," he told me, using an insider term that meant he had quintupled his initial investment. "It's one of the largest positions I have in my portfolio."

I sensed he was fishing for a compliment, so I congratulated him.

"Do you own it, too?" he asked.

When I said no, he looked disappointed, even offended. He asked me why.

"I'm concerned about their overmonetization problem," I said.

"What?" he yelled back at me.

"It's kind of complicated to explain," I told him. "But have you been to their website? People think it's a search engine, but that's not exactly true."

"Website? Search engine?" He looked completely lost. "I don't remember what the company does," he confessed.

Having been on Wall Street since the first day I left college, I had met many people in the industry who were less than competent. But owning a stock without knowing anything about its underlying business was something utterly new to me. I had heard the broker's joke that there's always a greater fool to sell a stock to, but it was the first time I actually had lunch with the phenomenon.

Over time, Knucklehead gradually ingratiated himself to me by always grabbing a seat next to me at the lunches. After a few IPO group dates, I had heard most of his story.

Once upon a time, Knucklehead was a successful trader on Wall Street, amassing most of his wealth in the 1990s when regulation was much less onerous. At the peak of his career, he had accumulated around a half billion dollars. But over the past 20-some years, he had lost 90 percent of his money. While he was still wealthier than 99.99 percent of Americans, he operated what bankers consider a modest family-sized business that managed around $50 million.

Knucklehead liked to think of himself as a hedgie. But unlike any true hedgie, he had never shorted a stock in his life. Shorting the S&P Index once in a while was effectively his only hedging strategy. Throughout his career, he had always taken long positions, betting that stock prices would rise and then leveling them up by borrowing from banks. In his mind, using leverage alone—borrowing capital to enhance his rate of return—meant he deserved the hedgie moniker.

More astonishingly, Knucklehedgie—as I now began to think of him—only bought stocks and never sold them. When a stock went up, he loved it more and therefore held onto it even tighter. When the stock went down, he loved it more because it was a bargain and so bought even more of it.

Knucklehedgie's way of picking stocks was haphazard. He would share some of his tips with me from time to time. He especially liked to make bets using gossip gathered from the A-list weekend cocktail parties at his country house in Connecticut and his golf outings to a country club in Darien.

It took me very little time to realize that Knucklehedgie had completely lost it. Playing with his dwindling pile of money was just a hobby to fill up his lonely hours. He was in way over his head with his China tech stocks. But he wasn't alone. He was just one of the casualties of a China gold rush that seduced even sophisticated investors. I was just beginning to find out how deep that story went.

* * *

One morning in early December, I got an unusual call in the office from a broker. The broker said: "Our analyst suspects a small company in China called China Little Fertilizer is going to miss its earnings estimates. He just spoke with the management, which told him business was affected big time by a flood in central China."

"Thanks for the heads-up," I replied, and hung up the phone.

Nine out of 10 trading ideas pitched by brokers are useless, but once in a while it pays off to follow through. With three computer screens in front of me, I pulled up a stock chart, a list of shareholders, and a map of China. The flooded area in central China was in Hubei Province, the home of about 5 percent of the company's operations. Instantly my hunch told me that the flood might have been a cover story for declining business. It's common for companies and governments of all nations to blame natural disasters for poor results so that none of the people in charge can be faulted.

Examining the shareholder list, I saw that some prominent Wall Street names and prestigious private equity firms were the primary investors in China Little Fertilizer (CLF). The stock chart showed that shares had fetched a higher valuation than CLF's American competitors. I assumed the premium was a reward for the growth that Wall Street automatically ascribed to any China stock.

My gut told me that CLF was another gold rush story, so I hurried to set up a conference call with the Chinese CFO, a guy named Jackie Lau. The call took place at 10 a.m. Eastern Time, 10 p.m. in Beijing. The executive must have been at a loud party or a karaoke bar, as there were thumping and whirring noises in the background. His voice was raspy, as if he'd smoked too many cigarettes that night. When I asked politely about his strategy in the face of declining business, he replied with some nonsensical muttering about tightening the company's payment policy from a 90-day grace period to cash upon delivery. It was an absurd answer: it's Business School 101 that reducing customer credit plans drives away sales rather than increasing them.

From our spotty conversation, I also learned that the fertilizer business in China was extremely fragmented among lots of small companies, much more so than in the United States. Since most of these mom-and-pop businesses didn't have enough money to invest in better technology than their peers, they competed with them solely on price.

After we hung up, I dug up information online about the CFO. There was no shortage of negative news about Lau. I carefully screened the information, and none of it improved my first impression.

Lau fit the profile of a new class of well-paid professionals who had emerged with the Chinese investment boom: IPO CFOs. Those CFOs were hired right before the companies went to the public market to raise money. They were not brought on as the permanent head of finance within a corporation, as most CFOs are in normal circumstances, but for a single purpose: to prepare and eventually sell the company to investors in a public market.

Their pay package was usually composed of two parts. They pocketed a base salary of around $100,000 to $200,000, a hefty price tag footed by oblivious IPO investors. But their real meat came from stock options. Options in Chinese companies typically have a two- to three-year lockup period—an amount of time during which company executives and other cornerstone investors are forbidden from selling their shares to protect the company price and limit trading volatility—which is much shorter than those of American companies. Once the lockup expires, the CFO can cash out his options to the tune of a few million dollars. The higher the stock price, the more value he or she can unlock from the option.

There is nothing wrong with making fast money as long as the money is clean—ask Mark Zuckerberg. But Lau had pumped up the valuation of the companies he worked on and then dumped them as if he were on steroids. Every company he touched had eventually crumbled.

All the facts suggested that CLF could be a fraud. The situation reminded me of Sunlight, one of our home-run shorts at my previous hedge fund. CLF had the same recipe of sketchy management, a highly commoditized business, and an overhyped stock. But most important, CLF's products were not selling, judging from the fact that the management was trying to cover up declining sales with excuses that didn't add up.

But here was the challenge. Unlike Sunlight, CLF was a retail stock, meaning private investors owned most of the shares, not institutions. Retail investors are slower to sell their shares when bad news breaks; they are more forgiving. That makes the stock difficult to short.

I needed a sounding board, so I e-mailed my old boss and mentor, Jason. "I need your advice on a stock," I wrote. "It's a Chinese fertilizer company fetching a 25× P/E multiple." The price/earnings multiple is one way to measure how expensive a stock is in relation to the amount of profit that company generates, and 25 times is a premium price. I also spelled out the other red flags: CLF was a poorly managed company in a commodity business that was shifting to a lower-margin product to fend off decelerating sales growth. Against common sense, it was making customers pay sooner, likely driving them away in the process. On top of it all, the CFO was the kind of guy who would take a conference call at a nightclub. "But it's a retail stock," I wrote. "How do you think this will play out if I'm right?"

In less than 30 minutes I had my response. Most people in my business are CrackBerry addicts (we still use the BlackBerry for its heightened security features). Jason had gathered all the basic information on the stock. As I read his e-mail, I was filled with the restless excitement that comes from uncovering a great play.

Jason wrote forcefully: "It sounds like a great short. This is how you short a retail stock. You short it, and every time it lifts its head, you hit it again. You have to save your firepower. Pace yourself. And if your thesis is right, the stock goes to zero."

That made perfect sense, so I took his advice. I started with a small position. Then, during the weeks leading up to the company's earnings report in November, I nibbled on it or added onto it each time the stock went higher.

The morning of the company's earnings release, I woke up one hour before the alarm. I went into the office at 6 a.m. to wait for the earnings release. At 7 a.m., the news flashed across my Bloomberg terminal. CLF's sales and profits had both come in at a fraction of analyst estimates, sending the stock tumbling 16 percent in pre-market trading. I had nailed it. While I was pleased, I was in no rush to cover the short position. I told myself, "The movie has just started."

The company's stock deflated further over the next few months. Then in February, a research firm issued a report alleging that CLF had falsified its 2009 revenue and earnings. The report featured detailed data and pictures demonstrating that the business was effectively a sham. In May, the Nasdaq hearings panel ruled to delist and suspend trading in its shares. Today, the stock trades not on an exchange but over the counter, where companies do not need to meet minimum requirements or file with the SEC, for a measly $0.16 a share. Just like that, in just six months, I had doubled my investment.

* * *

Normally I love New York in December: festive holiday parties, the Christmas tree in Rockefeller Center, ice skating in Central Park followed by hot chocolate. But this year was different. I felt like I was standing alone in the cold, with a thick pane of glass separating me from the happiness and excitement of New York's Christmas festivities.

Those who are single and working on Wall Street and who don't want to spend the holidays alone have two standard choices: going to glamorous beach parties at St. Barth's in the Caribbean or skiing in Aspen, Colorado. It had not taken long for word to get out that I was single again, but as I watched my e-mail inbox fill up with invitations to these two predictable destinations, I wasn't even motivated enough to open the messages and respond.

Rather, I wanted to be close to my family. Strangely enough, I needed to be with my father, to absorb a little of his strength.

I called Peter, my old friend from the education industry, to tell him that I was considering returning to Shanghai for the holidays. "Why don't we schedule a bunch of meetings for you around the holidays?" was his reply. "That way you can get some research done." I thought it was a great idea. I hung up and booked a last-minute trip to the place of my birth.

I wanted to see with my own eyes what was lying beneath all that fog and, I hoped, allay my doubts about the corporate governance and integrity of Chinese companies. Exploring a new investment frontier—and being among the people who knew me best—would almost certainly be preferable to facing the holidays as a newly divorced woman in New York City.

Shanghai

Stepping into the lobby of the Four Seasons, not long after I deplaned from my 15-hour flight to China, I was flooded with a sense of familiarity. The decor was just as luxurious as the hotel's Manhattan branch, with its silken table settings and crystal chandeliers. But the quiet New York sophistication was absent; the vast marble space was a hive of activity. At every table, a transaction was taking place. The crackling energy of the space evoked a sense of excitement and growing prosperity that was lacking on Wall Street.

There could be no doubt that this was China. The raucous hustle and bustle of businesspeople cutting deals was wreathed with the pungent odor of stale cigarette smoke. The coal bosses from the provinces and the flush local financiers yelled out to one another, oblivious to all the refinement around them, their jarring countryside accents drowning out their neighbors' conversations. An army of waitstaff stood ready to respond to the shouts of *"fuwuyuan!"* ("waiter!") from customers across the dining area. This was a new frontier, the Wild East, a place where rags-to-riches stories were unfolding before my eyes.

I was there to meet a friend, Robert, who had moved to Shanghai from New York a few years ago to join the private equity gold rush. I surveyed the room while I waited for him, and then I spotted a familiar face: Nick, a former investment banker and Ivy League graduate, now one of millions of unemployed casualties of the 2008 financial crisis.

"Nick! What are you doing here?" I asked after a quick embrace.

He was on his way to discuss one of the deals that was gestating around me. He briefed me on his latest venture: a boutique advisory shop targeting rural private businesses that needed cash to expand.

Nick's business model was to hire local analysts to scout out private enterprises far from China's booming coastal areas. These local hires, who work at one-tenth the salary of a comparable Wall Street position, would find private businesses operating in obscure locations, most of which had limited operating histories, no earnings, and no hard assets for collateral. Nick's trick was to convince these provincial company managers, many of whom didn't even need financing, that he could merge their businesses into an already publicly listed shell, therefore bypassing the usual stringent IPO regulations.

This was the model for the now-infamous reverse-merger deal, a loophole that gave companies a back door onto America's normally well-guarded stock exchanges. An advisory firm like Nick's would match a company seeking to list with a defunct shell company that still retained its ticker symbol. The first company would merge with the second, effectively going public while bypassing the SEC's strict auditing and disclosure requirements for IPOs.

Some legitimate companies did go public this way, such as Blockbuster Entertainment and Berkshire Hathaway. But many of the entities that listed through a reverse merger were evading SEC oversight for a reason. These firms were often too immature or poorly performing to attract investors—otherwise they would have chosen the standard listing route. Reverse mergers helped sneak hundreds of sketchy companies onto U.S. exchanges, including many Chinese firms that would not have passed muster for a traditional IPO. Between January 2007 and April 2010, a total of 159 Chinese companies took this back door onto U.S. securities markets—nearly three times the number of Chinese companies that conducted traditional IPOs.

It didn't take companies like Nick's long to exhaust the low-hanging fruit. As the China gold rush continued, banks began hunting down companies—IPO ready or not, with real earnings or not—to conduct reverse mergers. A few boutique investment banks in New York and California handled many of the reverse-merger deals. They sent employees to China's hinterlands to seek out new candidates, packaged them with promotional materials, and sent them down the assembly line to investors. Bankers weren't picky—there was too little meat and many mouths to feed. Likewise, many investors didn't know or care about the real quality of China-based companies.

They should have been more concerned. Some of these banks courted their Chinese clients by promising to use a light touch when doing due diligence. Investment banks are charged with verifying a company's financials before an IPO. But some American bankers sold Chinese executives by pledging not to contact their banks to check their cash positions—in other words, giving them a green light for fraud.

Reverse-merger production lines boomed, and Nick, ever the stellar salesman, became quite popular in China's business arena. Maybe even a little *too* popular—in less than six months after our encounter in Shanghai, both he and some of his clients would become targets of an ongoing investigation by the SEC.

By the end of 2010, fraud and serious accounting issues were being uncovered everywhere at Chinese firms, with the help of a group of independent research firms that began digging up dirt on fraudulent Chinese companies for their hedge fund clients.

Chief among these research firms was Muddy Waters, an outfit led by a former lawyer named Carson Block. Block drew the name of his company from an old Chinese proverb: "Muddy waters make it easy to catch fish." According to Block, the opacity of China's business environment had made it a breeding ground for committing fraud, cutting corners, and gaming the system. Block and his counterparts plunged into these murky waters and started catching fish.

His methods were simple and effective: Block would identify a target and dig in. His researchers spent months tracking down and interviewing insiders and delving into corporate structures. They would even travel to remote locations in China to videotape empty factories or count acres of farmland. Block's reports did not just tell their reader about fraud; they demonstrated it step-by-step with pictures, data, and insider information.

By September 2012, exposés by Muddy Waters and other firms had forced the auditors of 67 Chinese companies to resign. And 126 Chinese companies had either been delisted or had "gone dark," meaning they were no longer filing with the SEC.

Those results shouldn't have been that surprising. Many of these reverse-merger companies were low-end manufacturers or commodity companies in China's hinterlands. The management at these companies left a lot to be desired; many had built their businesses off local connections, as opposed to management or finance skills. It's unlikely that many knew enough English to say "Nasdaq" instead of "Na-si-da-ke," the Chinese transliteration— let alone understood and respected the mechanisms of first-world capital markets and their legal requirements.

Nick hurried off to his next meeting as I continued to scan the lobby for my friend Robert, who appeared a few minutes later, apologizing profusely for his tardiness.

"You must be really busy with all those listings," I said, as we sat down in a more discreet corner of the lobby, screened by a clump of potted bamboo.

"We had to push them out of the pipe because their four- to five-year shelf life was up," he explained. "Some of these guys are too hickish to go public. Their businesses don't make money, and they're burning cash. Banks won't lend to them because they're not connected with the Communist Party. So we have to push them out while the market is still hot."

Two Johnnie Walker and green teas later, he grew even more candid, confiding that one of the local sportswear merchandisers his firm invested in was in fact struggling. Sales objectives were met by channel stuffing—forcing products into retail channels so that the company could book the revenue, even though there was no customer demand for the products. The stores ended up stock-piling the goods or getting rid of them at a steep discount, sometimes by sending them back to the company or by unloading them on a gray market. In any case, the retailers rarely returned to the company for more orders, as the company's subsequent quarterly earnings demonstrated.

I couldn't help but think back to the IPO lunch scene at the St. Regis in New York. Nick wouldn't have been in business if it hadn't been for the insatiable demand for Chinese stocks. The demand came from such eager yet ill-informed American investors like Brian and those attending GET's IPO lunch. It started to make sense to me—a lot of sense.

I began to suspect, as I met with more and more people in Shanghai, that the entire financial food chain was laced with fraudulence. U.S. investors were sitting behind Bloomberg terminals daydreaming of striking gold but were either too lazy, too blind, or too hopeful to dig up the dirt and examine its contents. They would buy almost any stock from China, making the bankers seem like geniuses for financing the IPO.

But the real malfeasance involved the supply side—the some-times fraudulent, sometimes immature companies that private equity partners and investment bankers churned out as IPOs. It began with the delirious demand for all stocks Chinese, which drove enterprising bankers into China's less traveled regions in search of IPO candidates. There they found companies that were in need of capital but that also had unsophisticated management teams, limited operating histories, no earnings, and no govern-ment backing—and therefore no way to list domestically or in the United States. These companies were willing to pay the bankers' commission because having a New York listing gave them brag-ging rights in China. Several reverse-merger companies confided in me that after the fees to bankers, lawyers, and stock marketers, little of the IPO proceeds were left to grow their businesses.

Private equity had a similarly suspicious role in setting up fledgling private companies for IPOs. Bankers were pursuing companies, suitable or unsuitable, to cut them a check that would allow them to get listed in the United States.

When a hot investment theme begins to feed on investor greed, ignorance, and laziness—and is further inflated by unscrupulous, opportunistic investment banks—ugly things tend to happen. The Red Party was clearly a gold mine of shorting opportunities.

Beyond that, it prompted more questions. If Chinese stocks were mostly hyped-up myths, was the larger Chinese economy also not what it seemed?

Escaping New York for Shanghai this holiday season had turned out to be another rabbit hole of due diligence, and I couldn't resist jumping in. I had to learn more, the rank cigarette smell and coarse manners of these Chinese businesspeople notwithstanding.

I figured there was one way I could begin to find out. I called my sister and asked her to pick me up. I needed to talk to her and my dad. I needed an inside perspective—the truth about the reality of modern China.

CHAPTER 10

The New Chinese Reality Check

A S I WALKED OUT OF THE FOUR SEASONS, MY SISTER, JASMINE, pulled up in her brand new Mercedes—her second car. Jasmine, a marketing manager at the Shanghai office of a New Zealand dairy company, lives a typical Shanghai upper-middle-class lifestyle. She and her husband, a purchasing manager at an American multinational machinery company, take home healthy paychecks; they bought an apartment several years ago without taking out a mortgage.

Like most of her friends, Jasmine loves to drive to work, even though it means an hour's commute each way instead of the 20 minutes it would take by subway. Rather than fight through the crowds that swarm the trains and buses at rush hour, Jasmine prefers the luxury of sitting in the car, texting on her iPhone, and eating a tuna sandwich from Starbucks for breakfast. Because of the glut of cars that has recently appeared in China's big cities, it's often faster to walk than drive during rush hour. For locals, however, the novelty of such luxury more than offsets the inconvenience.

Sliding into Jasmine's front seat, I noticed a yellow tassel dangling from her rearview mirror with a Buddhist pendant promising lifelong protection. "When did you start to believe in Buddhism?" I asked.

"After having consumed enough, one desires some spiritual fulfillment," she said. "In China, there isn't much to believe in."

Sitting under the dangling tassel in a new Mercedes, I couldn't help but smirk at the hypocrisy. "Don't Buddhists believe in minimalism?" I restrained my tone so as to not offend, but she didn't seem to care.

"We buy fish from the wet market and release them in the river every Saturday," she said. "Buddhism has become really popular among the upper middle class."

The traffic in downtown Shanghai was total gridlock. We sat among shiny Buicks and BMWs at an intersection with Nanjing West Road, an ultracommercialized section of the city. Nanjing Road has long been a heavily populated, neon-lit shopping street, even when I was little. But only in the past few years have the world's most high-end luxury retailers taken over the boulevard's shops, turning this thoroughfare into an outlet for Shanghai's new spending power and the city's growing taste for ostentation.

The glitzy distractions were entertaining: fancy Cartier window displays, flashing movie screens with dancing Chinese characters, fashionable Shanghainese women sporting Louis Vuitton bags of questionable authenticity. Raggedy-looking salespeople twirled light-up toys on the pavement or hawked cheap scarves and sunglasses out of suitcases. Massive neon signs competed for the attention of potential consumers, the pedestrians laden with shopping bags who hustled around the hawkers with the exuberance and panic of Black Friday shoppers.

This was the China that grabbed the world's headlines. Its GDP growth and new wealth formed a sharp contrast with the aging infrastructure and mounting debts in the developed markets of

America and Europe, which were still struggling to heal deep wounds sustained in the financial crisis.

The car continued haltingly past a patterned Miu Miu store and then a gigantic, 100-foot-tall Louis Vuitton poster of a suitcase behind which the company was constructing a new store. I turned to Jasmine, eager to get her take on the growing luxury market, a perpetual area of interest for many U.S. investors. "Is it true that the Chinese are obsessed with foreign brands? Is it because the Chinese are so concerned with face?" I asked, using the Chinese term for keeping up appearances.

"Not entirely," she said thoughtfully. "A big part of the brand obsession is because the new rich are eager to show off their success. But part of the reason is also because the Chinese equate foreign brands with quality and reliability. Either you pay a very high price for quality, or you get knock-offs that fall apart a few months after you buy them. There's almost nothing in between."

The car came to a stop next to a digital advertisement showcasing a rare caterpillar fungus—a powerful traditional Chinese medicine. "Does that work?" I turned to my sister.

"Who knows?" she said. "Even locals like me can't tell the difference between fake and real products. So we just don't buy medicines outside of the major pharmacies. Don't drink Chinese milk or any dairy products, either. If you eat any fruit, make sure to first peel off the skin."

"Wow," I said. "It was a lot safer when we were kids. Remember we used to eat pan-seared pork buns from the street cart?"

"You can't do that anymore. They use oil from the gutters to save money. Chinese vendors think they have to cut costs in every way possible, or else they'll be out of business in no time."

It seemed counterintuitive. China had delivered impressive economic growth since I was a child. One would think that as a country gets richer, its people would no longer need to fight for their livelihoods. Shouldn't they therefore hold themselves up to higher moral standards, like the honor code we had at Middlebury?

Jasmine stopped the car on a narrow street, breaking my train of thought. "Where are we?" I asked.

She pointed to the street sign. "Tai Xing Road."

It was the street where we had grown up, a place I hadn't visited since we moved in 1993. The neighborhood had been completely altered: 20-story apartment buildings had replaced almost all the low-rise, plain concrete houses with corrugated roofs. And yet familiar vestiges remained: the clotheslines strung across the street, the same notice board with public announcements tacked up. Our old building was almost exactly the same, except for a new coat of paint and a few air conditioners sticking out of the apartment windows—signs of status in the new Shanghai.

"Are any of the old neighbors still there?" I asked Jasmine.

"Most of them. Let's go say hi to Grandma Yangyang," she said, referring to our old neighbor whom we called grandma as a term of endearment. "Last time I stopped by she asked about you."

"I thought everyone got rich in China and moved to nicer homes," I said, scanning the drab apartment blocks.

"Not all of them. Only 1 percent, at most," Jasmine explained as she skillfully maneuvered the car down a narrow lane. "But you Americans think the 1 percent is the whole of China," she added, with a slight smirk.

We got out of the car, and I followed Jasmine into our old apartment building, one of the only old-fashioned ones that remained in the neighborhood. We climbed the familiar stairs to a door on the third floor. The door to Grandma Yangyang's apartment was open, but we knocked to let her know we were there.

The inside of her apartment had been renovated, but it was still the same small one-bedroom apartment, about 300 square feet. The kitchen was so tiny that the half-size refrigerator stood in the living room, next to the TV stand. The decor was plain, just some faded curtains and an uncomfortable wooden sofa and chair in the traditional Chinese style. An assortment of plants that Grandma Yangyang had carefully grown from seeds was perched in the windowsill, brightening the room.

Grandma Yangyang greeted us warmly from her bed. She was reduced to skin and bones, and her mind seemed to drift in and out of her surroundings. Beside her on the bedside table was an assortment of pill bottles.

I sat by her bed for a while, listening to her stories. She informed me in a weak voice that her husband had died of cancer the previous year. She had been in perfect health until then, but just a few months after her husband's death, she too had become bed-ridden. Her five daughters, all in their forties, took turns staying over, feeding her, bathing her, and giving her medicine—not a cheap or easy endeavor. Medicines had become very expensive in China, and they cost more than Grandma's entire retirement income, so the daughters split the remaining cost.

This was a story not likely to be heard in America, where Grandma would probably be sitting alone in a home. People in China who send their parents to a nursing home, whether five-star or not, are often condemned by their extended family and communities. Taking care of one's parents is still viewed as an absolute duty in China, with some crimes of filial impiety punishable by law.

Her home was a reality check in more ways than one. I realized that, like many Americans, I had been misled by the glitzy Park Hyatt on the Bund and the proliferation of luxury flagship stores along Nanjing Road. That was not the average Chinese life. My old neighbors, with their rundown apartments and frugal lifestyles, were the real Chinese middle class.

The construction boom since 1980 had provided a portion of Chinese people with new apartments, washing machines, and refrigerators. But while their homes may have had new appliances and a coat of paint, most people were living in the same drafty buildings, with unpredictable plumbing and fuses that blew as soon you flipped on a hair dryer.

Compared with the people who now occupied the highest strata of Chinese society, people like Grandma and her family did not feel much better off than before. Grandma's family had some new possessions, but the major difference was that, unlike 30 years ago, they had far wealthier people around to compare themselves with. For the first time, they felt that they had been left behind.

CHAPTER 11

Walking with My Father

Phuket Beach, Thailand, January 2011

A
FTER A MONTH IN CHINA, MY LUNGS ACHED AND MY SKIN was breaking out. The oppressive pollution was enough to make me crave the pristine air, water, and amenities of New York; yet something was blocking me from booking my return ticket. Since the first dinner in Shanghai, Dad hadn't lectured me, even once. We were all being very cordial to one another, but I knew the trip would feel incomplete if I didn't allow him to say his piece.

In a masochistic impulse, I considered taking him back to New York with me, but just then an epic snowstorm buried the city. We needed a less harsh environment, without snow or pollution or traffic jams.

"Make sure you take a ferry to Phi Phi Island," my friend recommended when I asked her about Thailand, thinking a warm destination on a beach resort would be relaxing. "The water is calm and warm with beautiful coral. It's perfect for snorkeling."

She didn't need to say more. I booked the flights and hotel immediately. Dad loves swimming and so do I, although how I learned is an unpleasant memory.

It was a vacation of early bedtimes. Dad paddled about in the water every day as I watched from the beach, my head swirling with thoughts about education companies in China and the noisy crowd of businesspeople at the Four Seasons. By the third day, the roiling had subsided to a controlled flow, and my thoughts started to organize themselves. On the fourth day, I woke up so early that it was still dark out. I could see from the glowing line under my door that the sky was turning a deeper shade of rose by the minute. That meant it would a good beach day, so I texted my father, not knowing if he was up.

"Would you like to have a walk on the beach with me?" I asked.

It was a postcard scene. The white sand stretched into green hillside, and the bay yawned into an endless horizon. As I looked out over the scene, it was hard to tell where the sand became the water and the water became the sky. Strolling down the beach, I kept scanning back and forth, from water to stars, hills to sun, taking it all in. It must have put Dad in a pensive mood, because he suddenly recited a traditional Chinese saying:

"As long as there is life, there is hope, and a good man knows when to yield." He wasn't absorbed in the scenery as I was, but looking steadfastly at the sand beneath him, hands clasped behind his back.

I smiled at the quote. It's from a famous Chinese poem that we were required to memorize in high school.

"Success is never a straight line," Dad continued. "Deng Xiaoping was sent to the rice paddy, demobilized, dismissed by Mao, and then he came back to shape up the country and become one of the most respected leaders in Chinese history."

I looked back into the glowing horizon. His voice was not its usual didactic tone, not even matter-of-fact. It was soft. "How were your meetings in Shanghai?" he asked, changing the subject.

"Interesting, to say the least," I told him. "For some reason, I'm much more skeptical than my American colleagues who worship China for its hypergrowth. Maybe it's easier for them to dismiss America and look to the East for inspiration when things are tough there."

"America will recover sooner than people think. Talented people around the world still rush to that country, Chinese included. More Chinese parents are sending their kids to the U.S. now that they can afford it, unlike 15 years ago when one had to rely on scholarships."

He began talking about the nouveaux riches in Shanghai who were rushing to buy homes in America. Government officials too were leaving China in droves. Investing upward of $100,000 in a U.S. company or homestead ensured a fast-lane ticket to U.S. residency, and those who had money needed a safe place such as the United States for their cash. Most people, including those who worked for the Chinese government, knew that investments in China were not totally safe from the arbitrary whims of the state.

At the age of 64, Dad was as aware and well informed as ever. A lack of formal college education has never held back his intellect. The gold-mining Wall Streeters would do well to sit down with him for tea.

"That's exactly what I've heard," I broke in, excited to share these thoughts with someone at long last.

The wind had not woken up; everything was still, as if out of respect for the sun's triumphant return. For a moment, everything about this morning was utterly peaceful. Then Dad broke the brief silence:

"Junh, I apologize for being harsh with you when you were little. I hope you know that when I was beating you I still loved you. I didn't know a better way of making you strong. I didn't know I had any choice. I didn't know how to show you my love."

For a second, I thought about Andrew and my constant struggle to translate the language of love to him—one language I could never seem to master, just like my father.

"Your sister told me that you cried in her car the other day. It pains me to see you suffering this much from the loss of your husband. I was talking to your mother the other night. I told her if I could do anything, anything, to take the pain away from you, I would."

His words started to choke in his throat. I hadn't expected this. The zombie days, weeks, and months after Andrew left were still so fresh that I couldn't forget, no matter how hard I tried. I was walking in paradise, but it didn't assuage the dull throb of that wound.

"You are resilient, just like America. You've got the best education and training that both the worlds have to offer. You will come out of this tough patch feeling wiser. Americans will come out of this recession stronger. I know that."

Dad stopped walking and fished something out of his pocket, a debit card issued by the Industrial and Commercial Bank of China. It caught the light and glinted in the sun.

"I want to invest in your business. The combination of your China knowledge and Wall Street training is unique. The combination of your drive and courage is rare. I am very confident that one day very soon you will be a huge success."

"Thank you. I must have gotten my skeptical mind from you," I replied. Pointing to his debit card, I asked, "But what is this for?"

He cleared his throat, "I put all the money I made from my real estate business on this card. I've been meaning to give it to you for a long time now, but I couldn't find the right opportunity. This is perfect. Use the money to grow your own business."

Dad tried to put card in my hand, but I refused to take it.

"No, take it. You must! This is for me to show you my support, and for you to open a new chapter in your life. The timing couldn't be better."

In my father's eyes, I could see the confidence that I would succeed—a look that either he had hidden from me my whole life or I had refused to see.

* * *

I did not take the card. It represented years of laboring through corrupt state-run enterprises, lawless private practice, late nights, and early mornings. Dad deserved every penny he made.

Understanding the meaning behind that small piece of plastic helped me reconcile a lifetime of struggle with my past. Suddenly the burden of the childhood that had instilled in me such devastating insecurity, that cost me my self-esteem and marriage, began to lift.

CHAPTER 12

The Human Cost of the Economic Miracle

I T WAS GOOD TO SPEND TIME WITH MY FATHER ONE ON ONE—
healing, actually. I flew back to Shanghai to continue my
research, this time taking a special interest in modern Chinese
culture in order to understand what exactly had gone awry under-
neath this seemingly brilliant economic miracle.

* * *

Up until Mao's takeover, China had been a religious state. Whether
it was Buddhism, Taoism, Confucianism, or a local folk religion,
everyone had something to believe in. In feudal China, turning
your nose up at the local deities was considered suicide to your
fortunes. But after 1949, the Communists put an end to all things
religious (except for the religious reverence of Mao, of course).
Marx had proclaimed religion to be "the opiate of the masses."
For decades after Mao took power, religious people were heavily
persecuted.

Beginning in 1978, Deng's Reform and Opening Up focused
exclusively on economic development. If the Maoist era had not

been enough to squash the growth of spiritual beliefs in China, the crush of Tiananmen ensured it. After the 1989 massacre, Premier Li Peng made it clear that business would now be the only activity that Chinese people could safely engage in. And so, dismayed and heartbroken, and eager once again to put their past behind them, the Chinese turned to the one thing they knew to be secure, safe, and infallible: money.

The unstoppable growth that ensued made this proposition easy for Chinese people to swallow. As more and more people saw their wealth and their quality of life lifted beyond what they had ever dreamed of, it became reasonable to ignore any lingering gripes about the lack of shared beliefs and personal freedom of modern Chinese life.

In dismissing the importance of social rights in favor of uninterrupted economic growth, though, the government unwittingly signed a social compact. In effect, this compact promised that as long as the Chinese people focused on getting rich instead of building a fair and free society, they and their children could enjoy the ever-improving fruits of their labor.

Just as no one could have foreseen in 1980 the amount of wealth China would enjoy by 2000—the skyscrapers, the ever-present Audis, the iconic Rolex watches—no one in 1990 could have predicted the ultimate cost of China's singular focus on wealth. The result was that the Chinese people hold very few truths to be "self-evident"—there are no commonly agreed-upon values on which to base a constitution or belief system. Social values remain weak because the system does not encourage citizens to believe in a power higher than the state—and given the personal tragedies and inequalities that many Chinese have witnessed in the last 30 years, the state is hard to believe in.

The party sees the very existence of a higher moral authority as a threat—and with good cause, since spiritual beliefs are often what give people the confidence to oppose an earthly power. One of China's deadliest civil wars of the last 200 years was the Taiping Rebellion from 1850 to 1864, in which a man claiming to be the younger brother of Jesus Christ turned 30 million people against their Qing rulers. In modern China, joining religious institutions can still be dangerous: Chinese Christians still must register every time they enter a church, and joining "cults" as defined by the state can get them in serious trouble. While China's wealthier classes now have some freedom to quietly explore religion, the bottom line remains that the party is the highest law of the land—not a constitution, not absolute morality, and certainly not a god.

* * *

Most Chinese people have become too preoccupied with their own pursuit of wealth to value the spiritual. This trend has left a silent majority feeling disconcerted—including even my sister and her husband. Although Jasmine values her car and iPhone, she also seeks everyday ways to remind herself that there is more to life than luxury goods. So Jasmine and her husband study Buddhism and work some of its practices into their lives when they can, such as buying fish at the market and releasing them into the rivers near Shanghai so they aren't sold and eaten. There are still plenty of inconsistencies in trying to be a spiritual person in modern China—I'm not sure if the fish can actually survive the polluted water, for example, and Jasmine also happily goes to Morton's steak house in Shanghai for a porterhouse.

The focus on wealth has the unfortunate side effect of drawing attention away from ethics. Wealth does not always come at the expense of morality. In China, however, the singular focus on catching the mouse has robbed China of a societywide interest in fairness and decency. Cutthroat competition, starting in the classroom and carrying into the workforce, leaves little incentive for people to behave themselves unless it is in some way profitable.

The irony is that—as I've witnessed throughout my inter-actions with private business owners and managers—most Chinese want to make ethical choices. China's harsh business environment and lack of legal enforcement, however, means that the unethical choice is often the only way to survive. Cheating and corner cutting are the norm.

In industries where innovation drives growth and market share, such as technology and healthcare, China's culture of lawlessness hinders innovation. If you create something commercially compelling, it is nearly guaranteed that others will copy it and undercut your pricing. As I mentioned earlier, that is why most private companies spend a far lower portion of their revenue on R&D than American peers in the same sector. For example, off-patent drugs make up about 97 percent of the market in China. That proportion is less than 75 percent in the United States, even at the peak of a generic wave in 2012, when half a dozen major patents expired. The reason is that in China, it is far more lucrative to reverse-engineer, copy, or steal a drug formula than to create one from scratch and seek patent protection. In the long run, this atmosphere prevents Chinese companies from moving up the value chain in industrialized manufacturing to create more advanced and profitable products.

A Lost Society

Most Chinese people are quick to admit that something in the past few decades has gone awry in their country. The media and social networking sites are filled with stories that illustrate how lacking China is in shared beliefs and social trust.

In the early 2000s, an old woman became infamous for suing a stranger who found her lying on the sidewalk and took her to the hospital. The woman said that he had pushed her down while rushing to catch the bus. Her injuries cost tens of thousands of U.S.

dollars. While there was no evidence to convict him, the Nanjing court still ruled in her favor. The reason was that, according to the judge, no ordinary person would help someone whom he found on the ground unless he himself had caused her injury.

In 2010, a Xi'an college student ran over a young mother with his car, then flew into a fury when he saw her noting his license plate number. In order to avoid being sued, he stabbed her to death (he later received a death sentence himself). That same week, a drunk college student at Hebei University also hit and killed a pedestrian. He ignored the incident and continued on his way to drop his girlfriend off at her dorm. When he was finally forced out of his car by security guards, he invoked his father's status as a local official in a phrase that went viral on the Internet overnight: "Go ahead, sue me if you dare—my dad is Li Gang!" In the end, his father couldn't save him from a multiyear sentence in prison.

And while those young, wealthy drivers with fathers in power have solicited the most attention, they are not the only ones who are morally lacking. In 2011, a two-year-old girl in Guangdong was run over by a vehicle, then passed by nine other onlookers before her mother found her.

Every country has drunk drivers and murders. The United States is one of the worst models in that regard—it ranks high among developed countries for crime and homicide rates. What is special to China is the distance that strangers put between themselves, as if helping a stranger even on her deathbed were not worth the risk.

And so it is in business.

* * *

In the summer of 2008, tens of thousands of babies became violently ill from tainted milk powder. Subsequent investigations revealed that China's top dairy companies, which were enjoying inspection-free privileges from the government, were churning out contaminated products.

The backdrop of the milk scandal revealed yet another powerful example of how the government created distortions by intervening in the market.

In 2008, the growing costs of cattle feed and facilities began to squeeze profit margins in the dairy business, and farmers began to raise the price of milk. To keep consumers happy and control inflation, however, the government imposed price controls on the dairy sector.

Mengniu, a publicly traded Chinese milk producer based in Inner Mongolia, saw its share price fall 30 percent between mid-October and mid-November 2007 as the company's profit margin was squeezed by government price regulations and rising costs. To preserve their declining profits, milk suppliers in China resorted to an intuitive cost-cutting scheme: adding water to their liquid milk products. At the same time, a legal but harmful chemical called melamine was added to inflate protein levels and disguise that the milk had been diluted.

When the news broke that a dozen infants had died and tens of thousands had been hospitalized from watered-down, chemically adulterated formula, parents in and outside of China stopped buying Chinese dairy products. At least 11 countries halted all imports of them. Chinese consumers—including my sister, a mother with a newborn at that time—were too scared to touch any domestic dairy product. To be safe, they were more than willing to pay a big premium to buy imported baby formula. Leading Western dairy companies such as Wyeth, Mead Johnson, Abbott, and Nestlé profited from the Chinese consumer confidence crisis.

The melamine scandal became one of the largest food safety events in recent years, according to the World Health Organization, all for "simple, basic, short-term profits." Managers in the dairy industry were arrested. Several were sentenced to life imprisonment, and two were sentenced to death. Those held accountable were the highest-ranking members of the companies, CEOs and CFOs. No one who dealt directly with the product was punished.

The parents of the sick and dead children held a press conference in early 2009. For doing so, five of them were detained by the police and sent to labor camps, the typical punishment for someone bringing attention to embarrassing court cases in China.

China's food security issues extend far beyond milk products. Cooking oil bought in the store is often laced with oil and food waste gathered from gutters. Farmers overdose their fruits and vegetables with pesticides to increase the yield; some use dirty industrial water from paper factories to irrigate their wheat. Cottage industries have sprung up around creating "eggs" and "beef" out of paraffin, cheaper meats, and chemicals.

These disgusting practices have landed China in a paradoxical situation. Chinese people have more discretionary income than ever before. They spend more these days on everything: food, fashion, and entertainment. But at the same time, they have lost faith in domestic products. As a result, multinationals are perfectly positioned to seize the growing piece of pie. Global food brands including Nestlé, Mars, Dove, Kraft, and Heinz price their products higher, yet are met with unabated enthusiasm.

Like many visitors to China, I too experienced the effects of the poor environment. Even in China's cleanest cities, on the southern coast far away from the industrialized north, I felt the toll of the pollution. During almost every visit to China, I would come down with a sore throat—apparently my lungs had already been Americanized—and food poisoning, even though I was very careful about what I put in my mouth. Once I took a spotless, modern, and comfortable high-speed train, which zipped along from Beijing to Shanghai at an impressive 186 miles per hour. After eating a boxed meal—beef, cabbage, and rice—one hour later I was so deadly sick that I couldn't move. I figured later that what the sweet young train attendant had served me was a meal past its expiration date.

My parents and my sister repeatedly warned me not to drink milk from China, not to buy fruits or vegetables from the farmer's markets, and to avoid local pork or chicken even at the fanciest restaurants. I couldn't help but wonder: If one couldn't eat dairy, fruit, vegetables, or meat, what did locals live on? Jasmine and many of my local friends subscribed to delivery services to have organic vegetables grown on a farm outside the city sent to their homes every week. Even so, Jasmine wasn't sure of the quality—after all, in China it wouldn't be hard to pay a regulator to have your food certified as "organic." I was also advised not to exercise outside: according to my doctor friend, jogging in China's thick polluted air takes the same toll on your health as smoking a pack of cigarettes.

"How do you deal with this? It seems like China is no longer livable," I asked many friends in China, mostly young professionals and entrepreneurs.

"We try to make money here but live somewhere else!" They would laugh it off the concern with a shrug. Many of them bought houses in Hong Kong, London, New York, Vancouver, Melbourne, or California (recently, even Detroit has captured Chinese investors' imaginations)—especially after the housing crash in 2009 made overseas real estate much more affordable.

* * *

Unfortunately, deadly food products aren't the only shocking quality problems in China. A bullet train crash in Wenzhou in 2011 took the lives of 40 passengers and further showcased how corner-cutting can come at the cost of human life.

The accident was allegedly brought on by the perfect storm: negligence by the railway builders and inspectors, a design fault in the train's signaling equipment, and a thunderstorm. In their rush to build a domestic train manufacturing industry and fulfill the government's demand for indigenous innovation, the Chinese engineers had made fatal mistakes while reverse-engineering a Japanese signaling system. Only in retrospect did Chinese recognize the danger inherent in the hasty way the railways had been constructed. Liu Zhijun, a minister who was infamous for pushing his project teams to work around the clock, had led the build-out of China's high-speed railway. His workers even nicknamed him "Great Leap Liu" for his fervent commitment to the railway's rapid construction.

Authorities tried to minimize media attention by hiding the train cars almost immediately. Here too, their haste proved disastrous: while digging the graves to hide the train compartments, a little girl was found inside, still breathing. The authorities had been in such a hurry to hide the embarrassing equipment failure that they nearly buried a little girl alive.

It is not the lack of traditional Western-style human rights that angers Chinese people, as Western media would have us believe. Freedom of speech is an important source of creativity and innovation, but the lack of it is not the overriding issue in China. Rather, most people, from peasants to the middle class, are resentful of the government's failures to provide two other human rights: the right of equal opportunity to achieve prosperity and upward mobility and the right to be shielded against disasters like the crash at Wenzhou or the Mengniu milk scandal.

Blame it on a face-saving culture, or Mao's war on religion, or the education system, or propaganda—whatever the cause, China faces a crisis of ethics that has coincided with an increasing focus on wealth and little focus on anything else. In the breakneck speed of China's modernization, concern for anything but wealth has fallen by the wayside. Money, a thing to be celebrated in the 1980s, had become by the 2000s a very serious matter. It was all the Chinese had to believe in.

* * *

While the problem of corruption exists everywhere, China surely presents one of the world's most fertile environments for it. Economic research suggests that corruption results from three factors: the capacity of a certain minority, in either the public or private sector, to control the allocation of licenses, privileges, and other resources; a lack of transparency, including the absence of an independent media and a weak civil society; and a lack of accountability, due to the absence of an independent judiciary or the rule of law. China clearly fulfills all three of these conditions. Tracking corruption quantitatively is nearly impossible, but China scholar Minxin Pei estimates that kickbacks, bribes, and outright theft from the public coffers is equal to 3 percent of GDP—roughly equivalent to the central government's annual spending on education.

I've seen corruption in practice since I was in school, when I witnessed families bribing teachers so that their children would get better grades. It's hard to blame the well connected for taking advantage of their positions, given that cronyism is now so rampant in China. An individual makes a principled stand against this corrupt system at his own political, social, and economic risk. Therefore, few do.

While corruption is innate to all emerging markets, including Africa, Latin America, Eastern Europe, and the former Soviet Union, China is uniquely handicapped by its double status as an emerging and centrally planned economy. Many Chinese have observed that the spread of corruption is closely linked with China's massive infrastructure build-out, which was fueled by the 4 trillion RMB ($586 billion) stimulus plan in 2009. The stimulus triggered huge investments in megaprojects that temporarily staved off a recession in China, but also spurred a vibrant economy of corruption.

From an economic perspective, corruption is a form of rent seeking in which privileged parties in a system extract value from their political or social position. The Chinese government takes money from the population in the form of taxes and fees, as well as through less obvious channels, such as providing artificially low returns on deposits at state-owned banks. Much of this revenue is then channeled into government-led investments. But along the way, wealthy and connected politicians and businesspeople siphon off much of the money.

I believe that a big portion of government-led infrastructure spending in 2008 trickled out in the form of bribery, embezzlement, and kickbacks, all of which went to the connected and enfranchised. Interestingly, shortly after Beijing released its massive stimulus package, Macau casino stocks began to soar, led by those companies with the most exposure to VIP gamblers from the mainland. Between the start of the recession and the end of 2012, Galaxy Entertainment Group, Sands China, Melco Crown Entertainment, SJM Holdings, and Wynn Macau all saw their stocks appreciate 3,000 percent, 300 percent, 530 percent, 1,000 percent, and 100 percent, respectively. The observed correlation between infrastructure spending and Macau casino business supports my hypothesis that a big portion of the stimulus was wasted as corruption rent.

This government-led spending has not only wasted money; it has also embedded corruption from allocating contracts and approving bank loans into the engine of the state-driven growth plan. As a result, the party's economic objectives are deeply intertwined with the profiteering of its affiliates. Chinese people joke about why the government prefers fiscal measures to stimulate the economy: monetary expansion or tax cuts just don't offer the same kickback opportunities.

In developed economies, the private sector tends to attract talent, because it tends to be more entrepreneurial and efficient and therefore offers better financial rewards and more exciting career opportunities than jobs in state-owned enterprises (SOEs).

In China, however, the SOEs have the upper hand in attracting and retaining employees, due to hidden perks associated with corruption. Especially in recent years, China has seen a surge in the number of college graduates both taking the civil service exam necessary to get government jobs and applying to work at SOEs.

The government has thrown in with the crony class and has cut the many millions of hardworking people with fewer connections out of the profits of China's economic growth. This has worsened the already-wide income gap between the rich and poor in China and furthered social anxiety, causing the Chinese people to lose confidence in their government.

It is hardly a coincidence that as corruption blossomed with Beijing's stimulus package, the global fashion houses saw Chinese demand for Western luxury goods surge. Luxury sales in the mainland expanded an impressive 30 percent in 2011, making it one of the world's fastest-growing markets. High-end stores sprang up. Shin Kong Place, a luxury shopping mall that opened in Beijing in 2007, recorded store sales growth—a matrix measuring retail store performance—of 30 to 50 percent annually.

The hunger for luxury goods also spilled beyond the Chinese borders, as many Chinese went abroad to buy luxury goods to avoid high domestic taxes. Stores catering to the wealthy in major shopping destinations such as Tokyo, London, and New York began employing Mandarin-speaking salespeople and stocking Chinese teas. Chinese shoppers had become the world's preferred customers; by 2012, they consumed one-quarter of the world's luxury products.

Well-known luxury brands—such as Swiss watchmaker Richemont, the owner of Cartier; Swatch Group, the owner of Omega; LVMH, the owner of LV brands; and PPR, the owner of Gucci and Bottega Veneta—benefited handsomely from the stimulus, witnessing 20 to 30 percent sales growth year over year in Greater China (including Hong Kong and Macau) between

2009 and 2013. CEOs of high-end companies came to view their brand's China momentum as the defining source of their future success.

But events in 2012 and 2013 called that assumption into question. After occupying Nanjing Road in Shanghai and the trendy neighborhoods of Guomao and Chaoyang in Beijing, these brands couldn't wait to invade China's small cities, only to realize that few people in China's less populated cities could afford diamond watches or luxury handbags. At roughly the same time, global luxury brands discovered that their revenue was vulnerable to policy changes.

The reason had to do with the source of Chinese demand. It is impossible to get an accurate number of how many luxury items are bought for personal consumption as opposed to being given as gifts—often as bribes. JL Warren, my research firm, estimates that for high-end Swiss watches with price tags of more than 50,000 RMB (roughly $8,000), 40 to 60 percent of purchases are for gifting. Although most analysts attribute the surging demand for luxury products to the rise of China's middle class, these figures clearly imply that currying business favors is a powerful driving force in the market.

Another powerful source of demand for luxury items comes from what I call China's "mistress economy." A slew of sex scandals in China at the beginning of 2013 showed just how much power and sex go hand in hand in China. One Guangdong deputy chief was sacked after evidence emerged online that he had 47 mistresses, while sex tapes made by a property developer led to the firing of 11 officials in Chongqing.

In China's male-dominated culture, many officials keep a beautiful, refined mistress draped in Prada—or keep dozens of them if they can afford it. Infidelity is rife among all class levels in China, but among officials mistresses have become a de rigueur status symbol similar to flashy Cartier watches and luxury cars.

Chinese mistresses are unique in that they have far more material demands than their counterparts elsewhere. These young Chinese women are in a search not for love, but for cash, high-end apartments, expensive cars, and logo-emblazoned luxury products. They know that their affairs almost certainly have expiration dates; like everyone else in China, they are trying to amass as much wealth as possible before their luck—or their country's—runs out.

One company that benefited from both these trends was the high-end Swiss watchmaker Compagnie Financière Richemont SA (already mentioned above). After entering China around the onset of the global financial crisis in 2008, Richemont saw its sales grow 20 to 30 percent per year. The company owns many global leading luxury brands, including Cartier, IWC, Jaeger-LeCoultre, and Vacheron-Constantin. Due to its sky-high prices, almost all Richemont's brands were sought after as gifts to grease palms in Chinese business relationships. Richemont saw a surge in demand from Chinese consumers both in and out of the mainland that pushed the company's stock up 230 percent between 2009 and 2013.

But good things usually don't last, especially in China. Judging by consumer behavior—such as how many watches were purchased in bulk and how many watches were bought without adjusting the band size to the buyer's wrist—store managers and their distributors estimated that roughly 40 to 50 percent of purchases were intended as gifts. This high percentage of gift-driven purchases left the company's business vulnerable to changes in the political environment and policies. Richemont's revenue was what stock analysts call high risk, meaning it could dissipate unpredictably.

That is exactly what happened in 2012. The Swiss company experienced a slowdown in business around the time of the once-in-a-decade leadership transition in November. After realizing how much popular resentment their old bosses had caused,

China's new leaders, led by Xi Jinping, the country's president, launched an anticorruption movement. The government restricted or banned the giving of many extravagant traditional gift items, ranging from the ill-tasting Chinese liquor Mao Tai and the famous Longjing green tea to Hermès bags and Swiss watches with price tags of more than 50,000 RMB (roughly $8,000 at the time). To convince the masses that Beijing was serious about this new policy, Xi also required all senior officials to liquidate their real estate assets overseas or else risk being removed from the party.

Today, with nearly 50 percent of its revenue coming from China, Richemont is effectively a China story, a company whose sustainability relies largely on Chinese consumer demand. In a recent conference call to investors, CEO Johann Rupert was asked about the prospects of the company's growth globally. He answered, "I feel like I'm having a black tie party on the top of a volcano. . . . That volcano is China. . . . the food's better, and the wine's better, and the weather is great, but let's not kid ourselves. There is a volcano somewhere, whether it's this year, in 10 years' time, or in 20 years' time."

Richemont has felt the pinch of the anticorruption measures, but it is far from alone in that. Gucci's parent company, PPR, revised its China strategy and decided to hold back new store openings in 2013. LVMH, another popular luxury brand in China (largely because of its conspicuous logo, which appeals to a Chinese pack mentality), was also caught off guard by the unexpected slowdown and decided to call off its expansion into smaller cities.

Many analysts failed to foresee the slump because they didn't realize that the growth of these stocks came in large part from free-riding the corruption boom. Many sell-side firms ascribed these luxury names a high earnings multiple under the assumption that the demand came from the ever-rising Chinese middle class.

In reality, the demand came from a tiny portion of the population with concentrated power and privilege and therefore wealth.

But since this power and privilege shift with the change of bosses in Beijing and the policies they create, this demand should be considered risky. On Wall Street, risks should translate into a valuation discount. Analysts ought to assign this group of stocks a China discount, not a China premium.

* * *

Before I left China that summer, I had a conversation with an old friend, a former CFO of a few publicly listed companies. It drove home the point that the country was gripped by a crisis of confidence. I had stopped in Beijing for a few days, and he insisted on picking me up in the latest addition to his fleet of Porsches—a sleek black SUV. Given that our lunch destination was only a few blocks away, sitting in the snarl of Beijing's notorious traffic for far longer than it would have taken to walk was a bit over the top.

Over the phone, he had said he had some business to discuss with me. I was looking forward to hearing what he had in mind. After some idle chitchat over dim sum, my CFO friend cut to the chase so fast that he didn't even bother to remove the chicken foot he was gnawing on from his mouth. "Can you recommend some good hedge funds offshore for us to invest in?" he asked.

Even someone as connected and successful as my friend didn't feel safe leaving his wealth, mostly garnered from pre-IPO stock options, within China's borders.

At the same time that many American investors were trying to get their money into China to benefit from its economic growth, Chinese investors were trying to get their money out—even if they had to break the law to do so. A survey by Global Financial Integrity, a nonprofit research organization in Washington, D.C., showed that China was the source of nearly half of the world's $5.9 trillion in illicit capital flows, or money that leaves its home country illegally, between 2001 and 2010.

There is a gaping disconnect between the American perception of modern China's economic miracle and its reality. China's economy is buzzing, but it hinges on an institutional environment in which the rule of law and transparency have not kept up with its growth and success. Despite the vast wealth generated in China over the past 30 plus years, the country has begun to stall. Fear, uncertainty, and a sense of injustice and resentment toward the government are prominent, including among those who work for it and benefit from the unequal opportunity. This disconnect might take a while to travel to the Western world and reach U.S. investors, but ultimately it is sure to get there. It is just a matter of when.

CHAPTER 13

Muddying the Waters

February 2011

M Y SIX-WEEK TRIP TO CHINA WAS PRODUCTIVE FOR WORK AND for healing on a personal level. Being close to my family provided much-needed strength and confidence to start a new chapter in my life in New York. At the same time, everything I saw in China convinced me that both Wall Street and the rest of the world had gotten the China growth story wrong.

On the 14-hour flight from Shanghai to New York, my mind was buzzing with new ideas. The conversation with Nick and my private equity friend, enhanced by Johnnie Walker and green tea in the lobby of the Four Seasons; the visit to my childhood home and Nanjing Road, so transformed with its neon lights and luxury brand stores; the milk scandals, the high-speed rail crash, the rampant growth of Macau casino business, and the burgeoning corruption economy—all swam around in my mind.

The China miracle had happened all too fast, at the cost of the quality of the transformation. Those who have spotted the disconnect between the quality and quantity of China's growth are still ahead of the curve and stand to profit handsomely from this observation—or at least not crash and burn when the illusion crumbles.

* * *

My plane came to a halt outside the gate at JFK airport. I collected my luggage and wheeled it outside to wait in the taxi line. The New York air felt pristine and fresh compared with the thick Shanghai smog I had breathed in just hours before. I inhaled deeply. Then the ping of my BlackBerry brought me back to earth.

Skimming through the dozens of e-mails I had received during the flight, one caught my eye. An independent research firm had issued a report alleging that CLF was a fraud and detailing its dubious corporate governance and financial reporting. The report alleged that the company's managers pocketed most of the proceeds they raised from shareholders for personal use, rather than buying equipment to grow the business as promised. The report backed up its claims with photos of idle factories, empty store shelves, and interviews with purported clients who claimed they actually had no affiliation with CLF.

In the following months, CLF failed to file its annual report for 2010 and fired its auditor, Ernst & Young, one of the Big Four accounting firms. As a result, Nasdaq halted trading in the company's stock in May 2011.

The banker buddy I bumped into at the Four Seasons did not fare any better. Shortly after I returned, I read in the news that the SEC was investigating Nick's advisory firm regarding its activities in China, although I never heard any definitive results.

As in many other SEC investigations of U.S.-listed Chinese companies, no one was ultimately held responsible for these frauds. CLF's managers are still at large and living well on the money they stole from investors, just like many other Chinese executives who were involved in fraudulent dealings. The company's stock is still drifting on the Pink Sheets, an over-the-counter market with fewer restrictions than the Nasdaq.

CLF's downfall held an important lesson for investors: stick to sizable companies with proven operating records in major cities. The longer a company is around, the more historical information its investors have to base their analyses on. The company's location can also affect its performance. Small companies in obscure locales have a hard time accessing and retaining talent; therefore the quality of their employees and their management is often compromised.

Unearthing Fraud

CLF was just one of the many Chinese frauds that floated to the surface in 2010 and 2011. Several independent research firms had begun making names for themselves by uncovering suspicious practices at Chinese companies in a broad range of industries. These research outfits were mostly small or even one-person firms, staffed by forensic accounting nerds and former investment bankers who operated out of homes and coffee shops. They worked like a pack of lions, circling the herd and separating the weakest companies for the kill.

Muddy Waters, the China-focused research firm, emerged as the most influential of these outfits. Carson Block, its Harvard-educated American founder, had possibly been burned a few times doing business in China. Muddy Waters' business model is to uncover fraudulent business practices.

Block issues only one rating on the companies he covers: strong sell. Judging from stock price movements around the time he publishes his reports, most of Muddy Waters' clients are fast-moving hedge funds equipped with short-selling instruments—as well as perhaps some mutual funds, which subscribe to his research to avoid any stock in his radar screen. Here's how I believe the model works: Block typically sells his latest findings about a specific target to his inner circle of clients first, allowing them time to build a short position (or unload a long position) on a stock. Then he hands the evidence he has gathered to regulators such as the SEC, sometimes prompting an investigation and therefore investor panic. Finally, he releases a report, filled with data, pictures from on-site visits, interviews with related parties, and other supporting evidence, detailing how the target of his allegations has committed misconduct or fraud.

As Block built up his credibility, his attacks became self-fulfilling prophecies. Just by issuing a report, Muddy Waters would trigger panic selling and a sharp decline in the value of the stock, enabling his clients to make a handsome profit or avoid a deep loss. Although it has never been publicly stated, I suspect that this is his business model.

Block got his big break uncovering a company called Sino-Forest, which many American investors consider the granddaddy of Chinese frauds. Block's 40-page report described how the Chinese lumber company milked $6.1 billion from the Toronto exchange, essentially by erecting a Ponzi scheme. Block showed step-by-step, with photographs, charts, and diagrams, how the company fabricated its assets, inventory, and employee numbers, and booked phantom transactions. Sino-Forest's shares plunged by 82 percent immediately after the report was published.

Sino-Forest fooled several high-profile investors, including John Paulson, the hedge fund titan who reaped an estimated $3 billion to $4 billion betting against the U.S. housing market (believed to be the largest one-year payday in Wall Street history). But the ingenious Mr. Paulson was not able to avoid a loss of $720 million on his bet on this Chinese company, an expensive price to pay for his China wake-up call.

Paulson was not the only hedge fund titan who got burned by China: Hank Greenberg, the former CEO of insurance company AIG, had his fund Starr International defrauded by a company called China Media Express, a bus advertising company with a $400 million market cap.

Sino-Forest stirred market panic, but it was Longtop Financial Technologies that finally galvanized the SEC to go after Chinese criminals. The outing of the Chinese financial software company as a fraud provoked a vehement outcry from its outraged shareholders, among them some of the world's largest money managers.

Longtop was a seemingly first-rate company: Goldman Sachs and Deutsche Bank underwrote its 2007 IPO, and U.S. investors awarded the company a valuation of more than $1 billion. Longtop counted among its clients some of China's most prestigious financial institutions, including China Construction Bank and Agricultural Bank of China. But in April 2011, a short-seller firm named Citron published a report alleging that Longtop had fabricated its balance sheets. The company's auditor, Deloitte Touche Tohmatsu confirmed in its resignation letter one month later that the company's financial statements were inaccurate.

Deloitte, which had given clean audit opinions to Longtop for six consecutive years, alleged that it had been in the dark until it finally showed up at the bank to check Longtop's financial statements. Only then did the auditors realize that Longtop did not have the cash it reported; instead, it had "significant bank borrowings" not reflected in the company's books. When being questioned about its auditing quality, Deloitte defended itself by claiming that it had followed proper procedures to confirm the company's bank accounts (although via e-mail) but that it failed to detect the fraud because Longtop colluded with bankers at the branch level. Longtop's management later admitted to its auditor that the company had effectively been running a Ponzi scheme. But as of mid-2013, the CEO had not been prosecuted.

I personally met and interviewed Longtop's CFO a few times at various investor conferences after its IPO. I tried but failed to arrange calls with IT executives at banks alleged to be Longtop's clients. Typically, small companies in both China and the United States were eager to put me in touch with their supply chain, both as a goodwill gesture and as a means to convince a potential investor that firms should give them money to grow. But Longtop's clients, the state-run Chinese banks, mostly ignored investors' attempts to conduct due diligence because they considered themselves as bankers to be a strategic industry in possession of confidential government information. So instead I went to Longtop's competitors, other IT outsourcing companies that sold similar products to banks. No one I spoke with found Longtop's margins credible. Longtop consistently reported a 64 percent profit margin, almost double the average profit margin of 35 percent for the IT outsourcing industry.

My gut reminded me that if something looks too good to be true, it usually is. So I built a short position, even in the absence of perfect information. By that time, I had come to trust the instinct I had honed by analyzing similar situations. Whether American or Chinese, companies are run by people, and human behavior shares a lot of commonalities.

The case of Longtop demonstrated why investors, especially foreign ones, must have investigative due diligence capacity and a reliable network of contacts on the ground in China. In the United States, investors rely on reputable auditing firms to verify the integrity of a company's financial records. The Longtop case showed that even reputable Big Four accounting firms are not entirely adequate in China, and it also made it clear that having high-profile names among a company's investors or underwriters does not preclude the possibility of fraud.

If management cannot be trusted and if auditors and other institutional checks and balances are similarly tainted, investors must bear the responsibility of doing their own due diligence from the bottom up—for most, a daunting challenge. Performing exhaustive and meticulous channel checks is the only way for investors to penetrate China's many layers of opacity (government and corporations) and avoid being conned. Unless one has a network of reliable local intelligence as well as a thorough understanding of Chinese culture to decode the data, it is impossible to eliminate risk altogether. If investors lack the infrastructure and network to provide them with exhaustive due diligence, they are better off not investing at all.

Longtop's downfall triggered a flurry of investigations into China-based listed companies and auditors, as angry investors who suffered losses in the hundreds of millions of dollars turned to the SEC for "justice." But the SEC's ability to impose legal repercussions on foreign private issuers like Longtop was limited due to the conflicting laws of the two jurisdictions—China, where the companies were registered and operated, and the United States, where they raised financing by issuing securities. Foreign private issuers, including all China-based U.S.-listed companies, had never been subject to the same compliance measures as U.S.-registered entities. However, U.S. investors caught up in the China gold rush often ignored this critical risk. For its part, the SEC did not adequately highlight the risks inherent in investing in non-U.S.-registered foreign entities until after the damage was done.

Under U.S. securities law, the SEC was empowered to investigate alleged fraud and subpoena financial records from a company's auditors. Under Chinese laws, however, such records were deemed sovereign confidential material and sometimes even "state secrets," and therefore they could not be shared with a U.S. regulatory body (although it is hard to believe that a fertilizer company like CLF would possess any sovereign secrets). Without the cooperation of the Chinese government, U.S. regulators and prosecutors had no means to punish Chinese managers and their affiliates and bring justice to U.S. investors.

In the end, short sellers played a far more significant role than the SEC in unearthing fraud and encouraging transparency in China by exposing unethical and unlawful corporate behavior. Short sellers may be unpopular, but they help investors minimize risk in the long run by improving and maintaining the market's integrity.

* * *

The lack of transparency was a problem not just for stock investors but also for the American and multinational companies that bought businesses and assets in China. The financial crisis in the West prompted a cross-border M&A wave, and even some of the world's most notable international companies, including Caterpillar, were fooled into purchasing Chinese businesses rife with corporate governance issues or outright fraud.

The global recession was not contained in the West: as the factory to the world, China quickly saw its exports slow. But Beijing showed the world the upside to being a command economy: in an adverse environment, it could use its policy tools to boost economic growth far more quickly than could market capitalism's invisible hand.

Beijing released its 4 trillion RMB stimulus package at the end of 2008, which brought about approximately 10 trillion RMB in bank (and shadow bank) lending, to stave off the ripple effects from the crisis and bolster the economy. People in the West marveled at the resilience of the Chinese economy, and some even argued that the Chinese version of state capitalism was superior to the Western version of free market capitalism. Books like *When China Rules the World* by Martin Jacques (editor of the journal of the British Communist Party for nearly two decades) and *What the*

U.S. Can Learn from China by Ann Lee popped up in bookstores and on Kindle reading lists.

Corporate America continued to buy Chinese companies, some with dubious qualities, even as Muddy Waters was undermining investor confidence in Chinese stocks. Loaded with cash and facing gloomy prospects at home, the multinationals felt the heat from their investors and boards to deliver growth by jumping into emerging markets. When their competitors all rushed into China, they had to follow or risk being blamed for a lack of vision.

Generally speaking, a company can grow either by expanding its business organically or by acquiring or merging with other companies. Organic growth tends to be slower but healthier, because the company has better internal control of its operations. Growth by acquisitions delivers more immediate results but brings more execution risks, such as when cultural or organizational differences between companies complicate the integration process. China presented an additional challenge in that, just as in the public market, companies involved in the M&A chain had a tendency to inflate the value of local acquisitions.

Pearson, the London-based multinational education and publishing company, fell prey to just such a situation. As a public company, it was under constant pressure to deliver growth, even as its core publishing businesses, Penguin and the *Financial Times*, were declining. Meanwhile, China's English tutoring and test preparation industry was booming. So at the end of 2011, Pearson announced a deal to buy out Global Education and Technology (GET) at a generous price of "four baggers," the Wall Street term for four times a company's 30-day average share price (GET's stock had been hammered prior to the announcement). For each American depositary share trading at $5.37 on the day-of-deal announcement, Pearson would pay $11.01 in cash. When the deal was announced, GET's stock rose 97 percent.

Since the company's IPO lunch at the St. Regis, I had watched GET from a distance without getting involved myself—I didn't long; I didn't short. I didn't buy long because I didn't like the managers—they seemed provincial, and yet they intended to build a nationwide business. A big portion of the company's business was franchises, as opposed to directly owned schools. Adequately trained staff and management are the key to running franchises, but an industry friend told me that the couple who headed the company hated traveling, and the company's schools outside Beijing, where the couple lived and worked, were run-down and poorly managed. Even so, I didn't short. I knew the U.S. market at the time was crazy for Chinese education companies, and I didn't want to be killed in the rush.

Shortly after the deal was announced, the SEC sued four Chinese citizens affiliated with GET for insider trading. It seemed that GET's management had told the brother-in-law of the CFO (who was also the chairwoman of the board of directors) and his friends about the possibility of a deal before the takeover was announced. They started to accumulate company shares and doubled their money after the announcement. The SEC obtained a court order to freeze their assets only two weeks after the suspicious trading took place, but some of the insiders had already liquidated or transferred their illicit profits.

Despite the SEC investigation and vocal opposition from Pearson's shareholders, the acquisition proceeded, and the deal closed by the end of 2011. Almost a year later, the SEC brought charges against a new defendant in relation to the case. By mid-2013, no further information on the status of its investigation had been released publicly.

GET's case was an obvious transgression of corporate governance under American standards. The consolidation of power within the company created conflicts of interest and compromised the board's ability to protect the interest of minority shareholders.

In the case of GET, the CEO and the CFO—the husband and wife team that co-founded the business—also chaired the board. Many Chinese companies appoint a few individuals—sometimes family members and friends—to multiple senior executive positions. What Americans might call corruption, the Chinese call family values.

Besides Pearson, construction equipment maker Caterpillar also joined the China rush too quickly. And its executives also found out that they had not bought what they anticipated.

Caterpillar, the world's largest maker of tractors and excavators, was long held up as one of the biggest success stories for a foreign company in China, a huge market for construction machinery. It was also a highly successful stock, with a market cap of nearly $67 billion in early 2012. That is, until Caterpillar agreed to acquire Zhengzhou Siwei.

In June 2012, Caterpillar purchased ERA Mining Machinery Ltd. and its subsidiary Siwei, China's fourth-largest maker of hydraulic mine-roof equipment, for $887 million.

The Chinese company seemed like an excellent target: it was recording surging sales and offered Caterpillar access to the lucrative mining market. ERA Mining Machinery was also owned by two American entrepreneurs, which conceivably instilled the buyers with a sense of confidence and trust. Including Western faces on the board had become a common practice among Chinese companies seeking to boost their corporate image.

In January 2013, seven months after the deal closed, Caterpillar announced it would write down a noncash charge of $580 million against its earnings. The U.S. company had uncovered evidence that Siwei overstated its profit for years by fabricating nonexistent sales. Caterpillar was alerted to the possibility of fraud after it noted discrepancies in the company's routine inventory count, something its auditors should have discovered before the deal went through. Caterpillar's management defended itself to the board by saying that its due diligence was "rigorous and robust"—after all, the entire deal team, including the lawyers, auditors, and bankers, missed the blatant fraud as well.

It is my belief that most of the black-and-white frauds that originated in China have been largely flushed from U.S. exchanges. The majority of the Chinese companies left behind, however, still have some issues with corporate ethics and governance. These issues are common to all emerging markets, but they are more pronounced in China.

A story told to me by a former senior executive of Camelot Information Systems, an NYSE-listed provider of IT services for China's financial industry, shows that this degree of opacity and lack of corporate governance can be as destructive as outright fraud.

The executive found out, after the fact, that Camelot's CEO had been using the company's brokerage account, which was secured by its American Depository Receipts (ADRs), to fund his personal investments. When Muddy Waters' reports triggered a collapse in investor confidence and in the prices of ADRs across the board, the CEO got a margin call from his broker and was forced to sell millions of shares to bring the account back up to the minimum margin. Camelot's stock price plummeted. Today the stock trades between $1 and $2 per share, down 90 percent from its IPO price of $17 per share and 95 percent off its peak of nearly $27 per share.

The CEO kept the board and other members of the management team, including the CFO, entirely in the dark about his actions, and none of the loans from the company toward his personal investments were disclosed in the SEC filings as they should have been. After trying his best to explain and apologize to angry and confused investors, the CFO decided that he couldn't work for a boss who had deliberately misled him and the company's investors, and he resigned soon after. When even the CFO is kept in the dark about the company's financial situation, investors have no way to know what they are getting involved in.

To a large degree, China's weak corporate governance can be attributed to a lack of common values and moral standards. In the United States, education, religion, and social norms instill in most people some sense of ethical obligation and responsibility. Chinese business executives, on the other hand, seem to only respond to the prospect of punishment. And thanks to the structural loopholes, the U.S.-listed Chinese companies operating in two jurisdictions have little to fear in terms of reprisal. Corporate governance also has to be legislated and enforced by a strong, independent legislature and judiciary—neither of which is present in China. Securities litigation for Chinese capital markets did not even exist until 2001, when the Supreme People's Court of China began developing a framework for investors to sue listed companies for losses incurred through financial fraud. Today, the process is still slow and cumbersome, and the court can be bribed. It is not uncommon for Chinese lawyers to work out a "revenue-sharing scheme" with the judge to secure a ruling in their favor. Chinese investors have filed more than 1,000 cases against 14 domestically listed companies, but most remain in legal limbo and are unlikely to be settled in favor of investors.

Fabricating financial reports has become a serious problem among Chinese companies. In addition to a business culture that has long tolerated corruption, the problem stems from weaknesses in the accounting profession and lack of independent media. Recently, the Chinese media has made more progress than before in exposing corporate fraud, often after being prompted by vocal, outraged local investors on social media. However, red envelopes containing kickbacks still too often influence reporters and editors. Chinese accountants, meanwhile, have little independence from management, and the industry as a whole suffers from a severe shortage of qualified auditors. A CFO friend once shared a stunning story she experienced when interviewing someone for a controller position in her firm. She asked the interviewee,

"In a situation where you disagree with your boss, what would you do?" The interviewee answered with no hesitation, "I'm very flexible. I'll do the books however I'm told to." In many Chinese companies, this attitude is a prerequisite for a job.

Another common corporate governance issue relates to the lack of independence among boards of directors. This has been a heated topic in corporate America as well: Some say Enron's spectacular fraud resulted from the company being a one-man show under Ken Lay, in his dual role as CEO and chairman of the board. More recently, some blame J.P. Morgan's $6 billion loss in the London Whale trading scandal on the (potentially too) powerful Jamie Dimon serving as both CEO and chairman of the board. This type of arrangement is common in China, where many companies in private sectors are young and inexperienced when it comes to governance and shareholders' rights. Corporate boardrooms are supposed to protect shareholders by providing checks and balances on managers, but this safeguard is nearly absent from Chinese corporate boardrooms. In the end, it is usually the minority shareholders who suffer the consequences.

Corporate governance goes beyond the relationship between management and the board. It also includes the company's relationships with customers, suppliers, and the community. Problems with this kind of corporate governance are common even among China's biggest listed companies.

***

No discussion of U.S.-listed Chinese stocks would be complete without taking a close look at Chinese Internet plays, the most traded and volatile names on Nasdaq. Half the market capitalization of all U.S.-listed Chinese private issuers is concentrated among a few leading Internet names: Baidu ("the Chinese Google"), Youku ("the Chinese YouTube"), and Sina, a unique combination of Facebook and Twitter. But although these Chinese companies are often compared to Google, YouTube and Twitter, their business ethics differ significantly from those of their American counterparts. They tend to be so aggressive in monetization—the process of converting user traffic on a website into revenues—that it ultimately compromises users' experiences, driving them away to competitors and eventually undermining the companies' own future success. As such, these stocks tend to be volatile and can make for risky investments. They often sink or rise by a few percentage points within one trading day, indicating a distinct lack of conviction among investors.

The largest Internet name by far is Baidu, which was one of 2005's largest and hottest IPOs. Compared with Google's more moderate first-day pop of 18 percent in 2004, Baidu's stock soared 354 percent on its first day of trading, generating quick profits for investors like Knucklehedgie. Baidu had a market capitalization of $44 billion in July 2013, making it one of the largest Chinese ADRs.

Like Google, Baidu is a search engine based on keyword-matching algorithms. But Baidu is way "ahead" of Google in monetizing China's more than 550 million Internet users by utilizing an opaque bidding process and reportedly ranking its results based on the advertisers' bid price, rather than the relevancy of the information. China Central Television (CCTV), the country's largest and most influential state-owned broadcaster, shed light on the company's weak corporate governance in two major televised exposés in 2008 and 2011. In both instances, CCTV targeted unlicensed medical products, one of Baidu's most lucrative ad revenue sources, and revealed step by step how the ads sneaked into search results.

Ads for medicines, supplements, and body care products were a fast-growing and highly profitable portion of Baidu's business, accounting for an estimated 30 to 40 percent of its revenue. Drugs have become disproportionately expensive in China relative to average household incomes, and China is also an aging society with a weak and underfunded healthcare system. A long supply chain connects manufacturers to hospitals, with kickbacks paid each step along the way, the cost of which is passed on, either entirely or partly, to patients who may not have medical insurance. The invasion of American fast food such as fried chicken, pizza, and Häagen-Dazs into the Chinese diet means the demand for certain medicines, such as diabetes drugs and weight-loss supplements, has skyrocketed, and the ever-worsening pollution also makes certain respiratory conditions like asthma more acute. All these factors make purchasing medicines online for lower prices a compelling option, as more Chinese now have Internet access.

Baidu was well situated to take advantage of this trend— until it caught the media's and the government's attention. In 2008, CCTV aired an unexpected segment showing how Baidu carried ads from unlicensed and potentially dangerous medical companies with unproven claims for their products. Baidu's shares lost roughly half their value in the week following the exposé, as the company said it would no longer accept paid listings from companies that accounted for 10 to 15 percent of its revenue. Conspiracy theorists said CCTV had published the report because Baidu had not purchased enough ad time on CCTV's networks.

Baidu allegedly made peace with the broadcaster by spending a generous amount the next year on CCTV commercials. But CCTV apparently felt the pinch of shrinking ad revenues as corporations moved their budgeted allocations for advertising from traditional ad channels such as TV to online sources, and the TV network attacked Baidu again. In the fall of 2011, it aired another 30-minute program about an advertiser looking to post ads on Baidu for a miracle weight-loss drug. The situation was a setup: the would-be advertiser was an undercover CCTV reporter interested in documenting some of Baidu's more suspicious practices.

And document she did. When she presented her falsified documents, the Baidu representative recognized them as fakes. But rather than showing her the door, the sales representative advised her how to "improve" her fake certificates or even borrow another company's valid ones. Ironically, the representative also told the reporter that fake medical sites were receiving more scrutiny since CCTV had aired a related exposé a few years ago, so the Baidu employee suggested posing as a company in an industry with less supervision, like mechanical parts. The reporter followed his advice, setting up a website for mechanical components, but later had no problem switching the content back to promotional material for the weight-loss drug.

Some people argued that these salespeople were merely commission-based agents, not full-time employees, and that management was not aware of their poor decisions. In order to grow quickly, Baidu and many other companies had hired agencies across the country to sell online ads, especially in China's less populated areas. But that was no excuse: Baidu's senior management had plenty of time to clean house between CCTV's 2008 and 2011 exposés. And if senior management was indeed kept in the dark, that would indicate a lack of internal controls.

Domestic news reports exposed other unflattering aspects of Baidu's business. For one, the search engine allowed advertisers to purchase their competitor's brand names as keywords. Hypothetically speaking, KFC could bid for the keyword *McDonald's*, and as long as it outbid its rival, a KFC ad would show up when consumers searched for McDonald's. If that wasn't bad enough, Baidu sales representatives reportedly called up advertisers and asked them to increase their bids for keywords. If the company refused to pay more, Baidu could make the company's site disappear from its search results, regardless of the importance of the information provided (imagine if it were an effective cure for a rare disease).

Most Baidu investors were oblivious to these behind-the-scene dealings and continued to award the company a generous valuation. Only a well informed and rational investor would see that

Baidu's ad revenue was likely to become subject to greater regulatory and policy changes and therefore should be considered volatile. CCTV's media exposure had on two occasions reduced the company's healthcare product ad listings, causing Baidu's revenue to suffer. Events of this nature added significant uncertainty to the search engine's income stream. Beyond the effect on its stock price, the CCTV reports also prompted questions about the business's long-term sustainability. As more consumers were cheated online and bad-mouthed their experience on Baidu, how sustainable would the search engine's monopoly be?

The emergence of Qihoo, a new competitor that quickly grabbed market share, showed that Baidu's grip on the search market was not as secure as it seemed. Qihoo got its start making antivirus software similar to McAfee's and Norton's products. The company entered the search engine market in August 2012 and won over almost 10 percent of the market in just three months. Apparently Qihoo had learned something from the scammers and hackers it was used to dealing with. The company essentially tricked most of its users into making Qihoo's 360 Safe Browser their default web browser and search engine. Users of Qihoo's antivirus software would unwittingly click on pop-up windows, which would then change their settings to make Qihoo their default browser. The company's tactics were so brazen that China's State Administration for Industry and Commerce (SAIC) reportedly handed it a warning for unfair competition. SAIC called out the company for such offenses as making its antivirus software difficult to uninstall, giving users of non-Qihoo browsers security warnings suggesting their browsers were unsafe, faking incompatibility between its antivirus software and competitors' browsers to prevent their installation, and tricking users into thinking the 360 browser download was an official patch from Microsoft.

Although regulators disapproved of Qihoo's tactics, they clearly worked. The company stole many unsophisticated Chinese Internet users from Baidu, winning over U.S. investors in the process. As of July 2013, Baidu's market share in PC search had declined from almost 85 percent in 2010 to 67 percent, thanks to Qihoo as well as the vertical competition such as the search functions on e-commerce sites. Only time will tell which search engine will be the market leader in the long term. To monitor the competitive dynamics between Qihoo and Baidu, my firm worked with a group of computer engineers who continuously monitored traffic volume on PC, tablets, and smart phones. One interesting finding was that, despite the initial surge in Qihoo's market share from 0 to 10 percent, the company stagnated around that level. In addition, most of its browsing traffic occurred during the weekend, indicating that Qihoo's browser and search engine did not penetrate into the corporate world, where people tend to do the most browsing during the workweek.

Top Down Versus Bottom Up

Through the years, I've examined most hallowed wisdom about investing in China, and I've found much of it to be misleading to a fault. One example is the work of Jim Rogers, a quintessential China bull. Rogers cofounded the Quantum Fund with famed investor George Soros in the 1970s, retired from his fund in the 1980s, and traveled the world on his motorcycle. He fell in love with China, eventually moved to Asia, and documented his love affair with China in his book *A Bull in China: Investing Profitably in the World's Greatest Market*.

Rogers's 200 pages of empty-calorie analysis can be summarized in one sentence: buy every stock in every industry in China. The book exemplified a "top-down" approach to stock selection, which typically rests on shortsighted and overly simplistic logic. Rogers argued that America was in decline and China was on the rise, as clearly evidenced by GDP growth, and he urged investors to get in on the ground floor of "the greatest economic boom since England's Industrial Revolution" as fast as they could. Throughout the book, Rogers enthusiastically endorsed major public companies in every sector that was growing—pretty much all industries in China. He gave only a skin-deep overview of their businesses and historical growth rates, with little company-specific fundamental analysis.

This "macro call"—an investment strategy based on one's broad market view, a term that also signifies the top-down approach—is very common among institutional investors I encounter in New York. During corporate lunches and group meetings, where institutional investors are given access to a company's executives and can ask them questions, I often hear such investors focus on getting color and anecdotes on the state of the economy as opposed to updates on the individual company's businesses.

When selecting stocks using top-down analysis, investors first consider the strength of an economy as measured by its GDP growth, then look at industries within that economy, and, finally, analyze individual companies. This approach often does not work, for a simple reason: GDP measures economic activity, not profits. GDP is one driver of corporate profits but not the only one. A stock's performance is driven by the corporate profits available for distribution to shareholders, now and in the future. There are many steps between the profits earned by companies and the dividends paid out to shareholders, including governance, taxation, and administrative and regulator expropriation. Assuming that the growth data are even reliable, GDP alone bears little relevance to the return to shareholders—especially minority shareholders—in a company.

Moreover, China's reported macrodata are known to be fairly inaccurate. Most years, the total sum of the figures reported by individual companies, sectors, and industries does not match the overall figure released by the National Bureau of Statistics. There are many reasons why the data are so unreliable. Chinese bureaucrats do not have any interest in reporting anything that doesn't paint a good picture of their performance, and the statistics bureau remains woefully inadequate.

A friend of mine, the founder of a highly reputable U.S.-based provider of China macroeconomic data, told me he recently decided to halt the company's research offerings to its Wall Street and corporate clients. The founder, one of America's leading experts in data analysis and forecasting, confided that the data source his company received from its partner in China, an affiliate with the National Bureau of Statistics, was simply not workable. Data were often missing from the series the Chinese partner supplied, and the partner used a methodology for econometrics analysis that was 30 years behind what most Americans used, significantly diminishing the accuracy of the American company's analysis.

GDP forecasts issued by economists at major investment banks are equally untrustworthy. These experts are no more independent than the equity research analysts and stockbrokers who package IPOs and sell them to investors. The economists at major banks try to curry favor with Chinese bureaucrats in exchange for permits to open new branches. As such, their forecasts are essentially a point-for-point rehash of what the bureaucrats tell them is coming down the pipeline in terms of fiscal and monetary policies. This is repackaged and sold as euphoria to support those banks' profit-generating activities, such as introducing IPOs; underwriting corporate, sovereign, and municipal bonds; trading securities; and opening new branches in China.

This is not to say that the top-down methodology never works. It does occasionally, in situations where a single macrotheme overpowers other factors, such as the financial crisis in the United States or the ongoing crisis in the euro zone. But based on my experience and observation, by and large this approach tends to be less thorough than company-specific fundamental analysis—often referred to as "bottom-up" stock selection. Top-down approaches are also prone to too many errors, especially in a centralized economy where the government's plans and policies can change unpredictably. The latest example is the boom and bust of the solar industry in China, where government subsidies initially helped Chinese manufacturers wipe out their global competitors but eventually created so much overcapacity that subsidies were canceled and many domestic players were destroyed.

***

The online travel sector provides one example of why Rogers's top-down approach of picking stocks does not and will not work. Rogers was bullish on travel companies because he believed that Chinese people would want to travel more as disposable income increased. That thesis was proven correct: China's outbound travel market has registered double-digit growth for years, and the volume of online airline and hotel bookings has soared.

But even though demand for their services increased, online travel companies haven't benefited much from the trend. In fact, their profitability has declined as a result of a severe price war. As Chinese consumers gained access to transparent pricing information from different service providers, they actually became more sensitive to price. Relative to Americans, Chinese consumers have more free time and lower budgets and therefore are more likely to spend time searching among various online travel providers for a deal.

During the early 2000s, Ctrip.com International was the market leader in the online travel industry, with 52 percent market share and an EBITDA margin of almost 45 percent. The company's high profit margin inevitably invited competition. China's next biggest competitor, eLong, launched a price war to grow its 8.7 percent market share. eLong had enough financial resources from its major shareholders—it was owned 56 percent by Expedia in the

United States and 16 percent by Tencent, a Chinese Internet giant—to engage in a long and bloody war. In 2012, eLong slashed the commission fees for its suppliers, and its hotel booking service volume jumped to almost 80 percent of Ctrip's, from 20 percent in 2009.

Ctrip answered back by vowing to match the competition dollar for dollar using coupon programs, discounts, and other promotions. The online travel industry had been a cash cow, and Ctrip had plenty of money to sustain the price war. The companies' actions tipped into the irrational. At the peak of the price war, Ctrip decided to invest $500 million to accelerate its promotion programs, causing a significant 40 percent drop in its net profit in the third quarter of 2012. eLong's profits vanished, and it suffered a loss for the first time, as its marketing costs increased nearly 75 percent year on year.

At the beginning of 2013, as eLong's hotel booking volume neared that of Ctrip, investors wondered whether the pricing would reach a rational equilibrium, as standard game theory would predict. That didn't happen. Ctrip's CEO Fan Min said in 2013 that Ctrip had $800 million to $900 million in cash, which "can support the company to continue the price war for many years." In 2013, Ctrip's management confirmed that it would extend cash rebate programs to air tickets, an even more competitive market.

***

Another American titan of investment who fell victim to the top-down investment approach in China was Warren Buffett. He famously said, "The 19th Century belonged to England, the 20th Century belonged to the U.S., and the 21st Century belongs to China. Invest accordingly." With that, and a stock recommendation from Li Lu—a Chinese investor who fled to the United States after playing a prominent role in the protests at Tiananmen Square—Buffett began investing in China.

In September 2008, just after the collapse of Lehman Brothers pushed the financial crisis to new heights, Buffett's Berkshire Hathaway bought nearly 10 percent of a Chinese battery and electric car-maker company named BYD for HK$1.8 billion ($232 million), or HK$8 per share. The company's initials stood for "Build Your Dreams," and it was indeed a dream, both then and for years after Buffett invested. Buffett's reputation as the savviest investor of the twentieth century caused the stock to double on the day of the announcement to HK$16 per share, what was termed as a nice "Buffett pop." The Buffett premium helped to push the stock to a peak of HK$88 in 2010 before it finally started to fizzle.

From a top-down perspective, this investment made a lot of sense. China was the world's biggest auto market, and it would only get bigger as urbanization continued and the disposable income of the middle class rose. All these cars would exacerbate China's terrible pollution problem, leaving the government desperate to cultivate a market for small electric cars. In 2009, Beijing reduced the sales tax on vehicles with engines under 1.6 liters to 5 percent from 10 percent, abolished road maintenance fees, and subsidized clean energy cars in a bid to prop up the economy and limit pollution. BYD was a major car maker with high historical margins and a promising battery division, well positioned to lead China's electric vehicle (EV) market. Together, all these facts constituted a compelling investment thesis.

A bottom-up analysis revealed many flaws in BYD's business model. The company's past success was largely a result of free riding off the R&D of Japanese competitors. The Chinese government had also issued a subsidy for small vehicles in 2009, which created a bubble in car purchases. Many consumers moved their purchases ahead to take advantage of the subsidy, resulting in a drop in demand when subsidies were reduced a year later. Warren Buffett amassed his wealth through a highly selective buy-and-hold strategy, so when he bought into a Chinese company whose valuation was largely driven by electric vehicles, a product yet to be commercially proved, I was surprised.

The stock's value fell back to $8 by September 2011. Then BYD announced that corporate profit had fallen 94 percent to $13 million in 2012 due to weak car demand. BYD executives had reassured investors that the company could rely on its other business lines while it was waiting for China to build out charging stations for electric vehicles and for the still-tiny electric car market to grow, but that proved untrue.

In early 2013, the company was planning to raise $500 million in a rights issue to bolster its balance sheet and buy itself more time, putting further pressure on the stock. Four-and-a-half years after Buffett invested in BYD, the company's EV division—the part of the business that drove the stock's hype and investor hopes—was still a cash burner, and the stock had sunk to HK$22 from a 2009 peak of HK$85. Whoever bought into the Buffett bubble was likely sitting on a loss. That is, except for Buffett himself, who I believe had likely locked down and protected his profit from the trade by using sophisticated hedging strategies that are mostly beyond the reach of retail investors. The takeaway for investors? Don't join the Buffett party unless you are an invited guest.

Trading Versus Investing

China's economy has evolved quickly in the decades since Reform and Opening Up. The country has carried out its own Industrial Revolution in only a bit more than 30 years, a process that began in the United Kingdom in the mid-eighteenth century. The scale is also entirely different: The United Kingdom completed its Industrial Revolution with only around 16 million to 20 million people and the United States with maybe 50 million. China is doing it with more than 1 billion. This unprecedented speed and scale of change easily overwhelms investors in the public and private markets who are not equipped with the latest and most accurate data, information, and analysis. Therefore, for most people, China is not yet a market for long-term investments, but rather short-term trades.

Investing and trading in the public market both involve purchasing a security, but they are drastically different games. Investing refers to buying and holding a stock for a long period of time despite short-term share price volatility. Trading, on the other hand, is buying and selling a security relatively frequently to profit from the fluctuations in the share price.

Those in it for the long haul must have a conviction, typically based on thorough fundamental research on a company. Long-term investors then develop their own views on the intrinsic value (the actual, not the market, value) of the underlying businesses. Only with that conviction can an investor comfortably ignore the market noise and short-term fluctuations in the market value reflected in the share price.

Trading is a different game. An investor trades on a stock when he or she thinks the market value of the stock will increase or decrease. Changes in a stock's market value are typically driven by expectations of a company's earnings—profits distributable to shareholders—quarter by quarter. If an investor thinks the company will deliver better than the Street consensus—the median estimate of prominent sell-side analysts—he or she will "buy into the quarter," which stands for the quarterly earnings announcement in which all U.S.-listed companies are required to update investors of their operating performance. If the investor is pessimistic about a company's ability to meet the Street consensus, he or she may take a short position into the quarter. Either way, a trade is typically made only when the investor disagrees with the Street view on a company's near-term earnings.

For long-term investors, properly assessing the value of a business in China is a major challenge. Most value investors depend on what's called a "mid-cycle analysis" to assess the normalized earnings power before ascribing a value to a business. Normalized earnings or mid-cycle earnings are earnings adjusted for cyclical variations. To get that estimate, analysts look at the successive peaks and troughs in a company's earnings and adjust them to a moving average.

But for both Chinese companies and China's economy, mid-cycle references do not exist. Since the introduction of the market reform in 1979, the Chinese economy has only gone up, never down. Whenever the economy showed signs of slowing down, the government stepped in with fiscal stimulus and expansionary monetary policy. In other words, Beijing has so far defied the natural gravity of the economic cycle, with potential long-term structural damage.

In private, many economists argue that it is statistically improbable for any economy to have produced an economic growth trajectory as smooth as China has since 1979. In the 1980s, China's economy was still overwhelmingly agricultural, so it should have been subjected to Mother Nature's unpredictability in the form of bad harvests or bumper crops. In the 1990s, as manufacturing and industrial production grew as a percentage of GDP, business cycles driven by external demand and productivity fluctuations should have generated far more significant swings in economic growth than what reported Chinese economic data indicated.

Moreover, the structure of both the Chinese and global economy has evolved rapidly and unpredictably. China opened itself up to the global economy by engaging in international trade and accepting foreign direct investments, and therefore became more vulnerable to external economic shocks. Yet during this same period, Chinese official statistics show aggregate GDP advancing quickly and steadily, like a luxury car down an empty highway.

In the absence of a full cycle of growth, all projections of the intrinsic value of Chinese businesses are largely guesses. The tools commonly used on Wall Street to assess the intrinsic value of companies, mid-cycle and discounted cash flow analysis, are therefore not exactly applicable. This is another level of complexity to consider when investing in Chinese companies or the Chinese economy.

CHAPTER 14

The Power of
Investigative Research

B Y NOW, ALMOST EVERYONE KNOWS THAT REPORTED DATA COM-
ing out of China are not to be trusted, for various reasons.
Investing solely based on official figures—whether put out by the
government or companies—is a sure way to get burned.

For a long while, I had been strategizing how to develop a
proprietary system to acquire and collect more accurate data and
information for investment purposes. I had met with a few data
suppliers, but none quite fit the bill. Many of them were founded
and run by Westerners, mostly former American journalists. They
were typically small outfits whose primary research methodology
was journalistic investigation—sneaking into warehouses to count
inventory, interviewing the suppliers and customers, and visiting
department stores to assess foot traffic. Some of their work was
good, but most was mediocre, superfluous, or even controversial—one shop in particular was rumored to have accepted payments from companies in exchange for favorable write-ups.

Then, in the summer of 2012, a West coast–based hedge
fund manager and a friend from Middlebury College called me

unexpectedly to make an introduction. "You have to meet my friend Yifeng," he said. "He runs this data processing outfit with a group of computer geeks in China that could complement your business very well."

I said yes almost before he had finished his sentence.

I had realized from the very beginning that I wanted to partner with a native Chinese who operated on the ground in China, with a cutting-edge data acquisition and processing technology as well as a deep understanding of the country. I was convinced that data-driven fundamental equity research would be the future Ferrari of the research world. This is what I needed to take my business to the next level.

The kinds of journalistic investigations that most research outfits undertake in China are conducted by human beings and therefore subject to human bias and errors, whether conscious or not. But unbiased raw data generated directly from Chinese search engines, e-commerce sites, and social media—along with human fine-tuning to ensure relevance and accuracy—offer a far superior method of conducting equity research. Ultimately, that type of research can benefit not only stock investors but also corporations, governments, individuals, and research institutions that wish to gain insights into any particular company, sector, or subject.

* * *

One week later on a Friday afternoon, Yifeng flew in to New York from Shanghai for our first meeting. We met for coffee at the Tribeca Grill, Robert De Niro's downtown establishment. A Shanghai native in his thirties, Yifeng was casually dressed, with the typical low-key persona of a tech guy. He told me he had earned a computer science degree from Shanghai Jiao Tong University, the leading science and technology university in China. After graduating, he worked as an auditor at a Big Four firm, where he audited a few Chinese ADR companies, and then was recruited to open an Asia office for one of New York's largest hedge funds. The hedge fund went under during the financial crisis, just as mine had. Like me, he had thought about launching his own fund but decided a data services start-up was a more interesting and lucrative business model because of the underserviced market.

Thirty minutes into the conversation, I started to realize that not only did we share a similar background but the potential synergy between our businesses was too great to ignore. His company, Goldpebble, specialized in the kind of real-time processing of massive amounts of raw data that I was looking for.

Yifeng explained his unique methodology to me. As Internet use grew in leaps and bounds in China, more real-time data had become available online. Most analysts were still reviewing huge amounts of information one piece at a time, such as news stories, postings on social media sites, or reviews of products on e-commerce sites. The process was labor intensive and slow, potentially subject to significant delays if the information had to be translated from Chinese to English. But with its robust and sophisticated IT infrastructure, Goldpebble was able to tap into a massive amount of real-time data simultaneously, analyze the data, and spit out impressive patterns and insights.

For example, his company was way ahead of the pack on Sina, a U.S.-listed Chinese Internet company with a $4.5 billion market cap as of mid-2013. Sina gained press and investors because of its popular microblog Weibo, a social media service that (as mentioned earlier) incorporated elements of Facebook and Twitter and revolutionized the way information spread in China. Like social media companies around the world, Sina was still unsure how best to monetize its more than 500 million registered users. Even so, investors were typically kind to social media stocks, rewarding them a valuation based on their number of users rather than on the profits they currently earned from them.

Sina Weibo's 500 million followers fetched the stock a high valuation. Goldpebble's research, however, showed that many of these users were unlikely to ever generate value for the company, Yifeng told me. He and his colleagues developed an algorithm that tracked the number of users who logged in on a daily and weekly basis. They found out that among the 500 million registered accounts, nearly 80 percent were "zombie accounts," or commercial accounts set up primarily for spamming or third-party marketing. Only about 14 percent of the total registered accounts created at least one new post each month, and only 4 percent were doing so on a daily basis. The program also gathered much intelligence on how people used the service—such as how long they stayed online and what kind of device and operating system they logged in from.

"Data like that is immensely powerful," Yifeng said proudly. "We collect this real time, sometimes even faster than the company itself." He said his company's algorithm was reliable and robust, and the company had invested heavily in infrastructure. "The team is ready to go," he told me.

Yifeng's greatest asset was his team of talented programmers, whom he had hired and trained over the years to code algorithms to collect and analyze information available online. Over time, Goldpebble had also built a due diligence team, including a call center and a survey team that covered even remote locations across China such as villages in Xinjiang, Inner Mongolia, and Tibet.

By the time we finished our coffee, Yifeng and I had begun strategizing about a mutually beneficial partnership. With his high-powered data processing system and my rigorous analytics and expertise in Chinese businesses, we could identify and arbitrage market inefficiencies faster and more accurately than most.

One kind of inefficiency—valuation inefficiency—refers to a situation in which the value of a stock does not fully reflect timely and accurate information. This is far too common with Chinese

ADRs. With investors and the underlying businesses they are investing in separated by thousands of miles, an 11- or 12-hour time difference, and wildly different languages, cultural norms, and business standards, valuation inefficiencies prevail.

Inefficiencies in two groups of companies have the potential to be particularly advantageous for American investors: Chinese ADR companies and multinational corporations (MNCs) with exposure to China. For MNCs with significant exposure to China, more often than not the China segment of their business drives the price movement in the stock. I consider companies such as Yum! Brands, Mead Johnson Nutrition, Prada, Swatch Group, Richemont, BMW, and Caterpillar, which derive much of their revenue, earnings, and growth from China, to essentially be "Chinese" stocks—though they have the benefit of mostly hewing to Western standards of corporate governance.

These inefficiencies create opportunities for arbitrage based on disconnects in information and understanding. Most investors in both ADRs and MNCs are based in North America and Europe, physically disconnected from their investments in China. That means most portfolio managers acquire information about their investments predominantly from media and analysts' reports. Both sources are often inaccurate, biased (if not completely false), and delayed. Accurate information eventually reaches investors, but it takes time, sometimes months or quarters. In the case of hard-core frauds like Sino-Forest and Longtop, the truth didn't emerge for years.

Those with access to better information have a better chance of making profitable trades. But information alone isn't sufficient. The lack of or an incomplete understanding of China creates another source for arbitrage, what I term knowledge or analysis arbitrage. The knowledge includes proficiency with the Chinese language, familiarity with the Chinese culture and its nuances, and a realistic view of the commercial environment in China. China is a difficult place for outsiders to penetrate, it having been walled off from the rest of the world for decades by Maoist policies. If I gave one set of data or information to two analysts, one with local expertise and the other without, their interpretations would likely be drastically different or even opposite.

That first meeting with Yifeng piqued my interest. I realized that together we could yield perhaps the best results in the equity research world—especially given the worsening quality of sell-side research as Wall Street firms tightened their belts.

One month later, I flew to Shanghai to conduct my due diligence on Goldpebble. I spent a few days with Yifeng, checking out his IT infrastructure and meeting the rest of the team. I made sure that I met up with his compliance counsel, investigated the company's compliance methodology, and ensured everything was in line with U.S. procedures and standards. At the end of my visit, I had met my new partner.

Catching a Falling Knife

Our business is extremely humbling. No one is right all the time. Even reputable analysts can make very wrong calls. As Muddy Waters' reputation and influence in the market grew around 2012, the firm's impact started to outpace the quality of its research. The research firm issued a few unjustified "strong-sell" recommendations that sparked market panic and did lasting damage to those unlucky stocks and their shareholders. But for ready minds, those occasions also created special investment opportunities.

"Special situation investment" refers to an investment strategy that capitalizes on major movements in a stock. The special situation could be a major corporate initiative—such as a spin-off, a merger or acquisition, or bankruptcy proceedings. It could also be a shift in market perception—rather than the underlying fundamentals of business—due to the release of a media or research report.

Such a shift in market perception can be triggered when a prominent short seller takes a position against a stock—as in the case of Herbalife, when Bill Ackman, the activist investor in charge of the hedge fund Pershing Square, pushed down the value of the stock from $70 to $42 by labeling the company a pyramid scheme. A shift in market perception can also be caused by the announcement of unexpectedly positive earnings for a heavily shorted company, as in the case of First Solar. The U.S.-based solar company, which had nearly 30 percent of its float sold short, saw its stock climb from $27 to almost $40 when it surprised investors with its strong expectations for its performance in 2013. As well, a shift can be caused by the failure of a planned merger or acquisition, which forces arbitrage desks to dump their positions in target companies. This was the case with the unsuccessful attempt by Charles River, the U.S.-based drug developer, to buy WuXi PharmaTech, a China-based clinical research outsourcing company. The failed bid resulted in the collapse of WuXi's stock from more than $17 to around $11.

Like any other investment strategy, special situation investment requires solid, on-the-ground knowledge. Chasing ambulances or "catching falling knives," as investors say, can easily do more harm than good. For example, consider investors who bought Bear Stearns after its shares collapsed from more than $80 to $30 on Friday, only to find out the next Monday that J.P. Morgan had bought the company at a massive discount of $2 per share.

One such special situation in which I carried out a profitable long play was with New Oriental Education & Technology Group, the largest private after-school test preparation service provider in China. On July 18, 2012, Muddy Waters released a 96-page report alleging fraud at New Oriental and recommending a "strong sell" rating. Muddy Waters had apparently released its research to clients after the market closed on July 16, as investors woke up to a 32 percent overnight drop in the stock.

I had followed stocks in the education space for a few years by then. In fact, education was one of the top two sectors I always kept an eye on out of personal interest, the other one being health-care. I believed both sectors would enjoy secular growth in the foreseeable future, regardless of China's economic performance. I instinctively valued the two industries: one enlightened a coun-try's labor force; the other improved people's quality of life.

I became familiar with the for-profit education business model when I was a student in Shanghai, taking English test prepara-tion classes back in the mid-1990s. Students and their parents pay these companies tuition up front in cash for courses that last for a few months on average, and so the company's revenue model is relatively transparent and difficult to manipulate.

Some critics complain that New Oriental is structured as a VIE. As noted in an earlier chapter, a VIE is a legal structure that gives foreign investors de facto control of a Chinese operation but not direct equity ownership. In a VIE, the company sets up a web of contracts between entities in China and investors abroad to bypass Chinese regulations that limit direct foreign ownership in strategic industries, like education and publishing. Investors are rightfully suspicious of VIE structures because the investors have no claim on assets in the case of corporate restructurings. However, since New Oriental books most of its tuition and income to the overseas entity that investors have a direct claim on, I consider it a clean VIE.

I learned about the favorable macroeconomic trends at work in the education sector from my close friend Peter Winn, who had built one of the strongest for-profit language education franchise businesses in China. Over the previous decade, growth in the edu-cation sector has been consistently strong, with little dependence on macroeconomic conditions such as increasing inflation, unem-ployment, or falling industrial production.

The industry has also benefited from China's one-child policy, which ensures that the only child has the priority claim on the family's resources. As Chinese citizens become richer, more and more parents can afford the high price tag to send their children overseas to study. As of 2011, one out of every seven students studying abroad was Chinese—a figure that was up 17 times from a decade earlier, according to the Chinese Academy of Social Sciences.

Despite China's fast-growing economy, an increasing number of Chinese young people want to pursue a Western education abroad. North America, Europe, Australia, and New Zealand are the top destinations. The running joke is that the United States absorbs the smartest kids, while the rich but dimmer ones go to Europe. Australia and New Zealand have to deal with the leftovers.

Competition for spots in overseas schools is tough, and in order to win one, the students first have to learn English and achieve near-perfect scores on standardized tests such as the TOEFL, GRE, IELTS, and GMAT. So before sending their children abroad, most Chinese parents invest heavily in preparation courses, including online, after-school, and weekend classes.

As the largest and most established company in the for-profit education space, New Oriental Education benefits greatly from these trends. It is the most respected brand name in the sector. New Oriental is known for having a long operating history and high-quality teachers, and the high average test scores of the students who have taken its classes give it a strong reputation. This all allows it to charge higher prices than the numerous other private educational chains in China and still fill its classrooms. Although the competition in test preparation is heating up, New Oriental still enjoys a fair amount of pricing power as the industry leader. Chinese parents equate the New Oriental brand name with a fast-track visa and brighter future for their children.

The business is also highly scalable: New Oriental can sign up as many as 400 students per class for some of its most popular overseas test prep classes in Beijing and Shanghai. It packs hundreds of students into a large auditorium with television screens to broadcast the teacher's lesson to the back of the room; for each of these courses, it also records hundreds of sales of its proprietary textbooks. These classes can be very large because they are not aimed at teaching English as a method of communication, but rather as a specialized skill set to decode and conquer standardized tests.

Just like me when I first arrived at Middlebury, many graduates from test preparation classes don't really speak or understand much conversational English. However, they have learned the necessary techniques to unlock near-perfect scores on their TOEFL. Since the company's overhead, including the teachers' hourly salary and classroom rental cost, is largely fixed, high student enrollment per class directly translates into increasing profit margins.

I had met New Oriental's CFO, Louis Hseih, a few times at various conferences in New York and traded around the name a few times. I thought Hsieh was a bit arrogant but competent. Many investors were put off by his overly "promotional" air, but he struck me as highly intelligent and very familiar with his business. I considered Louis to be one of the most talented CFOs among the Chinese ADR companies.

Because of this background knowledge, I quickly realized as I read the Muddy Waters report on New Oriental that it was analytically sloppy. Unlike the firm's previous work, it was rich in conclusions and allegations but short on facts and evidence. At best, some of the allegations simply indicated a lack of understanding of China's commercial realities. At worst, the claims seemed exaggerated in order to intentionally trigger panic selling that would profit the firm's short-seller clients.

One claim in particular showed a lack of understanding of the commercial reality in China: the allegation that New Oriental had understated its auditing fees and that its declining auditing expenses per school over the years indicated accounting irregularities. The report pointed out that New Oriental's 2011 audit fee was lower than it was four years before, despite an increase in its number of schools. In Muddy Waters' thinking, that indicated either that the company was hiring a lower-quality auditor or that there were fewer stores to audit, despite what New Oriental claimed about its growing store numbers.

I have half a dozen former classmates working at various auditing firms, and after checking with them, I realized that this specific allegation was a shot in the dark. Operational scale, as indicated by the number of schools and learning facilities, is merely one of the factors and not likely the principal factor in determining auditing fees. An auditor decides what fees to charge a corporate client based on a combination of the complexity of a firm's business model and corporate structure, its strategic relationships with the client, and the potential for cross-selling different services to the same organization. I also learned that after the 2008 financial crisis, most Chinese auditing firms cut their fees by as much as 20 percent to retain customers in a slow business environment. These reductions may have been even deeper for large accounts, where auditors wished to cultivate long-term business relationships. With its annual revenue of $770 million in 2012, New Oriental is a large account by all considerations.

Even so, these realities didn't stop the Muddy Waters report from triggering a sharp decline in New Oriental's stock. Sell-side analysts were as clueless as the scared investors and jumped ship as quickly as they could, lowering their target prices for the stock and downgrading the company from buy to sell.

The other allegation that contradicted common sense, at least for a Chinese person, was Muddy Waters' suspicion about the fact that Michael Yu, the CEO, had transferred 26.4 million shares to his mother. In fact, gifting stock to immediate family is fairly common among Chinese managers. It's also often used as means to protect wealth in case of divorce, because a Chinese wife has no claim on assets that are in her mother-in-law's name. The experience of Tudou, a Chinese video site, demonstrates this point nicely: its 2011 IPO was delayed for almost a year because the founder's wife claimed a large portion of his equity interest in the company during divorce proceedings. If only Tudou CEO Gary Wang had transferred more shares to his mother! In addition, a mother would be considered a safer parent with whom to entrust such an interest than a father. In the case of a split between parents, the probability of an elderly woman getting remarried (thus giving the new partner a claim on the assets) is far lower in China's patriarchal society than for an elderly man.

The Power of Data

But the allegation that was most damaging and hardest to rebut was that many of the schools in New Oriental's network were franchises, rather than directly owned. Muddy Waters claimed that New Oriental had misrepresented certain franchise schools as fully owned businesses. In the view of Carson Block, Muddy Waters's founder, that allowed the company to maximize its store base growth, helping it to justify its fast revenue and profit growth, as well as counting its franchise fees as company cash.

To investigate this claim, Goldpebble developed a proprietary algorithm to sift through 107,517 of New Oriental's class records and 14,468 opening course records from its online enrollment website. To examine the potential for financial reporting fraud, Yifeng's team checked this database with schools and learning centers in China's major cities. The survey team also interviewed senior management of other nonlisted private schools, compared New Oriental's financials with those of other listed private schools, and performed on-site visits to private school associations, the

Ministry of Education, and the tax bureau to identify potential frauds in the corporate structure.

To ascertain the scale of its franchise network, Goldpebble conducted comprehensive surveys of 48 schools and 680 learning centers to verify the stated revenue and issued invoices. All 48 of the schools invoiced their revenues to New Oriental subsidiaries, indicating that they were directly owned. Thirty-five supplied bank details or postal remittances to prove that the funds went directly to New Oriental. Goldpebble received survey responses from 564 out of 680 learning centers, and those that answered all issued invoices to their local New Oriental branch. In addition, none of the 564 schools said they were aware of any franchise operations in their cities. Based on these data, we estimated that less than 1 percent of New Oriental's income was franchised and was therefore insignificant for New Oriental's operating and financial reporting purposes.

After completing this extensive investigation, we concluded that Muddy Waters' allegations were groundless. There was no trace of fraud, and all the issues Muddy Waters raised—from New Oriental's franchises to its accounting practices and corporate structure—appeared to be false. We urged our clients to buy the stock at less than $10 per share in July 2012. By November, it had bounced back to $20, a more than 100 percent gain in less than four months, our biggest win in 2012.

Our experience with New Oriental showcased the power of investigative research—in the words of Ayn Rand, "not to trust, but to know." This was the only way to invest in China, not through the "he said, she said" of analyst reports, unverified news, and rumors, but through exhaustive bottom-up research. Only with this rigorous methodology could an investor develop a level of conviction that would allow him or her to withstand market volatility and pursue profit-making opportunities by betting against the crowd. Of course, this type of research is beyond the reach of most retail investors due to resource constraints.

This is one of the main reasons that I suggest retail investors stay away from individual Chinese stocks. Again, losing money is a lot worse than not making money.

China's X Factors

On May 30, 2012, I sat down with a reporter from Bloomberg TV in the China World Hotel, a historic landmark on the western side of Beijing, for a televised interview on how to invest in China. I told him that I thought highly of Muddy Waters' work. Carson Block had shown, not just told, people how to conduct exhaustive and meticulous research, and in the process he had helped to combat opacity and generally poor Chinese corporate governance. Every serious investor should invest and build a research infrastructure capable of conducting this level of due diligence, but even so, there is no guarantee of getting it right 100 percent of time.

The interviewer asked how investors could capture Chinese growth. The best solution, I told him, was to invest in multinationals with defensible models and significant exposure to China. Multinationals give foreign investors a way to benefit from Chinese growth without investing in Chinese stocks directly, thereby circumventing Chinese corporate governance issues.

One of the multinationals I mentioned was Yum! Brands, an American quick-service restaurant (QSR) chain that operates 39,000 restaurants in 110 countries. Its brands include KFC, Pizza Hut, and Taco Bell, but its crown jewel is KFC China. With approximately 5,700 stores, Yum! China generated more than 50 percent of Yum! Brands' operating profits, and KFC China generated approximately 85 percent of Yum! China's profit. For this reason, the stock attracted the interest of global money managers and investors seeking a proxy for the booming growth in the disposable income of the Chinese middle class.

Since its first store opening in Beijing in 1987, KFC China achieved great success in branding itself to appeal to the swelling ranks of middle-class Chinese consumers. KFC in China managed to localize its menu but still have its customers think of it as a quintessentially American brand. The Chinese middle class was fascinated with American fast food, and unlike in the United States, the restaurant was considered an appropriate place to have a birthday party or even take a first date.

I was no different. I indulged in KFC in the mid-1990s, before I learned how unhealthy it was. The price tag, almost 20 RMB for a sandwich, was not exactly cheap, but I savored every bite of the delicious (and at the time unusual) combination of a fried chicken fillet, mayonnaise, and uncooked lettuce.

I have never bought Yum's stock. The valuation was above what I was willing to pay for a fast-food chain restaurant business. But it had been a darling for many global fund managers who wanted China exposure without China risks such as corporate governance and accounting issues. The stock took off from a level of $50 in October 2011 and ripped all the way to $70 in early 2012, as the company planned hundreds of new store openings in China. By late 2012, the stock traded at more than 20 times forward earnings, a huge valuation for a company that sells fried chicken.

I have been cautious of the stock for several reasons. The QSR industry is highly competitive. It has what analysts describe as a low switching cost for the customer: many consumers go to KFC one day, McDonald's the next, and Chipotle the day after, unlike other retail segments where consumers stay relatively faithful to one brand. That should ultimately spell volatile profits and leave the company vulnerable to competition in the long run. For such a segment, Yum had an extremely high valuation. In comparison, the stock of Swiss luxury watchmakers, another category in the retail space including Richemont and Swatch Group, is valued at around 12 to 15 times forward earnings—even though the luxury industry in theory provides a similar China growth story and even though the barrier to entry for companies, including brand equity and customer service, is much higher than in the fast-food segment. Even Apple, a great China discretionary spending story, typically trades at a multiple between the high single digits and the low teens.

By then, Yum had been hit by a string of events that prompted me to pay close attention to this "Chinese" company. It all started with the "45-day chicken."

On November 23, the Chinese media reported that one of KFC China's chicken suppliers, known as the Su Hai Group, had fed toxic chemicals to its chickens to accelerate their growth cycle from 100 days to a mere 45. On the same day, KFC China responded, denying the allegations and stating that a 45-day growth cycle was the industry standard.

Knowing that the chicken we consume in the United States is mostly, if not all, 45-day chicken, I wanted to understand why Chinese people were having such a strong reaction. I decided to delve into the nitty-gritty of the chicken breeding cycle. I learned way more than I ever wanted to know about poultry.

According to a study published by China's Ministry of Agriculture in 2003, China is home to about 100 chicken breeds: 95 native to China and 5 imported. The local breeds have yellow feathers, while imported ones have white feathers. Compared with the white chickens, the local yellow chickens require more feed to yield the same amount of meat, have a longer growth cycle, and command a higher wholesale price. In addition, white chickens are generally bred and raised in a more adverse environment to encourage them to gain weight. On average, white chickens are given only 130 square inches of farming space, not much bigger than a shoebox. Yellow chickens, on the other hand, are mostly free range and thus are considered more natural. So Chinese people have come to see yellow chicken as the premium product. In contrast, Chinese people often associate white chickens with chemical injections, poor nutritional value, cheap meat, and inferior taste.

After domestic media reported that KFC relied on the lower-quality white chicken, Sina Weibo and other social media networks in China lit up with consumer complaints. Netizens (a popular Chinese phrase for "citizens of the Internet") decried the added hormones, and a picture of a chicken with six wings and four legs, ostensibly the product of too many hormones, even went viral online. The chicken's defects could have just as easily been caused by China's polluted water, but that wasn't what mattered most for Yum. What was most important at the end of the day was consumer perception, and that had gone ahead of reality.

As the events unfolded, Goldpebble and I closely tracked the reaction to the story on social media sites. We realized that mainstream media and Wall Street analysts had greatly underestimated the public's disgust and outrage. Online, chatter about "KFC's 45-day chicken" multiplied. Three leading Internet services, Sina Weibo, Tencent, and MSN, surveyed their users on the safety of KFC's food. On average, nearly 80 percent of respondents declared that they wouldn't buy KFC in the foreseeable future, while 85 percent said they considered KFC food to be unsafe. Jokes began to circulate: "Next time I get sick, I'm going to KFC. I'll get my antibiotic fix from their chicken—it'll save me a trip to the hospital!" All the conversation was in Chinese, however. In English, the U.S. media and American analysts continued to report that concerns over KFC's performance were overblown.

I was rather surprised by the controversy the issue provoked. One would think that in a country where food safety practices are as infamously lousy as they are in China, the scandal would blow over quickly. With the huge number of food quality problems in China, from gutter oil to the sale of dead pigs for meat, why did the Chinese choose to care about this one?

To answer that question, I studied the KFC menu and those of its competitors. I started to realize that there was a critical difference between KFC in China and KFC in America: in China, menu items were viewed as luxury fast food. That might be an oxymoron to Americans, but it wasn't to the Chinese. The price of a KFC meal in China, perhaps 25 RMB, or $4 per head, was often double or triple the price at local fast-food chains with similar offerings, such as Country Style Cooking, a local KFC knock-off. KFC's claim to the premium segment lay in its environment—by Chinese standards, clean, spacious, well lit, and well staffed. KFC in China was not just a fast food but rather a dining experience that symbolized the quality and convenience of American life. So when Chinese consumers realized that the fried chicken they were paying a premium price for was the cheaper, fast-growing chicken rather than the 100-day chicken they typically ate, they felt extra disappointed.

Yifeng, who happened to own a takeout delivery service in Shanghai, pointed out another factor that had thus far gone unnoticed but was highly relevant to KFC China's future success. While most Wall Street investors considered the 45-day chicken scare a one-time event, a separate long-term trend was weighing on the KFC business model. Even more so than Americans, Chinese people were spending an increasing amount of their time shopping online.

One of China's most notable business success stories is Taobao, a shopping site that reached a record-high gross merchandise volume of 1 trillion RMB in 2012. Shopping on Taobao has simply become the new way of life, especially for young urban professionals. Yifeng connected the dots: online shopping means fewer trips to shopping malls, where most KFC stores in China are located. As the foot traffic in commercial areas falls, so will KFC's profits.

KFC clearly realized that it was losing business to the takeout services that were feeding China's growing couch-potato population. So the company responded by rolling out new value combos to go, with free delivery services. But Chinese customers weren't converted, for the simple reason mentioned above: they had gone to KFC not for the menu but for the dine-in American fast-food experience. For takeout services, consumers were more sensitive to price and therefore opted for cheaper local competitors.

I had started checking into the 45-day chicken scandal, but my research now led me to believe that KFC China could be facing long-term challenges that few people realized—least of all its management.

On November 29, one week ahead of a scheduled analyst meeting on December 6, Yum issued a press release after market close that lowered the company's estimate for its China same-store sales growth—one of the key measures that investors in the retail sector rely upon to assess a company's performance—to –4 percent for the fourth quarter, from a previous projection of flat or low single-digit growth. In addition, the company announced that it would open only 700 new restaurants in 2013, down from 800 in 2012. The management cited China's slowing economy as the reason.

Blaming slowing growth on China's macroeconomy can be a convenient catchall excuse used by many management teams for missing Street expectations, even though their problems are clearly company specific. Yum's press release did not even mention the chicken scare, suggesting to me that the company was still wishfully hoping the problem would go away. Regardless, investors could read the writing on the wall. Yum's shares plunged 10 percent the day after the announcement.

Without question, KFC had a nice run in China. As the first American fast-food chain to move into China in the 1980s, it had captured a first-mover advantage. Its success was also due to its rebranding strategy, including creating a menu localized for Chinese tastes with congee, egg tarts, more chicken wings and legs than the white meat that Americans preferred, and spicier flavors. It was also partly due to KFC's use of a decentralized supply chain, a practice that helped KFC become far more lucrative in China than McDonald's, which generated only 3 percent of its global profit in China in 2011.

But as profitable as this decentralized supply chain was, it was now posing a major threat to Yum's business. As I pored over the company's filings, I learned that Yum! China's supply chain consisted of more than 500 suppliers of products for its restaurant and just under 30 chicken providers, only one of which farmed its own chickens. The rest subcontracted to mom-and-pop chicken farmers all over the country for much lower costs. The quality control appeared to be very low: only 0.1 percent of the chickens sourced from contract farmers had been tested for safety. These lenient practices allowed Chinese farmers to become increasingly aggressive in abusing toxic chemicals such as antibiotics and antidepressants (used especially in the summer to calm down tightly caged chickens) to increase their yields and maximize profits. Farmers were also under pressure to find ways to offset rising feed costs.

Those who read Chinese newspapers or watch TV cannot miss the ever-more-alarming reports and exposés about dangerous food in China. Consumers are so anxious about food safety that they often stockpile foreign products: French food company Danone, for example, saw its baby food sales spike 17 percent in the first quarter of 2013, as Chinese consumers bought up all the infant formula they could get their hands on.

Danone also named Chinese demand for bottled water as a main growth driver. Many Chinese decided to begin shelling out for better-quality water when more than 16,000 dead pigs showed up in the river that was the largest source of Shanghai's drinking water. While authorities never clarified the real source of the pigs, journalists speculated that overcrowding had led to an outbreak of a deadly disease.

Similar quality issues also certainly affect poultry. Since big suppliers pay their contract farmers based on the size of the chicken, some small companies are known to sell unhealthy chickens as small or medium ones before they mature and their disease becomes evident. Big suppliers, such as Suhai and Dacheng, have relatively good control systems in place—Dacheng is even able to track each chicken online. Their contract farmers are far less disciplined, though, and the big suppliers do not test the contractors' products frequently enough to ensure compliance. A big KFC supplier like Suhai would provide these small farmers with fodder, medicine, and a feeding schedule and would require that after 38 days, no more medications could be administered to the chickens. My research showed, however, that one big KFC supplier tested only 3 or 4 chickens out of every 5,000.

In late 2012, as China's new leaders were sworn in, it seemed that the public outcry was finally forcing Beijing's new bosses to take food security more seriously. The government set up a food safety superregulator and tightened food safety practices, especially for mom-and-pop poultry farms. KFC China looked likely to face more frequent sampling tests and greater media scrutiny.

But all the new findings made me wonder about the company's long-term prospects. The 45-day chicken scare was unlikely to be a one-time occurrence for a fast-food company that drew half its business from a country haunted with food scandals, where it ran a supply chain that extended into remote areas with almost no regulation. Food quality issues are sure to come back to haunt KFC. That time it was the meat, but next time it might be E. coli on raw lettuce or hormonal eggs in the mayo.

If KFC suffers from food quality issues again, another media scandal is sure to follow. China's state-owned media, especially the all-powerful CCTV, is endowed with the power to cripple any company's business for whatever reason it deems fit—perhaps to "encourage" companies to spend additional ad revenues or to promote local brands over foreign businesses. Whatever the reason, recurring media ambushes are to be expected. KFC's management would have little to no control over the timing of such an attack or the way that events unfold and are resolved.

Wall Street analysts usually term destabilizing factors over which a company has no control as "x factors." It's common sense among investors that prescribing a valuation premium to a business plagued with multiple x factors is imprudent. But Yum! Brand had both a premium valuation and x factors everywhere I looked. The deeper I dug and the more data points I pieced together, the less Yum sounded like a stable business that would make good on a 20-times earnings multiple.

* * *

On December 6, 2012, I was in a crowded conference room on the forty-eighth floor of the Mandarin Oriental Hotel in Columbus Circle in New York. Hundreds of other investors and I were attending the Yum analyst day (the meeting referred to earlier), an annual event that the company uses to tell investors about its performance and strategy going forward. I spotted the legendary American billionaire investor Ken Langone sitting at the back of the room. A backer of Home Depot and the former director of the New York Stock Exchange, Ken was Yum's largest direct shareholder, with nearly 660,000 shares.

The walls of the ballroom were covered in posters and projected slide shows. Many of them featured pictures of China, shots of happy kids waving from the Great Wall, young Chinese couples giggling together over a meal at KFC, and Chinese grandparents smiling over soft drinks. It became even clearer to me that the energy in the company's story was China, and it would be Chinese growth that would make or break the stock.

The CEO, David Novak, took the floor, bounding around the room in the style of a motivational speaker. Thirty minutes into his flowery speech (which made no mention of the problems that

212

50 percent of his business was currently encountering), he had all of us standing on our feet.

"Let's do a Yum cheer!" he said energetically, with his hint of a southern drawl. "Give me a Y! U! M!" he chanted, moving his arms over his head to spell out the letters. The people in the crowd—all adults in suits with seemingly important job titles—waved their arms in response. "What's that spell?" "Yum!" the crowd yelled back. He then pointed to the new slide show—a group of Chinese kids in their red scarves raising their arms to do the same Yum cheer on the Great Wall.

I was dumbfounded. This was a $30 billion company, and the CEO was communicating with his investors and supporters as if he were running a cult.

Following a few more rounds of cheers—American motivational skills at their best—we were given a coffee break. I went straight up to David. After witnessing how things had unfolded in China in detail, I had quite a few questions for him.

"Excuse me, David. What are you going to do about the negative press in China regarding the safety of your chickens?" I asked politely, with a smile. Jason had always told me to try to put management at ease when approaching them with tough questions. Try to make friends not enemies, he would say— only then would they open up to you and share their views and concerns.

Unfortunately this strategy didn't get me the answers I needed. "What?" He seemed lost.

"Oh, you know, Chinese customers are concerned about the chickens that are sprouting five wings and four legs." I mentioned some of the other media reports about the scandal.

"It will blow over."

"Really? How and when?" I asked.

"It always has." All of a sudden, he looked confident again. "Don't you worry!"

"So you already have a comeback strategy," I responded. "Would you mind sharing a few points?"

"Go talk to my China hands." He pointed to the two Asian ladies sitting at the front row. "We are in good hands. That's all I know." He then brushed me off by looking behind me and taking questions from other investors waiting in line.

I went to speak with the China hands, but they just repeated their boss's line: "We'll be fine. These things blow over. Don't you worry!"

"Unbelievable," I told myself. This was definitely not a management that I was willing to pay a 20-times multiple for.

Jason used to ask me to "grade" every executive that I met. That grade became a critical factor in deciding whether an investment was worthwhile, and if so, how big a position to take in our portfolio. Without question, Mr. Novak had scored an F in my book. In fact, I was almost certain that if Jason were there, he would have called his trader to short the stock the minute he turned around (in retrospect, the trade would have worked out very nicely).

As I headed out to grab a water, I passed by Langone. I heard him say the words "A great China story. I love it" to someone next to him.

Thirty minutes later, the presentation resumed, with Novak's China hands taking over the show. The presenters gestured to a graph showing a steep upward line as they discussed the growth to be had from Chinese urbanization, the process of relocating China's massive rural population to its cities. The material was an exact rehash of the Communist Party line that appears in every mainstream state media publication. The China hands assured the crowd that, going forward, the company's growth would be led by expanding into China's smaller cities—cities few Americans had ever heard of.

The discussion of Chinese urbanization infused the crowd with energy. Everyone was excited about how many more cities Yum could enter, how many stores it would open in each, and how much new profit was waiting for it. The contrarian part of my brain started to whirl.

Many companies named urbanization as their major growth driver in China, just as Europeans talked of "growth" bringing them out of a recession. Unfortunately, neither urbanization nor growth is a policy, but rather the outcome of sensible policies that are executed well.

China had been urbanizing for the past 30-plus years, from the days when I was still a schoolgirl in Shanghai and witnessed waves of people flooding into the city from the countryside. Initially Shanghai was overwhelmed, as the infrastructure couldn't accommodate so many rural migrants. The crime rate, unemployment rate, and homeless population soared. It took a while for the city to digest these problems, and that only occurred as the economy soared as a result of mass production–driven industrialization. But that brought with it rising wages—and the question of what to do next.

Whether this process of urbanization could continue depended on how the economy industrialized—whether it could move up the value chain away from mass production driven by cheap labor and toward value-added services. As China's economic structure stood in 2013, there was little convincing evidence that this could take place. Furthermore, researchers had not produced the kind of detailed demographic profiling of rural areas that was needed to accurately assess the potential consumption power of those waiting to be urbanized.

China is a vastly diverse country, with much of its wealth concentrated in the big coastal cities. GDP per capita in Shanghai, for example, was roughly $13,500 in 2012, compared with $8,000 for China's 50 largest second- and third-tier cities. As companies like Yum focused on smaller-sized markets, it suggested to me that incremental new store openings would yield diminishing returns, as a result of both lower population density and lower income levels. What this meant was that the company's organic growth within China seemed destined to slow down or even come to a halt.

In theory, Yum could continue to "buy" growth in China. It had done this with its acquisition of Little Sheep, a popular Chinese chain that served the bubbling concoction that locals know as "hot pot." Yum inked a deal to buy a controlling stake in the Chinese company in 2011. But acquisitions in this vein to further localize Yum's food offerings would also involve operational and execution risks.

All this led me to believe Yum's prime growth stage had passed. Going forward, the company seemed likely to face diminishing returns on its continual investments, including new stores and new product offerings.

From there, things went from bad to worse for the company. On December 18, 2012, China's national broadcaster once again caught Yum in its cross hairs. CCTV reported that some KFC suppliers in eastern Shandong Province fed their chickens antiviral drugs and hormones to accelerate their growth. The report sparked an investigation by the local food and drug administration, and authorities in Shandong shut down two chicken farms. On January 7, Yum lowered its sales forecasts for its China division, citing "adverse publicity associated with a government review of China poultry supply." The company's shares plunged 5 percent in after-hours trading.

Issuing two guide-downs within a month, as Yum had done, was extremely rare for a multinational company, especially one with a market cap of nearly $30 billion. It showed that the management had little oversight and was unprepared to deal with China's challenging and unstable commercial environment.

On January 15, I landed in Miami to attend the annual ICR Consumer Conference, an event that features nearly every major company and investor from the retail segment. I was told that Yum had canceled its annual appearance at the last minute. Rumor had it that the managers didn't want to be confronted with the persistent questions about its China business.

By late January, the state-run Xinhua news outlet was still reporting on government findings of excessive levels of chemicals in KFC's chicken supply. As if this weren't bad enough for KFC's business, China was gripped in the spring of 2013 with a new strain of avian flu. The stock was pummeled in the next few months, as bird flu claimed more victims around China. By May, authorities confirmed that more than 130 people had been infected with the H7N9 strain, and dozens had died. In an effort to stem the outbreak, authorities culled tens of the thousands of domestic birds and discouraged people from eating poultry unless it was thoroughly cooked. Sales plummeted: high-end restaurants stopped selling chicken dishes, and Western restaurants in Shanghai all began serving their eggs Benedict over hard.

Yum announced that sales at KFC restaurants open more than one year plunged 13 percent in March after the outbreak turned many Chinese consumers off eating chicken. I issued a warning note to my clients that the drop in sales would likely persist in April and May as the public panic lingered.

China's Anti-Apple Campaign

Yum is not alone in facing enhanced state media scrutiny. Many other large Western companies have taken a turn under fire from CCTV, including Apple. Chinese people adore Apple products, and many professed their love for Steve Jobs after he passed away, but the country's state-run TV network obviously did not share their admiration.

On March 15, its annual World Consumer Rights Day, CCTV aired an annual evening special in which it claimed Apple employed a double standard for its after-sales service, offering far less comprehensive services to its Chinese than its American or British consumers. A series of attacks on Apple, presumably coordinated by some arm of the Chinese government, followed shortly after the CCTV special. *The People's Daily*, China's official government newspaper, weighed in, escalating the campaign by criticizing Apple on a variety of issues, including the "incomparable arrogance" of its initial response to the CCTV exposé, and the amount of tax the greedy company had likely avoided. Regulators even specifically mentioned Apple in a call to increase scrutiny and punishment of "illegal acts" by electronics manufacturers.

Westerners dismissed the state media reports as mere propaganda, but their long-term impact on Apple's China market share should not have been dismissed. The consumer tide in China was already turning toward Samsung's bigger mobile phones, and the bad press gave consumers another reason to avoid Apple. CCTV had launched a similar campaign against Hewlett-Packard on Consumer Rights Day in 2010 that triggered a roughly 50 percent reduction in its share of China's personal computer market. Over the next year, HP lost 42 percent of its market share in China, or roughly 0.3 percent of its global business. That caused investors significant pain: shares of HP fell from $52 to $42, even though the stock was priced cheaply to begin with.

Toshiba is another example. The notebook maker lost its top spot in the China market to IBM and Lenovo after it refused to compensate Chinese consumers for a disk drive flaw in its laptop computers that could cause a loss of data—even though it had compensated American customers for the same problem. Consumers launched a lawsuit against the company in the Beijing No. 1 People's Court, and Toshiba was lambasted by a series of media reports. The company's market share shrank to 12.6 percent in the third quarter of 2000 from 20.8 percent in the third quarter of 1999.

A Chinese Conundrum

The dramatic undoing of Yum! China in late 2012 and early 2013 should prompt any investor in China to ask a vital question: What is the right valuation for a Western multinational that conducts a significant portion of its business in China?

Generally speaking, investors reward stocks with high multiples when the companies deliver predicable earnings streams, as well as when they have reached or are near the peak of their product cycles. Yum's string of PR snafus and our detailed research revealed many big-picture issues that all multinationals operating in China should be aware of. The events also suggest that American brands are likely to lose some of their early-stage appeal as China develops. In the case of fast food, local Chinese competitors with or without government backing stepped in to erode the position of the established Western fast-food brands.

Companies generally attract high multiples after outperforming expectations for a few years. However, no company can sustain this forever (the hype that restaurant chain PF Chang's stock attracted in 2010 before falling nearly 50 percent is a good example). When hype dissipates for a stock, multiple years of underperformance tend to follow. This is especially true in industries such as restaurants that are highly competitive and subject to multiple regulations. This is why fast-food brands frequently fall into distress, such as Wendy's and Arby's.

It's not just individual Chinese companies that are headed for a correction. China powered through both the Asian financial crisis and the Great Recession, but every fast-growing emerging market in economic history inevitably experiences a severe economic correction. The United States struggled through multiple depressions while developing from the 1870s to the 1940s, and China will ultimately be no different—especially considering the government's efforts to stave off a recession have exaggerated structural imbalances between fixed-asset investments and domestic consumption. A correction is inevitable. It's not a question of if, but when and how.

For that reason, I believe Yum and some of the other multinationals—potentially the entire luxury group in China including Swiss watches—have passed their peak in China. I'm not saying that Yum is a terminal short whose valuation should be reduced to zero. However, the hype needs to be brought down to earth.

For those who aren't invested in Yum, the story still holds a valuable lesson. Yum is another example of how any investment in China requires close monitoring, since market dynamics change quickly and unpredictably. As many companies in China have demonstrated, past performance is not a great indicator of future success.

CHAPTER 15

What Keeps Me
Awake at Night

I ADORE BEIJING FOR ITS INCOMPARABLE SIGHTSEEING—THE
Summer Palace, the Forbidden City, and Sanlitun. But the escalating pollution and impossible traffic make it a very hard place to
stay for long. Thanks to my Americanized lungs, I now typically
break down with a cough and a sore throat after staying longer
than two weeks.

China's capital is also an inefficient city in which to conduct
business. The drive between Beijing's two commercial centers—
the Financial District on the west side of the city and the World
Hotel and Central Business District on the east side—can take as
long as two hours during peak times. Using the subway is out of
the question for me now since my BlackBerry was stolen, along
with all the photos and notes I took from the trip—I had thought
that the locals only liked iPhones. At other times, I was almost
knocked down to the ground by the crush of the crowd during
rush hour. Because of the sprawl and congestion, I've learned that
scheduling four meetings a day around the city is too ambitious.

In New York, I would probably do six meetings a day, jumping in and out of the subway with ease.

So whenever business doesn't require me to be there, I have gotten into the habit of retreating from Beijing to Shanghai and areas around it, where the air quality and amenities are better. In the summer of 2012, I was traveling from Shanghai to one neighboring city, Nanjing, on the new high-speed rail line that connects the cities.

I watched eastern China's industrial landscape zip past my window. Since I had last taken this same journey, more and more factories and new apartment complexes were crowding out the small farms that used to blanket the Yangtze Delta, one of the most densely populated places on earth.

I found myself eavesdropping on a conversation between two men behind me. After listening for a few moments, I realized they were loan officers from Industrial and Commercial Bank of China (ICBC), a state-owned company that became the world's largest bank with total assets of 17.5 trillion RMB ($2.81 trillion) at the end of 2012.

"The Nanjing government is running out of money. But we are still underwriting social housing projects. You get in trouble if you don't lend to those developers," one man said to his counterpart. I leaned in, my ear awkwardly pressed to the space between the seats, but I could only hear snatches of the conversation.

"Private sector? No, we are not allowed to lend to small businesses in this economic environment . . . I could get fired if they go belly up."

I was eager to hear their conversation because the men were discussing one of the biggest distortions in the Chinese economy: that China's so-called commercial banks are by no means commercial. Chinese banks lend at the behest of the government, giving the state the ultimate control over capital allocation and pricing. Investors in the United States had begun asking me about an unsustainable buildup in Chinese debt, and I was hoping to gain some insight into the risk this posed.

In China, as in most other emerging markets, banks have an outsized importance to the economy. Given China's relatively underdeveloped capital markets, bank loans fund 80 to 90 percent of all businesses. China's stock markets remain illiquid, plagued by dysfunctional corporate governance and the ineffective protection of minority shareholder rights, and both the sovereign and corporate bond markets are in their infancy. Almost all external financing for companies is provided by banks (and shadow banks, which are functionally similar and often controlled by real banks but are not subject to the same oversight—I discuss this later in the chapter). In this respect, China is more like Western Europe—where 70 percent of external funding of companies comes from the banking sector and 30 percent from capital markets—than the United States, where these ratios are reversed.

Banks are the dominant source of funding in China, and the biggest banks are all state owned. This puts SOEs and any private corporate entities that have good connections with the authorities at a huge advantage when it comes to funding their investment programs, regardless of the commercial and economic merits of these investments. This economic reality likely undergirded most, if not all, of the new construction sites I saw that day springing up between Shanghai and Nanjing. Companies with connections to the government and state banks were undoubtedly in charge of these projects and, because of these connections, had received heavily subsidized loans.

This reality also explained the effectiveness and timeliness of China's economic stimulus in 2008 through 2010 and again in the second half of 2012. Beijing launched a massive stimulus program in late 2008 that was successful at warding off the immediate impact of the global financial crisis on China's economy. China's fiscal stimulus seemed especially effective in comparison with the

limited effect of the U.S. Federal Reserve's quantitative easing policies and the modest fiscal stimulus of the Obama administration.

Once the Chinese central government approved the 4 trillion
RMB stimulus policy, banks immediately began lending toward
infrastructure projects such as roads, bridges, airports, subways,
highways, and railways. Except for the construction of the rail
network (including the high-speed network), which was funded
by the Ministry of Railways, local governments funded most of the
spending. Since the local governments were banned from borrowing from banks directly, special-purpose vehicles (SPVs) guaranteed by the local authorities were created to borrow directly from
the banks.

It is estimated that new bank loans rose to 17 trillion RMB in
2009 and 2010, while nonbank loans or private lending came to
approximately 5 trillion RMB—many times more than the 4 trillion RMB stimulus amount rubber-stamped by the government.

Economists warned that most of these investments would never
yield adequate financial returns and would ultimately result in
surging nonperforming bank and shadow bank loans, in addition
to excess capacity in sectors heavily subsidized by the government.
The Chinese government countered that the investments yielded
positive social returns, highlighting new toll-free highways and
subsidized housing projects constructed for migrant workers.

Yet even if the government's arguments are correct, the
resources to subsidize these socially worthwhile but commercially
not-so viable projects have been made available at the expense of
the rest of the economy—primarily, the Chinese taxpayers and
the Chinese people who receive benefits from the state. Resources
spent on subsidizing projects have crowded out other forms of
public spending, such as healthcare, education, social security,
retirement benefits, and R&D on socially beneficial projects.

Because banks are mostly state owned and state controlled, the
debt they rack up is essentially government debt. In principle, the

state is only an equity owner with limited liability, and it can avoid responsibility for servicing debt should banks become insolvent. But limited liability didn't stop the capitalistic United States from rescuing "too-big-to-fail" financial institutions such as Citigroup, Bank of America, AIG, Fannie Mae, and Freddie Mac, nor did it keep the governments of the EU member states from propping up dicey zombie banks in the United Kingdom, Ireland, Germany, the Netherlands, Belgium and Southern Europe.

There is even less chance that China will allow a state-controlled bank to fail. Chinese banks are huge. At the end of 2012, ICBC overtook Bank of America to become the world's largest bank in terms of Tier-1 capital, a measure of a bank's financial strength. As of 2013, China was home to 4 of the world's 10 largest banks for Tier-1 capital, the same number as America. This means that, regardless of the ownership structure of these banks, they are too big, as well as too politically connected, to fail. Just as was the case during previous bank recapitalizations, the Chinese government is not likely to let the depositors of the banks get haircuts if the banks become insolvent. Instead, it would likely write down some of the banks' nongovernment-owned equity.

Those in the bank lending chain, from creditors to depositors, know this, and therefore believe the Ministry of Finance implicitly guarantees their debts. That is why Chinese banks weren't that worried about piling up nonperforming loans with the lending spree in 2009 and 2010.

In return for that implicit guarantee, Chinese banks willingly carry out the government's bidding. When it comes to loan approvals, fulfilling political obligations is far more important for Chinese banks than a project's financial viability is. This is yet another fact that most investors coming from market-based economies find hard to comprehend.

Since the beginning of China's economic reforms under Deng Xiaoping in 1979, local governments have had to pay a dramatically rising share of total public expenditures, while the central government's share has fallen. At the same time, the local governments' share of taxes and fees has declined steadily. But as China's economy expanded at an unprecedented pace over the last decade, local governments found a way to close this growing gap by selling land.

Land prices rose quickly as China developed, giving the local authorities abundant collateral and resources with which to pay off debt or meet their obligations to the often loss-making SPVs they created to borrow on their behalf.

In China, the government technically owns all the land; however, land titles can be leased to private groups for periods of 40 to 70 years, depending on how the land is zoned. Local governments are responsible for auctioning off these parcels and make huge sums of money in the process. They often obtain these land titles, though, through a combination of inadequate compensation and intimidation or coercion, giving rise to social tensions among the very people whom developing is aimed at benefiting. But with few other revenue sources and such large sums of money available from reclaiming land at low prices and selling it to developers, most local governments find land sales hard to resist.

This financing model proved highly risky when there was an economic contraction. Local governments, rather than the central government, account for most of China's infrastructure expenditures. But when the Chinese economy began to decelerate as stimulus spending wore off, real estate and land markets cooled and local government revenues from taxation and land sales collapsed. At the same time, local governments faced increasing pressure to stimulate the economy by boosting investment. As local governments took out more loans through SPVs, their borrowing caught up with and then eventually exceeded their capacity to service, let alone repay, their debt.

As the global economy remained sluggish, the legacy problems from China's overinvestment in 2009 began to rear their heads, including the often-talked-about imbalance between domestic consumption and investment. Much of China's economic growth had been sustained by fixed-asset investments led by the government, resulting in an increasing role of the government at the expense of consumers and the private sector.

In China, domestic consumption lingered around 35 to 40 percent of GDP—dozens of percentage points lower than that of any other major economy, including the United States at 70 percent and Japan at 60 percent.

Some economists claim that capital expenditure figures for China overstate the real amount of investment in the economy, because China's investment figures likely include a high percentage of unrecorded "corruption rent"—income and wealth extracted from corrupt practices—which eventually is used to buy high-end luxury products or spent in Macao casinos. However, there can be little doubt that the Chinese system excels at pumping money into investment projects and that industries such as steel mills, chemicals, and high-speed railroads are experiencing selective but growing overcapacity.

Crowding Out the Private Sector

Economists widely recognize the danger of the structural imbalance between investment and domestic consumption in China. However, the inequity between the large SOEs and the small and medium-sized enterprises (SMEs)—the SMEs being the bedrock of China's real economy and engine of organic growth, innovation, and employment—represents a worse problem whose significance is often underappreciated.

In terms of long-run growth, the way credit is allocated in the economy is just as important as the total amount of credit. China's economic growth has been predominantly driven by low-margin and high-volume production, a system that favors SOEs in the manufacturing and industrial sectors that can obtain economies of scale. The service sector and private businesses in general have been starved of credit—one of the reasons that many private Chinese companies come to U.S. capital markets to raise funds. A further obstacle to start-ups and their subsequent growth is the fact that individuals and SMEs cannot collateralize land effectively, since the government technically owns all land in China.

As economies grow richer, structurally more complex, and more diversified, central planning and personal connections become less effective means of allocating resources, from natural and human resources to credit. The rule of law, markets, and arm's-length regulation are far more effective and efficient in this regard. It is clear that China has reached a point in its development where it should move toward a rules-bound market economy and away from the top-down micromanagement that served the country well for the previous 30-plus years.

Proponents of state capitalism argue that SOEs played a strategic role in driving the economy during its early catch-up growth phase, in which China's central planners took advantage of a surfeit of cheap labor and heavy capital investment to create the world's biggest manufacturing-driven export-oriented success story. This model eventually hit the wall, however, as overall inflation (including wage, rents, material and other resources) squeezed the profit margin—in many cases to negative earnings—for many industrial sectors.

As this model became obsolete, SMEs began to prove vital in transforming China into an innovative economy driven by domestic consumption and capable of making optimal use of scarce and skilled labor. SMEs—mostly small businesses that have sprung up since the start of market-oriented reforms in the 1980s—contribute more than 65 percent of China's GDP and are responsible for 75 percent of employment.

Innovations are rare among SOEs simply because innovation requires risk taking and a corporate culture that rewards it, something that is not encouraged in the central planning culture of SOEs. Executives who come to their bosses with innovative ideas can expect a small upside in the case of success, maybe a marginal pay raise, but a much larger downside in the case of failure—perhaps losing their job. Taking orders, not risks, is the unwritten rule of thumb for SOE employees.

Despite all the benefits they delivered to the Chinese economy, SMEs have not been given the government support they deserve. For one, SMEs are significantly handicapped in competing for cheap capital. This is partly because the government favors SOEs, but it is also because bank lending in China is collateral based. SOEs tend to operate in established and asset-heavy industries such as telecom, infrastructure construction, and steel, giving them plenty of fixed assets to put down as collateral. Because of their ties to local governments, SOEs also have much better access to land titles (rights to use the land), the collateral of choice for as long as banks have existed. Meanwhile, a high percentage of SMEs compete in service industries, with little or no fixed assets. SMEs also often have a short track record of operation and little or no credit history, a universal source of funding problems.

SOEs are far more likely to be able to obtain adequate capital on affordable terms, permitting them to expand their businesses. SMEs, cut off from bank loans, have to turn to the gray market to find capital. In Wenzhou, the capital of Chinese capitalism, SMEs borrow at interest rates as high as 85 percent, while SOEs often take out loans at single-digit interest rates. As the flood of bankruptcies in eastern China in 2011 demonstrated, borrowing at such high interest rates is an extremely risky practice for small businesses.

Shadow Banking

Until the summer of 2011, China's economic juggernaut seemed unstoppable. But starting in the fall, an acute credit crunch hit Wenzhou. A coastal city of 9 million about 300 miles south of Shanghai, Wenzhou had been a prosperous treaty port for centuries. It had earned a reputation as a hub of private wealth and enterprise, with a business-minded population known for its self-reliant and independent streak.

The city specialized in low value-added manufacturing, producing 70 percent of the world's cigarette lighters and 60 percent of its buttons, among other products. But since 99 percent of Wenzhou businesses were private, entrepreneurs didn't have access to affordable bank loans to fund their businesses. Therefore they had to borrow from underground banks and pawnshops, and the city soon became a nexus of shadow banking—and eventually an illustration for its risks.

Shadow banking typically refers to a system of credit intermediation between savers and borrowers involving entities and activities outside banks. In the United States, the main shadow banking players are hedge funds, venture capital, and private equity funds. Payday loan providers and money market funds are also considered part of the shadow banking system. Like banks, they borrow short and lend long, or else they fund themselves using short-term, liquid instruments while investing in long-term, often illiquid assets. Both banks and shadow banks experience mismatches in terms of liquidity, credit risk, and the duration or maturity of their assets and liabilities. Unlike banks, however, shadow banks often escape the close scrutiny of regulators and supervisors, even though many of them are owned or controlled by banks or bank holding companies.

In China, the world of shadow banking includes many smaller and less-regulated entities, including trust companies, pawnshops, guarantors, small lenders, underground banks, and wealth management products marketed at banks. Since these activities take place outside China's regulatory framework, figures on the scope of shadow banking are imprecise. But some economists estimate that total public and private debt, including shadow bank loans, could be as high as 200 percent of GDP.

In Wenzhou, private business owners took out loans from shadow banks to invest in their projects, sometimes expanding into unrelated and highly speculative projects such as real estate development. A credit bubble slowly grew in the city. With little or no regulation of underground lending and other forms of shadow banking and no required disclosures, shadow bankers were less able to assess risk and ultimately lent to riskier businesses. The shadow banking system was vulnerable to several potential stress points, including the deterioration of the real estate market, the weakening of exports or manufacturing returns, or even the investments of individual entrepreneurs going bad.

It wasn't just one of these factors that was Wenzhou's undoing—it was all three together. These financial arrangements worked fine when there was optimism, confidence, and trust between parties. But those sentiments didn't survive the financial crisis. As the global recession deepened and demand for exports plunged, the whole town began to default. Optimism, confidence, and trust turned into pessimism, fear, and distrust, and the complicated layering of credit and debt created during Wenzhou's good times imploded much faster than it had grown. Loan sharks disappeared in the middle of the night, construction ground to a halt on half-completed apartment blocks, and property prices plunged. More than 80 prominent local businesspeople committed suicide or declared bankruptcy as they found themselves unable to pay back their gray market loans. China's high-speed economy appeared to be running off the tracks, with Wenzhou leading the way.

The situation continued to worsen in 2012. In a note uncharacteristic of the typically bullish nature of most sell-side analyst reports, one bank analyst issued a report that summer describing in detail the desolate streets and empty department stores of a now-bankrupt Wenzhou. The analyst noted that factories had shuttered their doors for a month or more after seeing orders decline by one-third, year on year, and that owners said this was the hardest time they'd seen in 18 years. Prices at a luxury riverside residence dropped to 50,000 RMB per square meter from more than 70,000 RMB in one year. "Fiddling with iPhones, reading newspapers, playing cards and sewing have become the favorite pastimes. . . . It isn't what I expected at all," the analyst wrote. "I was hoping to be overwhelmed by skyscrapers like Shanghai's or roads like Beijing's. But Wenzhou is disorganized. Debris and waste dot the city."

This account showed the deplorable consequences of the triumph of China's unique form of state capitalism, characterized by the distorted allocation of capital and human resources and the consequent uneven playing field. SOEs were still surviving and even thriving because of their monopolistic positions and government support. But private enterprise, the source of most of China's GDP and jobs, was struggling, with slim access to financial and human capital.

One facet of shadow banking—wealth management products, or WMPs—has deeply penetrated the ranks of retail investors around the country. Many Chinese, including friends and families I know in China, purchased these financial products at one time or another, since they offer a significantly higher yield than saving accounts do.

WMPs are bank-generated investment products that are sold to the banks' retail and institutional customers. Similar to money market funds, WMPs pool funds with a relatively short investment horizon (as little as five days) and invest them in longer-duration assets to arbitrage the difference in returns. Disclosure on these products, including the assets they invest in and the likely returns of each, is limited. WMPs essentially circumvent China's tight control of interest rates by rewarding investors with higher returns than deposit rates.

Everbright Bank first pioneered this form of shadow banking in September 2004 as a way to attract retail deposits—the bank would require a customer to open a savings account before buying WMPs. Other banks followed suit, and competition among WMPs heated up. WMP issuance surged in 2010 as inflation accelerated; real interest rates dipped into the negative, and depositors who realized they were actually paying for the privilege of depositing their money in the bank moved money out of their savings accounts in droves. As China further tightened monetary policy in 2011, banks scrambled to attract deposits to meet their required loan-to-deposit ratios, and WMP growth accelerated further. Ratings agency Fitch estimated that China had around 13 trillion RMB of WMPs outstanding by the end of 2012, an increase of over 50 percent on the year.

In principle, with authorities capping deposit rates at below-market levels, the emergence of financial products that circumvented the cap and offered a higher rate of return did not necessarily compromise stability. In other words, the excess return on a WMP over the officially controlled deposit rate did not necessarily imply that the WMP was riskier than a bank deposit. Instead, the higher return could be a reasonable approximation of what the real deposit rate would have been without an artificial ceiling.

However, WMPs rapidly moved beyond that point, offering returns well in excess of an appropriate level for a depositlike investment. The trust funds and other providers of WMPs invested in high-risk projects in order to offer spectacular returns. Most investors in WMPs—typically, average middle-class households—didn't realize that these returns included a significant risk premium. Like so many before them, in different times and places, these investors considered "excess returns" to be evidence of their acumen as investors—what financial pundits call alpha—rather than compensation for increased risk that would likely materialize at some point—what financial pundits call beta.

Central to the WMP structure is the pooling of investor funds. The general pool will fund a variety of assets across the risk spectrum, many in the shadow banking sector. The average Chinese people who buy WMPs basically have no idea what they are buying. Xiao Gang, the chairman of the Bank of China, wrote a controversial op-ed in the state-run *China Daily* newspaper in October 2012, in which he called WMPs a Ponzi scheme. But most investors overlooked these warnings until several WMPs started to default.

One WMP in particular became infamous. The Chinese investment vehicle known as Zhongding promised investors a short-term return as high as 11 to 17 percent, many times what Chinese investors typically earn on bank products. Even though the investment threshold was at least 500,000 RMB, customers still flocked to the product. Huaxia Bank, which marketed the Zhongding product, provided exceptional service for the VIP clients the product targeted. Those interested in the product would be ushered into a VIP room for a pleasant conversation with the lobby manager and only had to sign on the dotted line.

Banks sold all kinds of WMPs, but they guaranteed roughly only half of them. Many WMP investors realized this fact for the first time on November 25, 2012, when Ms. Wu, one of those well-served Zhongding investors, was told that she wouldn't get her money back. The managing partner of the product, Tongshang Guoyin Asset Management Company, told the banks that had marketed the product that the company could pay customers neither the interest nor the principal. Crowds of angry investors who had bought Zhongding and other WMPs formed outside the Huaxia branches in Shanghai. State media quickly painted the default as a one-off event: according to the press, the fault lay with Chengyang

Wei, who ran the Zhongding Wealth Investment Center and who had spent seven years in prison due to financial fraud in the past. Huaxia Bank's management was outraged and put the blame on "a rogue salesperson" for selling those problematic products without permission from headquarters.

Other defaults soon followed the Huaxia incident, calling into question the safety of other WMPs. That same month, customers at a branch of China Construction Bank in the northeastern province of Jilin suffered a loss of 30 percent of their principal claim from a WMP. Soon after, Citic Trust Co, a unit of China's biggest state-owned investment company, missed a biannual payment to investors in one of its trust products after a steel company failed to make its interest payments on the underlying loan.

I began to investigate the WMP offerings from various banks as investor anxiety over WMPs grew. My company started to monitor the websites of banks and third-party marketers to track new issuances, including the volume, rates, and maturity dates. We also registered with major banks as WMP clients so we would get the updates on their promotions. We regularly called their hotlines, and we monitored online discussions on WMPs from all major social networking and news sites. Based on this, I believe that default risk is significantly underpriced for most WMPs. Retail investors who view them as a safe deposit with higher rate of return stand a good chance of losing their money. For Chinese retail investors, the lesson should be clear: if something looks too good to be true, it almost surely is. The lessons for foreign investors should be clear as well: U.S.-listed Chinese banks are simply not suitable investments. The stocks may look cheap compared with the companies' book values, but the book value could be miscalculated. I often call China's economy a black box, but the banking sector is the darkest part of all. Chinese banks need to be cleaned up, be recapitalized, and become much more transparent before they can be investible.

In fact, the leading American banks recently sold stakes in Chinese banks. Bank of America sold part of its stake in China Construction Bank, while Goldman Sachs sold a $2.3 billion stake in Commercial Bank of China last year, following a similar sale of its holdings in ICBC. The American banks claimed they were just raising cash, but I believe opacity and corporate governance issues played a major part in their decisions.

By 2013, anxiety over a bubble in China's economy was beginning to grow in the United States. The TV show *60 Minutes* aired an exposé on the Chinese real estate bubble, and known China bears like hedge fund manager Jim Chanos and economist Michael Pettis gained airtime. The world was tuned in to see whether China's economic miracle would crash and burn.

* * *

The shortcomings of China's financial system pose potential near-term risks that could trigger a deep recession with profound global implications—what traders like to term a high-frequency risk. I believe that the real source of China's long-term vulnerability, or low-frequency risk, lies in the country's education system, which undermines the integrity and creativity of young minds and ultimately the nation's labor productivity. Many people in the West believe that China is rising because Chinese kids are more competitive than kids in America. But I view the education system as China's Achilles' heel.

When foreigners visit China, they are often impressed by the country's spectacular hardware: the modern architecture of the coastal areas, the fancy international hotels and luxury shopping malls, a high-speed railway that is faster and more comfortable than Amtrak in the United States, the brand-new subways with Wi-Fi access. The continuous news cycle on America's economic stagnation and Europe's structural decline reinforces this shortsighted view. Visitors to China leave after their short stay, thinking that China is going to take over the world.

What they do not see is the lagging "software" beneath the surface. China scores very low when it comes to the rule of law, accountability, governance, and most importantly the quality of its citizenry. China's educational system has failed to produce either an honorable or an innovative society.

Investing in a business is ultimately about investing in the people who run it. I often say to investors that a business is first and foremost about its managers. The integrity and quality of management should be an investor's top concern, above all other factors including the business model, market opportunities, and competitive landscape. If the manager is a crook or has a defective character, none of the other factors will make the target a good investment.

China has succeeded based on a single economic mode, that of mass production of low-value manufacturing products. But the country's changing demographics make this system increasingly unsustainable, as China's aging population and rising wage costs eat away at the abundant supply of cheap labor. To continue growing, the country needs to transition to a more value-added, service-oriented economic model. In order to do so, however, China needs stronger institutions and more dynamic and innovative workers.

China's ultracompetitive education system, which prioritizes propaganda and memorization above critical thinking, is ill suited to meeting that demand. The country needs to undergo major institutional changes—some of which will compromise the state's tight control over its citizens—to produce a labor force compatible with the advancement of the economy.

The process of upgrading China's software, or its human capital, must start with the educational system. In the years since I left China, the overall structure and content of a Chinese education has remained basically the same, despite the dramatic changes in Chinese business and society.

Instead of encouraging independent thinking, education is first and foremost a device for drilling party ideology into impressionable minds. The stories told in Chinese textbooks exemplify and glorify the party—how it takes care of its people, the way a parent does for a child, and how society should therefore be appreciative and obedient, ready to put self-interest aside when the party asks.

One story that recently went viral on Chinese social media— a hypothetical comparison of how *Cinderella* would be taught in China and in the West—demonstrates the rigid and painful way literature is taught in Chinese schools. In the Western school, students would be encouraged to speak their minds after reading the story. Some of the kids would remark that Cinderella's stepmom was horrible, while some would say the lesson was that a girl should dress up so that she can catch the attention of a prince. Others would notice that at the end of the story everything, from the mice to the pumpkins to the rags, turned back to its original form, except for the glass slippers—a potential error on the author's part. Then they might put on a play based on the story. The kids would come away from the lesson with the impression that learning is fun.

In comparison, the teachers in Chinese schools would divide the story into a few major parts, boiling down the events of each into a thesis that students could memorize for a test. One thesis would be that capitalistic society is superficial and divided by class—after all, Cinderella had to exchange her maid's rags for a ball gown in order to receive love. If the students were to question this conclusion, the teacher would tell them not to worry because other answers wouldn't show up on the test. The students would all soon be so bored, they would fall asleep in the middle of the lesson.

Teaching ideology in itself is not a problem, but dictating which idea is right or wrong is a problem. Every school in the world teaches some sort of ideology. American schools normally prioritize freedom of choice and individualism, for example. They encourage students to dare to be different, to think outside the box, to take risks, and to lead. The products of those ideologies include some of the world's greatest innovators, such as Bill Gates, Mark Zuckerberg, and Steve Jobs.

My sister Jasmine has a toddler, Audrey, about whose education she is already agonizing. Living in the modern, international city of Shanghai, she sees that more skills are needed in life than just rote memorization and militaristic discipline. She is concerned that Chinese schools will all but extinguish Audrey's sense of creativity and passion and has begun thinking about enrolling her in an international school.

To assist my sister with her decision, I called up a close friend who is a senior executive in China's private education industry to get her opinion. A mother of two teenagers, she cited the government's conformist ideology as a major factor influencing her choice to switch her children out of the local public schools to privately run international schools featuring a liberal arts curriculum—an increasingly desirable option for Chinese parents who have the required foreign passport and can afford the tuition, which can range in the tens of thousands of U.S. dollars.

"The government worries that if we don't build a universal Communist ideology, their control over citizens will be significantly weakened," she told me. "So Chinese textbooks are designed to indoctrinate students to serve the party—not for our children's edification. That's my main problem with the Chinese system."

The government, represented by the Ministry of Education, still holds onto Marxist and Maoist teachings because it is afraid to part with the bygone era—parting with it would mean reform, and the party inherently fears reform. The party also wants to ensure that certain lessons regarding loyalty to it are continually enforced, especially among liberal, imaginative college kids, such as those who led the Tiananmen protests.

The members of the younger generation are bored of these tedious lessons, but they do not complain. Since their educations have been dictated to them from an early age, few feel they can protest; nor do they know how to protest. They come away from these lessons believing that the purpose of education is to pass tests, no more, no less. Education is a series of hoops to jump through, not a process of self-improvement or self-discovery.

To be fair, the Chinese system does have some merits. For example, Chinese schools excel in knowledge-based teaching. My friend was quick to point out that she did not idealize the American system, which lags behind the systems of East Asian countries in imparting some basic skills. "For some subjects like math and grammar, this is very important, especially during a child's early years of schooling," she said. "However, when it comes to teaching how to learn, not just what to learn, Chinese schools just cannot match the liberal arts approach of most private schools."

Her words resonated with me, as I have experienced both worlds firsthand. My father and my Chinese education gave me discipline and perseverance, but Middlebury taught me integrity and curiosity. I don't know what I would be without either experience. But I do know the combination of the two gave me the strength, audacity, and intelligence to compete on Wall Street and advance my career as a leader, not just a follower.

As I've faced down my fair share of challenges in life, I have always reminded myself of that steamy summer in Shanghai when I biked an hour and half every day to get to my TOEFL class and spent the evenings memorizing the entire dictionary to pass a test in a foreign language I did not really speak. "Where there's a will, there's a way," my father drilled into me. His teachings were the source of my courage to achieve the seemingly impossible: to break into both the white-male-dominated world of Wall Street and the Chinese-male-dominated sphere of corporate China. But it was my American education that gave me the courage and skill set to question and dare to be different, to embrace new ideas, and to take risks to turn those ideas into a business practice.

Another strong point of American education is its emphasis on collaboration, whether group work in the classroom, or teamwork on the sports field. A friend who is a partner in the Shanghai office of an American private equity firm conducted an experiment with two groups of MBA interns. He gave the same project to a team from the Wharton School of the University of Pennsylvania and to a team from a leading business school in China. One group of students gave a well-balanced and coherent presentation. The members of the other team took turns upstaging one another for personal glory and ended up with contradictory conclusions.

Most Americans would predict that the Chinese group would give the organized report, while the Americans would be out for themselves. After all, books like Amy Chua's *Battle Hymn of the Tiger Mother* have emphasized the high caliber of performance given by many second-generation Chinese students. But no one should be surprised that it was actually the reverse. Chinese students—from China, that is—have been taught only how to work for their own good, not how to cooperate to ensure the group's success.

Sports provide another example. China is rightly proud of having won 51 gold medals at the 2008 Beijing Olympic Games, the most of any country. However, its only teams to win gold were in gymnastics and fencing, both intensely solo sports. American expat friends who play pickup basketball and ultimate Frisbee in China have told me that they have trouble with the go-for-glory playing habits of Chinese teammates. As one American friend explained to me, "In a moment of pressure, they go for the big shots, never for the smart side pass. They rarely nail that shot." I cannot help but think that even the sports culture reflects deeper flaws in China's education system—that students are raised to be so competitive that even a basketball game cannot be shared equally with friends.

The gaokao system—the countrywide college entrance exam that is almost the sole factor determining where a student goes to college—has contributed to a cutthroat competitive learning environment. For years leading up the gaokao, students are frequently tested and ranked on a narrow set of subjects, leading to incessant backstabbing and bitter competition. This engenders a society bent on self-promotion, lacking almost entirely in any community values beyond the immediate family. This legacy persists into adult life as well: a suspicious, zero-sum ethos pervades most Chinese work environments, limiting collaboration.

The costs to the Chinese economy are considerable. The wealthy spend millions of U.S. dollars overseas for private, international-style education. The long-term consequences of this trend are frightening. Graduates from international schools and universities often choose to remain abroad after graduation, unable to stomach returning to China once they step outside the country's constrained political and social system. At home, meanwhile, the children who rise through Chinese schools to the top universities in China—an achievement that paves the way to the top jobs—are likely to be the yes-men with uncannily good memories and little mental flexibility. Instead of pumping money into sky-high tuition fees and passport-earning overseas investments, the Chinese should be investing in their own education system.

Rigid, lackluster schools are also the origin of China's long-standing culture of cheating and corner cutting. In a 2008 survey of 900 college students by *China Youth Study*, 83 percent of students admitted to cheating on their exams. Whether the figure is accurate or not, the practice of copying from each other's papers, sneaking information into tests on their calculators, or plagiarizing essays from the Internet is undoubtedly prevalent.

And as more Chinese students study abroad, these practices expand beyond Chinese shores. The number of Chinese undergraduates in the United States climbed to 57,000 by 2012, up from only 10,000 five years before. A significant number of these students use forged transcripts or ghostwritten essays to beat out competitors and win coveted positions at American colleges.

The Chinese Internet abounds with consultancies that promise to "guide" the student through their college applications for a hefty fee. These consultancies often hire foreign expats to write the entrance essays (about $45 an essay, a significant amount in China), and they use special relationships with admissions counselors to guarantee students' admittance. In 2010, Zinch China, an education consulting company, interviewed 250 Beijing high school students headed for American colleges. The survey found that 90 percent of Chinese applicants had submitted falsified recommendation letters, 70 percent had others write their college application essays, and half had forged high school transcripts.

Chinese schools should do much more to crack down on these behaviors. I believe honesty should be the foremost value taught in schools, before comradeship, citizenship, and even compassion or love. Without the existence of an honest culture, all these other values are cheapened. Cheating should result in severe repercussions, including expulsion—such as at Middlebury, which successfully implemented an honor code and self-regulating system, not only for students but also for teachers and administrative staff who accepted bribes.

Teaching materials should also reflect these values, in China and the rest of the world. Chinese history textbooks are far from this ideal, portraying the country as either a victim or a hero in international affairs. The history books emphasize the wrongs committed by colonialists during China's "Hundred Years of Humiliation" after the Opium Wars and by the Japanese during World War II. However, the Great Leap Forward—the period from 1958 to 1961, where 30 million people died of famine as Mao Zedong tried to transform China's agrarian economy into an industrialized one— is remembered as the "Three Years of Natural Disasters," with only nature to blame for millions of deaths. I didn't learn the reality of the Great Leap Forward until I watched Zhang Yimou's historical drama *To Live* at Middlebury College. Nor would I have been informed of the unspoken facts of the Tiananmen Square "episode"—modern China's most significant event and best-kept secret—if I hadn't left the country.

Granted, Americans also dress up their own history—for example, by including rosy portrayals of partnerships between Pilgrims and Native Americans in textbooks. But there is a difference, both in a matter of degree and in the consequences one faces for speaking the truth. Americans have gradually accepted and begun teaching the truth about how European colonizers destroyed native civilizations through warfare and disease. Even Plimouth Plantation—the living museum where the first meeting of the Pilgrims and Native Americans in Plymouth, Massachusetts, is reenacted—has changed its museum to reflect this reality.

China, however, shows no interest in changing the way its history is taught. The only way for Chinese citizens to learn the facts of their home country is to leave China and go somewhere with a free and unbiased media.

This culture of denial and dishonesty begins in Chinese schools, but it has infected almost all other aspects of society. If truth telling is not mandated in schools and espoused by the media, how can one expect honesty to be observed and honored in business dealings or even courts of law? Old habits die hard, especially those formed at an impressionable age.

* * *

Investors outside China often fail to appreciate this dangerous imbalance between the country's hardware and software. Many people living in China, from the top leadership in Beijing to corporate executives to average citizens, believe the country is nearing an inflection point that will force it to reflect and reform. The country's singular focus on fast growth and the bottom line in the past ought to be shifted to the quality of economic growth, of the country's citizenry, and of the society. But wresting control from vested interests and carrying out the dramatic reform to institutions necessary to make this shift will be very difficult.

For investors, this imbalance should send a clear message: *buyer beware*. Assuming that China's past rate of growth will continue to be the norm will only invite costly mistakes. For Americans, the realization of this imbalance should also help alleviate the prevalent and unwarranted sense that America is in decline. With its principles, beliefs, and checks and balances, America is well equipped to continue to lead the world and thrive throughout the century, even with some structural problems it must address at home.

China today is essentially caught in a prison of its own success—the staggering and unprecedented achievement of lifting 500 million people out of poverty in a bit more than 30 years. Chinese people are energized and anxious at the same time. Outsiders are awed, and they assume past glory is indicative of future achievement. But the country's trajectory seems similar to that of an athlete on steroids. As with most athletes on steroids whose temporary outperformance is inevitably followed by a long period of underperformance, the truth will eventually find its way out.

China is a special case in the speed and magnitude of its emergence and its ability to sustain GDP growth of roughly 10 percent for so long. However, many transitional economies have gone through a period of brilliant growth—Japan in the 1960s and 1970s and Korea in the 1980s and early 1990s. The rich history of the developed world gives China an advantage: it can learn from other countries' history and avoid some of their mistakes—should it choose to do so.

CHAPTER 16

From Shanghai to New York and Back Again

NOWADAYS, I TRAVEL REGULARLY BETWEEN NEW YORK AND Shanghai, cities I think of, respectively, as my residence by choice and my hometown by birth. I consider New York to be calm and orderly in comparison with the 24/7 action and frenetic pace of Shanghai. I enjoy watching people's jaws drop when I tell them with a little exaggeration that compared with Shanghai, New York is rather sleepy.

My family's life goes on with Shanghai's transformation. Dad continues to work on various real estate projects, and one way I keep tabs on the state of the Shanghai property market is by noting how busy he is. He also keeps up with his violin practice and enjoys traveling whenever he has downtime. After touring around Europe last year, he decided that Switzerland is his favorite destination because of its peace and quiet. So we plan to meet up there this year. Since our last father-daughter vacation in Phuket, Thailand, I haven't spent much one-on-one time with my father. I am very much looking forward to it.

Mom happily volunteers as my sister Jasmine's full-time unpaid nanny, babysitting Jasmine's three-year-old daughter, Audrey. I have never seen or heard my dad, nor anyone else in the family, drill Audrey on her multiplication tables, but Audrey is clearly quite smart. She can already recite an ancient Chinese poem, Li Bai's famous "A Quiet Night Thought." She can also count to 10 and name all the fruits in English. Whether Audrey should attend grade school in China or in Australia, where my sister and her husband are permanent residents, is an ongoing topic of family discussion.

On the other side of the globe, I am expanding my business and building my team as the track record of our due diligence–based research company strengthens. To cater to the needs of large institutional investors in the United States and Europe, our research today goes beyond Chinese companies to include multinationals with meaningful exposure to China. We are also developing and testing proprietary macroeconomic indexes. Today, I spend half my time as a research analyst and the other half managing a growing and exciting business. My life continues to be filled with exciting challenges and opportunities, as it should be.

After having lived in New York for a decade now, I am still mesmerized by what the city has to offer. I love New York for the top-notch talent and fascinating characters it draws from all over the world. My life has been defined by the group of friends, colleagues, teachers, and mentors whom I have been so fortunate to have met around the world. They inspire and motivate me every day to reach beyond my limits and to venture into the impossible.

In the midst of chaotic city life, I have fallen in love with yoga. In moments of calm and solitude after each practice, I often reflect on the journey I have made so far, from perching on the washboard for my father's multiplication drills; to learning English in the dank dorms in Shanghai; to having an authentic American college experience in Vermont; to years of tireless learning, burning, growing, and succeeding on Wall Street; to carrying what my American and Wall Street education taught me back to China as a stock analyst today.

I can attribute much of my achievement to an intense focus on and discipline in my work. My father's quintessential tiger parenting ultimately resulted in an American success story built with Chinese strengths. Unfortunately, my single-minded focus on succeeding in my career has also come with some painful personal lessons. From these, I have learned that unbalanced growth is never sustainable. When I analyze China and its economy today, I often remind myself of this life lesson.

Note to Investors:
Do Your Homework

I am in the equity research business because I firmly believe that the equity market is *not* efficient. The efficient market hypothesis asserts that financial asset prices fully reflect all available information at all times and that therefore no one can systematically outperform the market by using an informational advantage. The efficient market hypothesis says that you can beat the market only through luck. The spectacular and repeated failure of the efficient market hypothesis has barely dented its popularity, even following the financial crisis that erupted at the end of 2007.

Market inefficiency exists when any of the following four forms of knowledge is missing or misunderstood:

1. Raw data
2. Gleaned information

3. Tested understanding
4. Creative intelligence

Investors derive information by making connections and finding patterns in data. They form an understanding by testing these patterns in the light of hypotheses and theories. They then make the leap from analysis using established facts and theories to new, original insights or creative intelligence to form investment decisions. Investors can and will outperform the market if and when they identify and explore inefficiencies from any of the four levels of knowledge. The best way to do this is to thoroughly research and ferret out what the Wall Street consensus has not yet taken into consideration.

If you want to invest in a consumer products company, try to get on-the-ground information firsthand. As I have done on many weekends, spend time at Best Buy, lululemon, and Apple stores; touch and try out the products; talk to people on the floor; and read customer reviews online. If you want to invest in an aesthetic laser company, book an appointment at a local med spa and ask the doctors questions about its efficacy and safety as if you were going to be operated on yourself. If you want to invest in an online travel agency, register yourself as a user not only on its site but also its competitors' sites and experience firsthand how the agency's services differ from each other and what drives the decision to pick one over the other.

For most investment ideas, you can find many creative ways to research a company. Only lazy minds refuse to see and explore them.

If you can't do firsthand research on a company, do not invest in it. For example, banks are very hard to research because of the complexity and opacity of their on- and off-balance sheet activities. Many people think that U.S. banks are still cheap on a book-value basis. But it is difficult to ascertain the accuracy of the market value of bank balance sheets, including the number, extent, and characteristics of nonperforming loans and other toxic assets. This is true when thinking of investing in American and European banks—it is essential for Chinese banks.

Bank stocks are among the hardest to dissect. They are also largely influenced by policy, politics, regulation, and macroeconomic factors, all of which are beyond the control of the management. Company-specific research might not be sufficient to tackle this group of stocks. You may well need the advice of a political scientist specializing in the impact of populism and popular reactions on legislators and regulators before considering investing in the financial sector.

The globalization of the capital markets has meant a surge of new and unfamiliar investment candidates for analysts and portfolio managers. Foreign issuers—regardless of their listing destinations—provide analysts and portfolio managers with access to investment opportunities outside the United States. These are likely to be beyond the knowledge base of most investors (including the professional money managers). Some opportunities that sound compelling initially may offer poor risk-adjusted returns.

Understanding risks is at least as important as understanding opportunities, if not more so. Market valuation tends to be particularly inefficient for stocks that are less followed, poorly covered, misunderstood, and traded on illiquid exchanges. Generally these are small-cap stocks and the stocks of companies in emerging markets such as China.

One reason that small-cap stocks have more alpha (the risk-adjusted return above the market) is that they are often too small for the large funds to invest in. Small caps tend to be less liquid, as defined by daily trading volume. Large funds cannot get in and out of a position in a small-cap stock without influencing its price significantly, and it may take investors days to build or exit a position. The absence of big players in the game eliminates competition in due diligence, furthering market inefficiency and creating a sweet spot for smaller investors.

Stocks Are Not Companies

The most commonly made mistake by investors is confusing stocks with actual companies. People tend to have a positive bias about the stocks of companies that make products and offer services that they know and use, such as Facebook, Apple, Netflix, Starbucks, Ford, McDonald's, and GE. It's important to remember that stocks and companies are distinctively different: stocks literally have lives of their own. Companies do not change every day; stock prices do. Good companies—companies making good products and offering good services—can be bad stocks. Apple's stock, which fell from $800 to $400 in mid-2013, is an excellent example. Poorly managed or financially distressed companies, including near-insolvent banks, can sometimes make good trades: Citigroup's stock, for example, ripped from around $9 in March 2009 to almost $47 in May 2013.

The reason for this is that companies are evaluated based on business performance, but stock prices are driven by investor expectations. For stocks with lofty expectations that are already factored into the price, a small execution hiccup can trigger a sharp sell-off. Seeking out the humble stocks that are overlooked and underestimated is a better strategy than chasing the hyped-up ones.

Sometimes the stock price of a company will move in a direction against the wisdom of its business management. What's good for the long-term growth of the company may be bad for the short-term performance of the stock price. For example, stocks typically do not perform well when companies are in a heavy investment mode, even though this helps to ensure future growth. Investors typically want to wait and see the return on the investment before they put their money in the stock. It is a prove-it-to-me-first mentality.

Earnings Estimates, Surprises, and Revisions

Generally speaking, stocks move the most during earnings season. This is especially true when there are earnings surprises followed by revisions in the projections of future earnings, which usually happens concurrently with sell-side upgrades or downgrades on a stock.

Public companies are required to file quarterly reports with the SEC within 40 days of the end of a fiscal quarter, and most listed companies announce earnings within one month of the end of the quarter. Investors—both institutional and private—and analysts play this earnings game once every three months. What investors like me live for are surprises.

To capture the potential big swing in a stock due to a surprise, you have to be in the stock ahead of time. You need to buy a stock before a positive surprise sends the price soaring, and you need to short a stock before a negative surprise triggers a sell-off. By definition, surprises are not predicted by the market, except by contrarians. To catch the surprise, you need to have done sufficient homework to hold a conviction on a stock's future earnings that is different from the Street consensus.

Investing Anywhere, Including China

My research philosophy applies to investing anywhere in the world, including China. To be a successful investor in any stock, you must do your homework: perform due diligence and unearth misunderstood information. The nature of business in China means that you must take your game up one notch and be even more exhaustive when performing due diligence on the company's business and on its executives, including their professional track record, character, and integrity.

In addition, investors need to be mindful of the China-specific risks arising from the weak rule of law and the discretionary power of state bureaucrats, which can result in corruption, predatory behavior, and other abuses by state entities and their functionaries.

In global equity markets, premium valuations are rewarded to companies with predictable earnings streams and good governance, including a track record of respecting and protecting the rights of minority shareholders. This is why a subscription-based software company with recurring revenues typically receives a higher multiple than a hardware company with lumpy sales that swing unpredictably from quarter to quarter.

When the China craze that I call the Red Party was in full swing, investors ignored these factors, and undesired consequences followed.

Because of the unpredictable commercial, policy, and political environments, the revenues of both Chinese companies and multinationals in China can be at risk from time to time. Past crackdowns on medical ads, for example, have shown that Baidu's advertising revenue can be volatile. Yum, the parent company of KFC, saw sharp sales declines in late 2012 and early 2013 after the Chinese FDA expressed concerns about its food hygiene. These sudden changes in the enforcement of government regulation had dramatic consequences for Yum.

Few investors like companies with dramatic swings in earnings. And when these swings are caused by factors beyond management's control, they compromise earnings predictability.

Every publicly listed company faces what economists call a principal-agent problem between the managers (often the majority owners in China) and the minority shareholders. The problem: How does a shareholder (the principal) ensure that a manager (the agent) acts to advance the principal's interests, rather than merely empowering and enriching himself or herself? This universal problem deserves more attention from Americans considering investing in China; they would be separated from their investments by 12 hours in time, thousands of miles in distance, and vast differences in languages and cultural and legal norms. Unless investors can find ways to overcome those challenges by collaborating with or developing their own local expertise, they are unlikely to generate alpha in a sustainable way.

What makes China even harder to invest in is a tradition of lousy corporate governance, rampant corruption, and the consequent economic distortion and waste, often as the result of local and regional governments being partial owners of the business. Because of these irregularities, the future earnings of Chinese companies can be difficult to predict. Under normal circumstances, that should warrant a substantial valuation discount.

During the Red Party, investors dismissed these risk factors, and in some cases actually rewarded companies with a valuation premium based on the idea that Chinese companies would experience rapid revenue growth because of the size and rising prosperity of the country. A company's rate of growth alone, however, does not reveal the quality of growth, and revenue growth does not equate to distributable earnings growth. Distributable earnings inside China to Chinese shareholders are not the same as the actual distributed dividends to American shareholders, because of different taxes imposed on foreign recipients of dividends and exchange rate and currency convertibility risks. Dividends due to foreign shareholders can also be at risk as a result of poor corporate governance and the absence of the rule of law, as we discussed before.

Assuming that past growth is indicative of future growth is yet another common mistake—one with grave consequences. Luxury Swiss watch sales in China have grown by 20 to 30 percent per year since 2008. But a substantial portion of that growth comes from purchases for bribery aimed at corrupt officials, business owners, and mistresses, and it is therefore vulnerable to a government crackdown on corruption, as we saw in China in 2013.

Consider another example: KFC China had a nice run in China since the 1980s. This does not mean that future expansion into less populated and less wealthy small cities will garner the same rate of return that we have seen elsewhere.

Another issue for investors is the difficulty of properly assessing the long-term value of a business in China. Most value investors depend on what's called a mid-cycle analysis to normalize a company's earnings power before ascribing a value to a business. Normalized earnings are earnings adjusted for cyclical variations. To get that estimate, analysts look at the successive peaks and troughs in a company's earnings and adjust them to a moving average.

But in China, for most businesses, mid-cycle references do not exist. The Chinese economy has only gone in one direction— up—since the Reform and Opening Up movement of the 1980s. Whenever the economy showed growth fatigue, the government stepped in with stimuli and pumped the growth to double digits. We simply do not know how the Chinese market will act in a down cycle, as the government has not yet allowed it to happen.

In the absence of a full cycle of growth, all projections of a stock's intrinsic value become guesses at best. The tools commonly used on Wall Street to assess the intrinsic value of a company, such as discounted cash flow analysis, are compromised.

* * *

There is only one sustainable winning strategy for all investors, whether in the United States, China, or anywhere else. Do your homework, explore market inefficiency, and exploit it. When and only when the inefficiency is identified and verified by meticulous research can you invest with conviction. Conviction allows you to tolerate market volatility and to maintain a sound mind when the stock behaves differently from your expectation. Only a sound mind can exercise intellectual and emotional discipline, without which rational investment is not possible.

Active investing is work—hard work. It is not a game; nor is it gambling. It is not for everyone. Only those who are willing and able to commit to the intellectual and emotional discipline it demands will excel. Everyone else is welcome to watch the market from a safe distance. There is no shortcut—no effortless road to riches—for the active investor.

Notes

CHAPTER 3

18   urban youth
http://press.georgetown.edu/book/georgetown/
chinas-sent-down-generation

19   August 1968
http://dangshi.people.com.cn/GB/85039/14329784.html

CHAPTER 4

26   early 1980s
http://www.chinatoday.com/data/china.population.htm

29   foreign investments
Ezra F. Vogel, *Deng Xiaoping and the Transformation of China* (Cambridge,
MA: Belknap Press, 2011)

CHAPTER 5

38   state-designated prices
http://www.china.org.cn/features/60years/2009-09/16/
content_18534471.htm

39   27 percent in the middle of the decade
http://www.suomenpankki.fi/bofit/tutkimus/tutkimusjulkaisut/
online/Documents/bon0108.pdf

47   in 1942
http://www.insidevoa.com/content/a-13-34-beginning-of-an
-american-voice-111602684/177526.html

CHAPTER 8

97   Alibaba's board
http://dealbook.nytimes.com/2012/01/23/a-loophole-poses-risks-to
-investors-in-chinese-companies/

103   the codes
http://www.bloomberg.com/news/2012-03-15/china-corporate
-espionage-boom-knocks-wind-out-of-u-s-companies.html

103   have filed for bankruptcy
http://money.cnn.com/2013/03/21/news/suntech-solar-bankruptcy/
index.html

110   first quarter of 2009
http://online.wsj.com/article/SB123984767545423661.html

CHAPTER 9

117   in 2008
http://www.renaissancecapital.com/ipohome/review/2010review.pdf

117   same period
http://www.dailyfinance.com/2010/12/05/a-new-record-six-chinese
-ipos-to-hit-u-s-markets-in-a-week/

127   traditional IPOs
Public Company Accounting Oversight Board, Activity Summary and
Audit Implications for Reverse Mergers Involving Companies from the
China Region: January 1, 2007 through March 31, 2010, Research Note
2011-P1 (March 14, 2011). Accessed through http://www.sec.gov/
news/speech/2011/spch040411aa.htm#P77_41374

128   no longer filing with the SEC
PCAOB, http://pcaobus.org/News/Speech/Pages/09212012_
FergusonCalState.aspx

CHAPTER 12

147   Qing rulers
Stephen R. Platt, *Autumn in the Heavenly Kingdom: China, the West, and
the Epic Story of the Taiping Civil War* (New York: Knopf, 2012)

148   market in China
http://www.nextgen-china.com/admin/Southidceditor/1.pdf

149   in prison
http://www.chinahush.com/2010/10/21/
sue-me-if-you-dare-my-dad-is-li-gang/

149   tainted milk powder
http://www.telegraph.co.uk/new s/worldnews/asia/china/3074986/
Chinese-ordered-cover-up-of-tainted-milk-scandal.html

150   inspection-free privileges
http://www.bloomberg.com/apps/news?sid=aenM_612o.4c&pid=ne
wsarchive

150   Chinese dairy products
http://www.ndtv.com/convergence/ndtv/story.aspx?id=NEWEN2008
0066441&ch=9/23/2008%208:19:00%20PM

150   short-term profits
http://www.voanews.com/content/a-13-2008-09-26-voa45/403825
.html

151   court cases in China
http://www.reuters.com/article/2009/01/02/
us-china-melamine-idUSTRE50112220090102

152   signaling equipment
http://www.nytimes.com/2011/12/29/world/asia/design-flaws
-cited-in-china-train-crash.html?_r=0

153   railway's rapid construction
New Yorker, 2012, http://www.newyorker.com/
reporting/2012/10/22/121022fa_fact_osnos

153   little girl alive
http://www.forbes.com/2011/07/27/china-train-crash-opinions
-contributors-rescue-xiang-weiyi.html

154   on education
http://carnegieendowment.org/files/pb55_pei_china_corruption
_final.pdf

156   at SOEs
http://www.chinadaily.com.cn/bizchina/2012-08/22/
content_15694719.htm

156   30 to 50 percent annually
http://europe.chinadaily.com.cn/business/2013-05/31/
content_16550756.htm

156   world's luxury products
Bain & Company's China Market Study, 2012, http://
www.scmp.com/news/china/article/1109728/
chinese-consume-one-quarter-worlds-luxury-goods-says-report

157   47 mistresses
http://www.guardian.co.uk/world/2013/jan/05/
chinese-corruption-crackdown

157   in Chongqing
http://news.xinhuanet.com/english/china/2013-05/07/c_132365731
.htm

159   20 years' time
http://www.richemont.com/images/investor_relations/results/
annual_results/2012/annual_results_transcript_fy2012_ui36ze82bna
.pdf

159   to call off its expansion
http://www.marketwatch.com/story/china-luxury-apparel-and
-accessories-market-report-2012-2015-2013-07-18

160   between 2001 and 2010
Illicit Financial Flows from Developing Countries: 2001–2010, http://
iff.gfintegrity.org/iff2012/2012report.html

CHAPTER 13

167   $400 million market cap
http://www.wantchinatimes.com/news-subclass-cnt
.aspx?id=20110322000107&cid=1102

167   $1 billion
http://www.nytimes.com/2011/05/27/business/27norris
.html?pagewanted=all&_r=0

167   were inaccurate
http://www.sec.gov/Archives/edgar/
data/1412494/000095012311052882/d82501exv99w2.htm

168   preclude the possibility of fraud
http://newsandinsight.thomsonreuters.com/Legal/News/2013/04
_-_April/Deloitte_s_China_unit_wins_dismissal_of_fraud_claim_over
_audit/
http://www.reuters.com/article/2013/05/28/
us-usa-auditing-china-deloitte-idUSBRE94R0RG20130528

172   insider trading
http://www.ft.com/cms/s/0/0b916fda-202f-11e1-8462-00144feabdc0
.htmla

172   By mid-2013
http://www.sec.gov/litigation/litreleases/2012/lr22508.htm

173    $887 million
http://online.wsj.com/article/SB1000142405297020435800457702955325247909414.html

173   against its earnings
http://www.bloomberg.com/news/2013-01-18/caterpillar-to-take-580
-million-writedown.html

173   Caterpillar was alerted
http://www.caterpillar.com/cda/layout?m=393518&x=7&id=4326216
&mode=noNav

175   Today, the process
http://books.google.com/books?id=n-IwJdFn3JYC&pg=PA157&lpg=P
A157&dq=Supreme+People's+Court+of+China+securities+litigation
+2001&source=bl&ots=7sVYFNfXjA&sig=rS8SQ6v-mYKEuSRPezwDF
k1mUHg&hl=en&sa=X&ei=f8a0UcbDB83LqQHTr4CIDQ&ved=0CC0Q
6AEwAA#v=onepage&q=Supreme percent20People's percent20Court
percent20of percent20China percent20securities percent20litigation
percent202001&f=false

175   in favor of investors
Roman Tomasic and Neil Andrews, "Minority Shareholder Protection
in China's Top 100 Listed Companies," p. 5

185   year on year
http://www.iresearchchina.com/views/4611.html

185   price war for many years
http://www.morningwhistle.com/html/2013/
commerce_0201/217015.html

186   HK$8 per share
http://www.byd.com/na/aboutus/milestones.html

187   car demand
http://online.barrons.com/article/SB5000142405274870483620457836
2533369655220.html

CHAPTER 14

193   mid-2013
Nasdaq

193   500 million registered users
http://news.xinhuanet.com/tech/2013-02/21/c_124369171.htm

197   pyramid scheme
http://money.msn.com/top-stocks/post.aspx?_blg=42&post
=fa0a9db0-f8cd-4ad8-a69d-932c47dbb7a0

197   "strong sell" rating
http://www.muddywatersresearch.com/research/edu/
initiating-coverage-edu/

199   Chinese Academy of Social Sciences
http://www.theepochtimes.com/n2/china-news/china-sends-more
-students-abroad-than-any-other-country-295022.html

204   110 countries
http://www.yum.com/company/

209   as the reason
http://www.yum.com/investors/news/ir_112912.asp

210   outbreak of a deadly disease
http://www.reuters.com/article/2013/04/24/us-china-farming
-pigs-idUSBRE93N1C720130424

216   poultry supply
http://www.reuters.com/article/2013/01/07/us-yum-outlook
-idUSBRE9060UX20130107

217   dozens had died
http://www.who.int/influenza/human_animal_interface/influenza
_h7n9/WHO_H7N9_review_31May13.pdf

217   13 percent
http://investors.yum.com/phoenix
.zhtml?c=117941&p=irol-newsArticle&ID=1809994&highlight=

218   British consumers
http://news.cntv.cn/2013/03/27/VIDE1364383682319950.shtml

218   of 1999
http://english.people.com.cn/english/200006/01/eng20000601_42067
.html

CHAPTER 15

225   same number as America
http://www.economist.com/news/
economic-and-financial-indicators/21581768-worlds-biggest-banks

226   at benefiting
Henry Sanderson and Michael Forsythe, *China's Superbank: Debt, Oil and Influence—How China Development Bank Is Rewriting the Rules of Finance* (Singapore: Wiley/Bloomberg, 2013)

227   Japan at 60 percent
http://www.international-economy.com/TIE_W10_
ChinaEngineGrowth.pdf

229   of employment
http://finance.ifeng.com/news/special/zgfzlt_2012/20120317
/5764772.shtml

231　200 percent of GDP
http://online.wsj.com/article/SB1000142412788732433860457832596270
5788582.html

231　gray market loans
http://www.reuters.com/article/2011/08/10/
china-loans-idUSL3E7JA03T20110810

233　on the year
Fitch Ratings: Chinese Banks—Issuance of Wealth Management
Products Heats Up as Year-End Approaches, December 5, 2012

234　Ponzi scheme
http://www.chinadaily.com.cn/opinion/2012-10/12/
content_15812305.htm

242　their exams
http://www.theepochtimes.com/news/5-9-8/32106.html 00

243　five years before
http://www.nytimes.com/2012/02/05/education/international-
students-pay-top-dollar-at-us-colleges.html?ref=global-home&_r=0

243　high school transcripts
http://www.nytimes.com/2012/02/05/education/international-
students-pay-top-dollar-at-us-colleges.html?ref=global-home&_r=0

Acknowledgments

This book is truly a product of teamwork. I want to thank Ana Swanson and Hannah Lincoln, my "China hands," for their tireless editing on the book. These two extraordinarily talented American women's unique experiences, insights, and endless fascination with China were truly inspirational. Thanks to my agent, Esmond Harmsworth at Zachary Shuster Harmsworth Literary and Entertainment Agency, for his vision, dedication, and confidence in me. I also thank Tom Miller at McGraw-Hill for his skillful editing, crafting, and guidance. I also want to thank Samantha Marshall and Gwynn Guilford for their contributions to the book.

Index

INDEX

INDEX

INDEX

INDEX

INDEX

About the Author

Junheng Li runs JL Warren Capital LLC, a China-focused equity research firm based in New York. Her firm utilizes bottom-up, fundamental research to seek variant views and to explore market inefficiencies. In the near future, she plans to expand the firm's platform into economic analysis and forecasts, aiming to provide solutions to investing in China's largely opaque business environment.

Prior to founding JL Warren, Junh was a senior equity analyst at Aurarian Capital Management, a long and short equity hedge fund best known for its investigative research into companies mispriced by the marketplace. She focused on the technology, medical devices, and renewable energy industries globally, becoming highly conversant on a myriad of complex and controversial investment subjects.

Before joining Aurarian, Junh was an investment officer in the global small/middle capitalization team at Franklin Templeton Fiduciary. Before Fiduciary, she was an investment banking analyst in the Media and Telecommunications Group at Credit Suisse First Boston based in New York.

Junh received an MBA from Columbia Business School and a BA in economics from Middlebury College (summa cum laude, honors in economics).

Junh is a Shanghai native who speaks fluent Mandarin and English and some Japanese. In her spare time, she practices yoga, travels, surfs, reads, and writes.